THE CONSOLIDIST MANIFESTO

THE
CONSOLIDIST
MANIFESTO

Kadey Tonick

Matador
9 Priory Business Park,
Wistow Road, Kibworth Beauchamp,
Leicestershire. LE8 0RX
Tel: (+44) 116 279 2299
Fax: (+44) 116 279 2277
Email: books@troubador.co.uk
Web: www.troubador.co.uk/matador

ISBN 9781783061792

British Library Cataloguing in Publication Data.
A catalogue record for this book is available from the British Library.

Typeset by Troubador Publishing Ltd, Leicester, UK
Printed and bound in the UK by TJ International, Padstow, Cornwall

Matador is an imprint of Troubador Publishing Ltd

Quite simply, dedicated to You the 99%.

CONTENTS

PART 1

THE PRESENT INSANE REALITY

CHAPTER 1

Politics…Vile?

In your world. During your day. From your eyes. What do you see? The planet functioning in a state of complete perfection? A state providing the optimal environment in which 'all' we deserving humans can live our lives to the fullest? Do you see anything even remotely approaching that? After your hard day's work is done, does the News on the television leave you Sanguine or Saddened? Aghast or Optimistic? These are quite the easiest questions to momentarily consider, then swiftly answer. You are correct. The World is a Mess. But the fact that those in charge have botched our countries, our World, is not the most concerning issue. Far more worrying, is that if they're left to continue with their bungling, it will get worse and worse, until the complete collapse of Civil Order and all of our lives.

'We' have Nil time to squander. As is the Consolidist Way, we will immediately expose and confront the flaws and foibles which are handicapping our prosperity. This is not a complex novel which builds and rises to a crescendo, but rather a focused, concise, unswerving map, granting us extrication us from the maelstrom that is our 'Present Insane Reality'. Whether we like what are about to be identified as our problems or not, it's a reality that they are the reasons we currently find our societies in such extreme distress.

We all have a part to play in creating, not perfect, as perfect is not possible for human beings, but near perfect societies within each of our respective countries. Societies that are fair and laced with 'Common Sense'. Societies where everyone exhibits thoughtfulness and selflessness when considering the effects that their actions are having on those around them. Who is it that has the greatest part to play in creating such societies? Those who hold the power. It's the Politicians. This mess every one of us finds ourselves in today, is largely the fault of the Politicians that are 'running' our countries. If they ran our countries like you have absolutely no choice but to run your households every day, 99% of people on the planet would live significantly better lives than those which we're presently experiencing. The filthy rich 1%, owing their fortunes to, and sometimes sharing them with the Politicians? Their lives could hardly get any better.

Under Consolidism. No, people do not live 'Under' Consolidism, as they live 'Under' Politics. If Consolidism were implemented, the 1% would still enjoy great lives, but, 'Common Sense' must be applied to how our societies and economies function if they're to be fair to everybody. Is it Common Sense to allow somebody to amass and hoard billions of currency, when crime is rampant and those billions could be used to protect all deserving humans, you, from the negative elements of our societies? Does that make sense to you?

As you'll see throughout this Manifesto, in complete contrast to Present Day Politics, Consolidism asks You the 99% for Your opinions, and more importantly, takes heed of them. It's You the 99% who should make the decisions and laws that You have to live by. Not a couple of hundred Well-Off, Detached from Reality Politicians. If the Politicians woke up to our problems 'and' ceased to be selfish, amongst other things, we would live, not just exist. Does it ever feel to you like you're not living, but simply existing, day to day, nothing but existing? Just about managing to breathe? Craning your neck to keep your head above the bills, taxes, inflation. Every day is a fight to prevent yourself from drowning beneath the ever-rising cost of living. Our lives, our journeys, take us all on our own individual quests for 'real' happiness. Not just the kind of happiness where you accept that things will never be anywhere near fantastic and you simply make the best of what you've got. We all dream of 'real' happiness don't we?

Consolidism. The World's newest Socio-Political Ideology will give You lives. You will live, because we Consolidists want You to. Not just that, but because we Consolidists, and You, are one and the same. The Consolidists are the People, and, the People are The Consolidists. In the current setup, our Politicians and Governments are some otherworldly entity, far removed from, and totally callous towards the needs of its citizens. Do you feel the Politicians care about your lives or just their own? After all, quite amazingly, their job is to make our lives better. Do you feel the Politicians speak on your behalf? How many of your daily problems has a Politician ever solved? More easy questions to answer. For the 1% they've solved them all. For us remaining 99%, they've either solved a miniscule amount, none at all, or heaped more upon us. Consolidism asks, Does the latter apply to you? Exactly.

Up to this point in the tumultuous life of Planet Earth, the process whereby groups of people make collective decisions has been termed "Politics". There's no doubt that an 'entity' such as Politics is required. It 'ensures' justice and equality across a society, and subsequently maintains civil order. An 'entity' such as Politics 'ensures' each and every one of us has voice, and this is indisputably a good thing. What's the major reason for the planet's turbulent history? The manner in which its Politics has been conducted. With sensible Politics, the world would have experienced far less upheaval, chaos and death. What is this sensible 'Politics' that could have provided for, and saved so many? Consolidism.

Politics is a 'business' that has demonised itself. The vast majority of the Low to Upper-Middle Class, including even some Politicians, detests Politics. The Politicians have brought this upon themselves, and they're well aware of this. Again, Consolidism asks you, Do they care, as long as they're just fine? Politics has always been seemingly inextricably linked to scandal and controversy.

Would you agree? Or would your opinion be that Politicians are honest, trustworthy individuals, having your interests forever within their hearts? Exactly. "Political Machinations". "Political Wrangling". "Political Scheming". "Political Division". "Political Incompetence". The word Politics, and all its strains and variants, marry perfectly with words of deep negativity. They are intrinsically linked, working with a synergistically lethal perfection to sully the quality of every subjugated citizen's life. Why do these terms sound so right, so familair? Because, down your years, you've heard them over and over again? What you hear or see with regularity becomes normal and goes un-noticed, but, when you think about things from a different angle, there's a whole different story to be found.

What about, "I don't know why we have to do it this way. There seems to be some Political reason behind it". I'm sure you've heard that phrase spoken by many of your fellow, hard-working citizens in your life. You've probably even used it yourself. It points to some underhand activity or clandestine plan being hatched in the shadowy background, often in the name of the Self-Advancement of the Instigator.

There are three words which can be used to describe the conduct of all Politician's behaviour. Sinister, Cowardly & Idiotic. It cannot be put any simpler. And it is a Consolidist's belief that it has to be put. If a problem ails us, it must be identified without the fear of being labelled this, that 'and' the other. Without trembling beneath the weight of "Phony Human Rights – PHR" or "Political Correctness – PC". These the creations of the Politicians. Creations that are bringing our countries to their knees as we disappear up our unmentionables trying to adhere to these farcical, unwritten, highly ambiguous rules.

In everything we do throughout our lives, we should seriously consider any 'genuine' negative effects we're having on those around us. We're not talking about something minor, such as 'hurting people's feelings', which the Politician's "PHR" & "PC" have been invented to prevent. We're talking about genuine, physical, negative effects. If you pander to people when they say "that hurts my feelings" or "you can't say that to me", you open up an arena for the lazy, dishonest and foreign persons among us to play our systems. This will result in society wasting time and money on what should be non-existent issues. Lazy people claiming State benefits play on PHR & PC. As societies, we can't speak the truth and confront them with what should be their reality. Instead, we have to pussyfoot around, worrying about not 'hurting their feelings'. The result is less money in the pockets of you, the hardworking element of society. Criminals sue Governments for 'mistreatment' in prisons, usually the most trivial of things. It's ridiculous.

As an example, name-calling is childish, no doubt. Just as childish though, is to take it with anything other than a pinch of salt. Thanks to the Politicians, the term "Racial Abuse" now has such nasty connotations within our societies. It's basically Name-Calling. Something that happens a million times a day in the playgrounds of our schools all over the world. How many times have you seen a Police Officer arresting an 8 year old for calling somebody "Milk Bottle Face"? How much time and money have our governments spent dealing with 'Name-Calling', also known as 'Racial Abuse'? The pandering and subsequent waste has to stop. What is currently waste under the Politicians would be used by Consolidism to improve your lives. But the Politicians won't stop the waste. Are we not nations of free speech? The precious blood spilt on battlefields by our heroes, in the name of 'Freedom of Speech'. If we create laws stopping people from being able to speak their minds about those who undermine their countries, we are spitting on the graves of all who have fallen for us.

If people within our societies use violence against anybody, that cannot be allowed and must be severely punished. But Name-Calling? Under the Politicians' rule, you don't even have to 'call somebody names'. You may just be respectfully voicing your opinion on an element of society which you're not approving of.

That's deemed Politically Incorrect, or possibly even Racist. Should it be unacceptable, or "Politically Incorrect", for someone to quite respectfully voice their opinions? What do you think? Should we make it a criminal offence for someone to identify those who threaten the prosperity of their children and fellow citizens? The hands of the people are tied by the Politicians. You're not free to identify those who are a drain on your taxes because you fear being labelled a "Racist" or "Politically Incorrect". It has to end. Should we really be wasting time and resources on Name-Calling? Is there a law against calling Ginger people names? Or White people? Or Midgets? Or the Handicapped? Of course not. Then why other classifications of people?

If a child is getting called names in a playground, what do we say to them? "Just ignore it. Sticks and stones can break your bones but names will never hurt you". Yet across society we're wasting time and money cracking down on Name-Calling. All the while, it's going unnoticed as being a major contributory factor in the bankrupting of our countries, as people take advantage of the timidity of our societies. If a shopkeeper in Pakistan doesn't want to let a Christian into their shop, then it is absolutely their right to take this stance and point of view, and voice it openly. If an Eskimo wishes to not trade fish with someone who has a turn in their eye because they believe it brings them bad luck, it is entirely their free choice.

No matter what a person's opinions and beliefs are. No matter how wrong or ridiculous they may seem to us, they should be able to do and say whatever they like. If you're having 'real' negative effects on those around you, such as committing crime, then this cannot be allowed. That is the belief of a Consolidist. Stating any opinion is acceptable. Shouting abuse, or, disturbing the peace, i.e. having an actual negative effect on those around you. This is not acceptable and should be stopped at once by law enforcement personnel. Whilst an individual can voice an opinion and choose perhaps not to interact with ginger people, a Consolidist

Government would not discriminate and would provide fairly for all 'its' people, be they Ginger, Gay, Black or Muslim.

It's bad enough that the Politicians waste your time and money even considering policies we can all see will create problems in our lives. It gets worse when they actually enact these policies. As they witness the havoc their policies wreak, it's galling that they stand by and do nothing to change course. The icing on the cake though, is when they make it unacceptable, also known as 'Politically Incorrect', or even illegal to openly identify the problems that they have created. Can this really be happening to us?

Our societies would tell an Alcoholic, "You have to openly admit to and identify your problem before you can cure yourself of it". It is this unfettered honesty, and identification of our problems that will improve the health of our societies.

★★★

Is it the Politician's lives that suffer due to their Sinister, Cowardly & Idiotic behaviour? Precisely. It's you who will eek out existences of a far lower quality than you're entitled to, and much deserving of. If you asked each of the Politicians if they believe they're wholesome and virtuous, do you think every single Politician would answer "Yes"? Would you believe them? Exactly. Those holding posts of Political importance use Politics as the theatre for Self-Gain yes, but also for what seem to be two other passions of theirs. They partake in them so much, and they're so incredibly apparent, it surely must be intentional behaviour? One of these passions is "Dithering Ineffectiveness". With the other being "Making Decisions of Pure Stupidity". Does it sound blunt or rude? That's because it is. The actions have effected the verdict though. It has to be spoken as it is. A Consolidist believes in the truth being spoken, immediately. If we all speak the truth, immediately, we can all start to live better lives, immediately. This is what Consolidism wants for all of us.

The clocks of our lives are ticking, and we need to start calling things as they are, thus enabling us to tackle issues head on. If "Dithering Indecisiveness" & "Making Decisions of Pure Stupidity" are the intentional passions of politicians, why would that be? As many propose, is there some conspiracy simmering beneath the foundations of our societies? Who knows? We could ask the Politicians, but do you think we'd get a straight answer from them? Precisely. Is a hidden agenda working toward some large-scale, fantastical goal, or is it perhaps just Self-Advancement at the expense of the 99%, with decisions being made to satisfy and gain favour and funds from rich businesspersons?

Cherish the thought, if we the people got the Politicians in the dock, and the judge asked us to provide an example of this alleged stupidity of the Politician's decisions, what evidence could we present? Could you think of an example which would condemn your current gaggle of Politicians? Consolidism would guess that you could come up with many, and it asks, Could You? In the West, how about, the UK & US Governments sending their armed forces half way across the world to die in the fight against Terrorism, when, the threat lies directly within their borders. To a Consolidist, it's unimaginable that anybody could put forth a policy such as this, let alone be serious, and worse still, follow through with it. Do you think this is a decision oozing and dripping with 'Common Sense'? There is an incredibly simple solution to Terrorism, and it will be discussed in a later chapter.

Would you agree that, when you witness the decisions Politicians make, when you hear the Policies they put forth, the assessment you're cornered into, is that they're either dim-witted or likely have some undeclared, hidden agenda, or both? 99% of you would surely agree, but, if not, Consolidism asks you to take a closer look, from the different angle, at the Politicians running your country today. Day by day they eat up the hours of your lives. Seemingly feeding on your suffering and gaining the strength they need to make poor after shocking decision. Do they get a buzz out of it? The tawdry, sickening grins on their faces would indicate so, as they implement watered down, ineffective measures that never actually change anything for any significant good within our Societies and Lives.

As already identified, the word Politics is used almost exclusively with depressing & divisive connotations. When the word Politics is spoken, it immediately conjures up a downturn in one's outlook on whatever subject is being discussed. The word Politics is interchangeable with the phrase 'At Loggerheads'. The word Political can be seamlessly replaced with 'Underhanded'. And in the name of the progress of the people, the frank nature of Consolidism identifies that the word Politician has precisely the same meaning as the word 'Imbecile'. This is all true due to the behaviour of those involved in the 'Business' over the years. Politics now has the irreversible, set in stone status of a dirty word. Would you agree?

As filthy a word as Politics is, it pales into insignificance when compared with quite probably the lexicographical leader of filthy words, 'Politician'. Politics might be a dirty word, but Politician is positively disgusting word.

Within Politics, the business of ineffectiveness, incompetence and Self, Self, Self. Beneath the facade of "We're working to improve your lives", is an interwoven network of seedy, self-interest driven machinations. Every day, this weave smothers what little positivity we have inside us. Do you think we should all work together in a concerted effort to completely overhaul Politics so that it works for us? So that it works for the 99% of Law-Abiding, Hard-Working Citizens of the World? With Consolidism, those that currently fall under the classification of the 1%, the mega-rich, would be included in the above-mentioned 99%. The remaining 1%, that would have no say in Consolidist Society, are the Criminal & Lazy among us. A Consolidist doesn't think we should change Politics. Politics doesn't need to change. It needs to be banished to the history books.

THE CONSOLIDIST MANIFESTO

A Consolidist's proposal is that we start afresh, totally eliminating Politics from our societies. In place of Politics, we implement "Societics". Societics is an entity that actually makes decisions and formulates Policies for the good of its people. Not just pretends to. In Societics, a problem is identified, the truth is spoken. Sharp, decisive, 'Common Sense' action is taken, and the lives of the honest & hardworking are improved. The way Politicians currently run the 'business' is to identify what 'they' see as problems, when actually they're having entirely the wrong conversation. They then have time-wasting, lengthy discussions about whether or not they are actually problems, amongst themselves it must be added, without consulting the people. They then consider at length how any action they take would affect everybody except their own good citizens. The feelings of State-Dependents & Foreign Persons (PHR & PC) seem to come before those who go out to work every day and live by the law. That's You.

Thrown into the Politician's discussion, "What would be the best decision to make for my own Political & Financial gain". After they've finished their cocooned discussions, whilst you've been suffering all the while, they eventually either do nothing at all, deciding rather idiotically that there is no problem, or they implement money wasting, watered down measures that they know will never have any positive effect, but which they feel they have to implement in order to be seen as doing 'something', thus increasing their chance of re-election. Though, to the Politicians, it really doesn't matter if the problem isn't solved. It's not negatively effecting their lives, so why should or would they care?

Predominantly, the trend is that their decisions, which involve 'action' or inaction, usually result in having exactly the opposite effect they should be. The decisions Politicians make are meant to be continuously improving your lives, society and keep everything humming in harmony. Do you see this around you? It is excusable and absolutely justified to think that Politicians do have this hidden agenda we sometimes hear society's "loons" talk of. These "loons" are labelled so by the Politicians, with the rest of society, being formed by the Politicians, jumping on the bandwagon. Whatever the reason may be, is there an agenda to dig the societies they should be aiding, into an inescapable hole? With their brilliant, 'apparent' stupidity on display every single day, you have to entertain the hypothesis. Especially maddening is the very rare occasion when a Politician does speak sense on a subject, identifying a problem and promising 'Common Sense' action to put it right. But, we all know full well that it's much more likely than not, they won't follow through on their promise. It's just a soundbyte. They're just speaking these rehearsed, empty words as a means to an end. With the end goal being Power, and the subsequent financial rewards that come with it.

'Politicians focusing on and discussing entirely the wrong issues'. This is absolute key to why we find ourselves in such trouble at present. There are 6 key issues/reasons that are killing our economies and societies. The Manifesto will lay them all out for you. One has already been identified. Pandering to PHR & PC.

★★★

Do you feel that "stupidity" is a harsh, Politically Incorrect word to use in our nowadays societies, when referring to Politicians and the decisions they make 'on your behalf'? ?

After winning power in the summer 2010, the UK's new Coalition Government announced that the £55 Billion, 20 Year 'Building School's for the Future' programme would be scrapped due to lack of funds. UK, that's the lives of your children suffering due to the bungling of the Politicians. They may blame the necessity to cut this important public spending on the previous Government, as every Government that comes into power does. Do you find this incredibly childish and annoying? Exactly. Even if the culpability does lie with their predecessors, if You, proletariat of the UK, were making the here and now decisions, and had to cut public spending, would the first spending you cut not be State Benefits and Healthcare for Foreign Persons within your country? Would you then not secondly say "We don't have the money to spend on fighting wars against terrorism in foreign lands. We'll have to find some alternative strategy"? Would those kind of decisions strike you as 'Common Sense', first stop actions in an attempt to solve this debt problem that confronts you?

Not only do they not say that, but on the latter, they continue to insanely propose that the Foreign Wars are the best strategy to combat Terrorism. In summary, they spend billions providing free Benefits & Healthcare for Foreign Persons, some of which are posing a possible terrorist threat. They spend billions sending your loved ones to die in a dusty nightmare. They then pull money out of your child's education, which has the added negative effect of massively reducing construction industry jobs that could have been created if the billions was spent on building new and refurbishing old schools. All this is your money that they're squandering. This is quintessentially illustrative of the miscreant that is the Politician.

Cut education spending, cut construction jobs and borrow money, which you the hardworking, "Average Josephine" will have to pay back, plus interest, to send British Soldiers to their death, while foreign persons enjoy a comfortable, effortless life, free money and reign back in the UK. These kinds of decisions are also virtually identically mirrored in the USA. The only difference being that 'alot' more of your brave soldiers perish in your Politician's 'Wars of Fancy'. Would you agree out there, people of America?

Consolidism asks you again, Good Person of the World. Do you feel that "stupidity" is a harsh, Politically Incorrect word to use in our nowadays societies, when referring to Politicians and the decisions they make 'on your behalf'?

Their minds are either devious, with this hidden agenda, or staggeringly illogical. And in telling you the above is what they're going to be doing, they somehow manage to keep a straight face. Quite a feat. Up until now, we've all had no choice but to somehow deal with the Politician's stupidity and total disregard for the welfare of you and your families, because even though Politics has different parties, the parties are all full of Politicians. Now you have a different choice, Consolidism. To a Consolidist, it wouldn't even matter if one school in the country had to miss out on a new box of pens, your money would not go 'abroad'. If your own are in need, anything you have available that doesn't go to help them, is wrong. Full Stop. Is that how you would see the situation in your home with your children?

As is the Consolidst way, let's bring one thing immediately out in the open. There are many, including Politicians, who would already be saying, "Consolidism sounds Racist". The Politicians especially, would say this for Self-Gain. They've planted the PHR & PC seeds within our societies and will play on them to keep themselves in power. Do not be fooled by the creature that is a Politician. It's obvious that they would throw any dirt they could at any opposition party, whether it was true or not. We can all see that, and do every day on our News Channels. If an opposition party wins power, they're obviously out of power, so they'll profess that the other is incompetent, racist, or whatever they think will work to undermine the opposition.

Their decisions, stances and statements are not driven by a desire to help the people, but rather by a desire to remain in power and advance their own position in life. Those who aren't Politicians, but who say "Consolidism is Racist" have been programmed and bullied into reeling off this judgement by two elements, Politicians and the Foreign Persons currently enjoying the free Benefits, Healthcare and all the other perks of developed countries. Again, rather obviously, they wouldn't want your taxes to cease coming in their direction in the form of free Benefits & Healthcare. The sooner everybody stops screaming "Racist". The sooner everybody stops cowering at the sound of "Racist", or whatever the PC & PHR blocs want to unjustifiably get on their high horses about, the sooner each country's citizens can start to live, actually live.

Consolidism is not about Racism, it's about 'Common Sense' and looking out for its own. This goes for Swedish people who live in Thailand, or Thai people who live in Sweden. Whichever combination of Nationalities & Countries are involved, your own come first.

Politicians continually inflict upon us their idiocy, with their decisions resulting in higher taxes, rising costs of living and reductions in our public services. They can see it all around them every day, but still do not change the course of their actions and decisions. What's your valued opinion? Hidden Agenda, Cowardice to enact vital policy changes or Stupidity? A poisonous blend of all three? A Consolidist Government will do whatever it takes to safeguard its population and improve their lives, right across the board. Absolutely whatever it takes.

It's incredible that when the Politician's goal is to improve their citizen's lives, they make so few good decisions, so many utterly bad ones and even more involving the 'implementation' of watered down, half-hearted measures to tackle the very serious problems and deficiencies faced by the people. With the suffering all around us, as will be discussed, does it seem impossible to you that the Politicians are actually trying to help us prosper. Politician's are the antithesis of prosperity. So why aren't they willing to take the serious steps toward actually helping the people who pay their salaries? A few hypotheses have already been put forward for your consideration, but it is the belief of a Consolidist that the reason is a mix of stupidity, greed, inability to look at problems from a different angle to that which has been used previously. This can also be described as an unwillingness to jump from the bandwagon. There's also some Cowardice involved. They fear any backlash that may arise from the Criminal, Lazy and Foreign 1% if they proposed such big, but necessary changes. Changes that will be discussed throughout the Manifesto.

Initially, some of the changes may seem drastic, but they are compulsory if you grafting, tax-paying people are to enjoy a good quality of life. Of course, the Politicians already enjoy a good quality of life, so why would they choose to roll up their sleeves and do some hard work? The measures that a Consolidist Government would implement, should be feared by criminals who negatively affect others. By lazy and foreign persons currently living off your taxes. By the mega-rich, hoarding millions or billions. And of course Politicians. A Consolidist Government will implement Consolidsm & Societics. With Politicians securely imprisoned within the history books, Consolidist Societicians will get down to the serious work of ensuring that You, the 99%, the good people of the world, are inordinately better off.

We must all finally take this long overdue, unwavering stand against Politics and reject it wholeheartedly with all that we are. The choice is ours, the ball is in our court, we can make it happen. Together we can make Societics emerge from the putrefying carcass of politics. Emerge like a pristine, fluorescent butterfly from its ragged, mishapen chrysalis. Societics is, and always will be, an entity that works relentlessly towards improving the lives of you, the diligent & dutiful, the responsible & conscientious citizen of your country. The number one priority will always be absolutely all of you and your families, nothing and nobody else. Societicians make decisions and take bold steps that 'actually' make a difference to you, your family and your community.

Consolidism will free you from the hole that the Politicians have dug you deep into over the years. To escape this hole and be able to view a new horizon, to view 'something' in front of you, will take some hard work and more importantly a radical change in our way of thinking. We'll have to start looking at situations from entirely different angles. Assess situations and effect changes using methods never previously adopted. This different frequency of thinking that we all need to tune into, will be laid out in great detail as 'The Consolidist Manifesto' progresses. If we don't make this change, right now, then nothing will ever change. Mark these words, Consolidists will not be talking about the change a Politician touts at every election, but never ever delivers. Consolidists will promise change, and actually deliver it, right to your doorstep.

Countries, the world, humankind wouldn't be entangled in this current insane mess, hurtling at a trillion miles a second towards oblivion, if Politicians had just acted with 'Common Sense'. The kind of 'Common Sense' that you have to adopt everyday of your lives in order to run your household and bring up your children. If you don't adopt Common Sense and act appropriately in accordance with the world around you, you and your family will be constantly visited by nothing but insurmountable difficulties. Even as hard as it is for you, you still make the sensible decisions required to stay afloat, just. You make sensible decisions, so why haven't the Politicians been able to do it?

You see, a country is analogous to a house. That's all a country really is, a big household. As our discussions move forward, progressing with focused purpose and vigour, towards the goal of actually bettering your lives, this analogy will be referred to in very simple terms as the "Home Analogy". Just as in a country, within a household, everybody belongs to each other. They're of the same family. In a household, decisions have to be made adopting 'Common Sense', such that they avert the catastrophic outcome of you and your family finding yourself buried up to your furrowed brows in debt. In a household, all the members of the family are looked after above those outside your home who are not your family. The family members are helped, and rewarded, as long as they are responsible and do their fair share. Does the above describe how you how you run your household? Would the above be a 'Common Sense' way to run a country? Precisely. Not to a Politician though.

As depressing as it is, we must analyse how Politician's have brought the world to such a calamitous position. Both to learn lessons of the mistakes which we should never return to, and to expose their idiocy and underhandedness. With the stories in the news every day, you very probably will not need too much help in the illustration of these dastardly and dunce-like shenanigans.

However, it's important that we all have the full story in our minds, thus ensuring we embrace solidarity, and ensure that politics dies. Once the lessons and expose are complete, we can cast Politicians and the carcass of their farcical business of Politics into a 100% inescapable hole, just where they belong. Their bedfellows in this hole, a Consolidist believes, amongst many others, treating Women as second class human beings, as is believed ethical in some countries and religions. This is of course disgusting. Also, the casting of judgement upon somebody's sexuality. What right do Politicians feel they have to draw up laws solely against Homosexuals or Lesbians? Only if the survival of the human race was at stake and procreation needed to be encouraged, should Homosexuality or Lesbianism be a problem. We as a society should only take action if something is having a genuine negative effect on others. A final example, Racist Violence. The idea of forming beliefs and opinions on people, without any reasoning whatsoever, 'and attacking them', simply for the race of human being they are. That is downright wrong.

So, as we stand, our countries are in a mess. Financially, Morally, Public Services, Infrastructure, absolutely everything. Top to Bottom, Tip to Toe. If you're household found itself in this state, what would you do? Would you continue to make ineffective, clumsy decisions? Exactly. Of course you wouldn't. Because if you did, you'd be homeless and destitute quicker than a hiccup. What you'd do is start tightening your belt, cutting out un-necessary spending. Ensuring your money is used only to provide for you and your family.

If you and your family found yourselves in the abovementioned undesirable position, would it be 'Common Sense' to give $1,000, or 1,000 of whatever your currency is, to House No. 26 in your street so that they could fit a new garage roof? Precisely. With that in mind, why did the UK Government give India £295 million foreign aid in 09/10, considering the UK was hundreds of billions of pounds in debt? Is that 'Common

Sense'? Is that the kind of decision that would keep your roof over your head? It's not that anybody should have anything against India. It's a beautiful country full of wonderfully pleasant, gentle human beings, but, "Sorry we just don't have the money to give you anymore. We're in serious debt ourselves, and have to start making spending cuts that put the citizens of the UK first and foremost". Do you think that would have been a sensible position to take on the matter? Would that have been fair to the British people? That's how a Consolidist Government would view the situation.

To send that amount of taxpayers' money abroad, when you could have spent it on their public services, is to put it very politely, a scandalous decision. When you consider that India are the 4th largest economy in the world and the United Kingdom come in at 8th position, it's ludicrous. How can somebody give the go ahead for this to happen? It's mind-boggling.

Is it as a gesture in the hope that India will continue to do business in some way, shape or form with the UK? Are the Politicians pocketing some of this 'business'? Putting that question to them would be futile, a total waste of breath. The truth would not be forthcoming. No doubt there are instances where aid like this swings favour with countries and benefits the people of the donor country. Of course, it should be the case that the people's prosperity is at the top of any Government's agenda. With this in mind, such foreign aid should be considered. But there are no doubt cases where the return business does not form part of the equation. It's these cases that the Politicians should be ashamed of.

Not just Foreign Aid, there are literally tens of thousands of examples of the poor attributes of Politicians, examples of their lack of backbone, bad policies and decision making strewn throughout our Government's History. With no time to waste in improving your lives, we will only be able to touch upon a few, but we all know the rest exist.

So why would you make the 'tough' decisions to get your

household back on its feet, but the Politicians won't do the same for a country? There are, as already discussed, a few reasons. A major factor is that they're unable and unwilling to approach society's problems and attempt to solve them from a different angle. The inability can be attributed to two things, a combination of stupidity and a fear to break away from the conventional paths of thought that have brought us all to this catastrophic point in the world's history. Then there's the unwillingness. They and their families are not negatively affected by the detritus that is currently passing for your country, so there's no need for them to worry. Yes, maybe their taxes could be less if they rectified problems, but they have enough money not to notice the difference of the small amount of additional currency that leaves their earnings each year. Would you notice the difference if your taxes were lowered by any amount? Exactly. It would make a big difference to you, and a Consolidist is acutely aware of this.

It's a fundamentally obvious decision to make when anybody, any business, any country, any household finds themselves in financial troubles, you have to change your ways. Do you see the current batch of Politicians changing their ways, or is it more of the same? Politicians need to change the way they conduct themselves and how they treat their citizens. But you can guarantee they won't. Just as countries of the world were discussing what ails them 40 years ago, we're all still having the exact same conversations 40 years on, and we'll be cogitating the same issues 40 years from now, unless, we reject Politicians, their flaws, stupidity, cowardice and disdain for their people.

A Consolidist Government, Consolidist Societicians, would propel a country forward, not be a bystander watching it and its people drown. Politicians are supposed to have been remedying our problems. Do you see society's problems being set right around you as the years pass you by, or do you see virtually nothing changing for the better?

Let's analyse more specifically how the political machine works in our countries nowadays. Does the following sound familiar? Election time in your respective countries rolls around. Renewed Hope & Fresh Promise. Relief, as change appears on the horizon. Each candidate & party vowing with all their hearts to get tough on crime, improve your healthcare, tackle immigration, reinvigorate your economy. When a leader and their party is voted into power, they spend the term of their Government bumbling around, implementing lacklustre, diluted policies, having little or zero effect on improving what they swore blind they would.

Change' was the keyword of the incumbent US President, Barack Hussein Obama's campaign. America, a Consolidist asks you, has anything really changed? As pleasant a human being as he seems, after the multi-million dollar campaign hype, with the same old lines and pauses for applause, it's bad business as usual for you USA. There's no doubt, he has intelligence within him, so why hasn't he brought about the 'Change' for the better he promised he would? Many years ago, he was infected by the disease that is politics. Once a carrier, you will never have the ability, gumption or foresight to effect change for the good of your people. You will always waffle, without ever actually detailing precisely what you intend to do. Politics instils within a person an inability & fear to break away from convention. Add to this that he's living a good life, and always will till the day he passes on, there's no need to go through the hard work of taking what initially seems like drastic, difficult action.

At the time this Manifesto is being written, the 2012 US Elections are just a month away. Let Consolidism make this prediction. It doesn't matter which of the 2 Political Candidates you choose America. Neither of them will solve any of the problems they're swearing to. Have they? Even if, as the President of the United States of America, you don't have it in you to exact life-improving change for your people, you'd still surely stop throwing away your taxpayer's money on wacky 'scientific' experiments? Wouldn't you? Not a chance. The President is a Politician. The people within his administration are all Politicians.

This is why in 2010, they allocated $239,100 to a Stanford University Professor, enabling him to study how Americans use the internet to find love. Is that 'Common Sense'? Or do you think the money would be better spent putting some more Police onto the crime-ridden streets of America? Not only would this help in the fight against crime, it would create jobs. That makes no sense to a Politician though. None whatsoever.

After they've spent their term quaffing expensive wine at the plethora of free functions that flow their way. After they've spent their term spewing forth predictably flawed policies with unflinchingly metronomic proficiency. What happens? The farcical cycle begins again. All the while you're suffering in either tepid squalor or complete penury. How many free meals do you receive over the term of their Government? Exactly. As one imbecile gets ready to leave office and live comfortably for the rest of their lives, never having to worry about money again, the next batch of wannabes saddle up, vowing that their party "will be tough on crime and will not waver in our commitment to protect the hardworking citizens of this country".

Prisoners in most countries have their own bed, a television and a games console in their cell. That's how tough a Politician is on criminality. It's unbelievable that anybody actually votes these people into power, but, thus far, there's not been an alternative in our Democracies, until now. Do you find this farcical cycle frustrating? Would you like to have the power to change it? Consolidism? To become President of the United States of America you need hundreds of millions of dollars to assemble the kind of campaign that has a chance of winning. Where does this money come from? Donations mostly from the 1% mega-rich. You're cornered into voting for these candidates who are now in the pockets of the 1%. Once in power, the Politicians are duty-bound to look after the 1%, because that's who got them where they are, both in terms of monetary donations and media exposure, courtesy of the filthy-rich media moguls.

A Politician would tell you Consolidism won't work. But then Politicians lie alot don't they. Would you agree? They lie and complicate issues just to keep themselves in power. Everything in our lives and societies can be simplified. Don't let the Politicians tell you any different. A Consolidist Government would keep things simple and improve your lives immeasurably. As you read on, you be the judge of Consolidism. Fend your ears from the inane claptrap that every Politician will attempt to confuse you with.

It's not just crime or healthcare or international aid. The Politicians reward your hardwork and paying of your taxes with a veritable smorgasbord of woefully idiotic decisions that degrade your existence and pare away your joys in life. They are doing nothing towards the betterment of your communities. How often over the years do you see members of the public being interviewed on television, rightfully voicing their complaints about the state of the public services they're paying their good money for? Or the Crime and Anti-Social Behaviour in their communities. It's the same subjects, the same problems, recurring over and over and over again. A Consolidist is cognizant of this and even more cognizant of the desperation of the people to have the problems put right. After listening to, and feeling great affinity with the interviewee, you switch channels to find a narcissistic, self-aggrandising Politician giving some vague, vacuous speech about how they're going to bring about change for the better. Exactly the necessary change the member of the public was just speaking of. Though the Politicians never actually say how they'll achieve the change they promise. They simply ramble on, identifying that 'something' needs to change, and the fact that they plan to make that change. Why don't they explain absolutely specifically how they will deliver the change?

It's because they don't know how to. Inevitably, what will happen? The change is never realised. Does a Politician's vagueness incense you? They have no sense nor backbone to set a course for the ship, and cure what ails our societies. They won't suffer though, you will. It's you, the proletariat that needs your taxes reduced before your Government sends hundreds of millions of currency abroad to countries on the other side of the world. Those countries must be laughing at us. Would you find it a joke if a family living across the other side of town gave your family free money when they were deep in debt themselves? Precisely. Our countries are many billions or trillions in debt, but some are still giving free money away? What the Politicians are doing with your money is a joke. But are you laughing? A Consolidist certainly isn't.

Politicians aren't desperately in need of a tax reduction like you are. They earn a handsome wage, and also have their fingers in many an inappropriate pie. Whether it be fraudulent expense claims or using their position to win business for family members, or through some scheming or loophole, even themselves. Their bank accounts are full of money, albeit tainted. But that doesn't bother them, as long as they're comfortable. They've got no worries financially. Have you? The worst aspect in all of this, is that Politicians pocket this money, receive lifelong nods and winks, all while displaying a great incompetence in their jobs. What would happen if you kept failing at every task you were given at work? You'd be out of the door within 3 months.

Even with the evidence of our broken societies all around us, smack bang in everybody's face, how many times have you heard a Politician say they're in the wrong or yield to claims that they haven't done a good job? Exactly. They use the invidiously slimy tactic of never giving a straight Yes or No answer, but instead sidestepping the question and spinning off the subject with some tangential drivel in the hope we'll be blinded by their waffle. Are you blinded by their attempt to confuse issues, or can you see straight through them? A Consolidist concurs with your answer to that question. The other tactic they use, is to blame the previous Government. It has to be said, it's pathetic. Like 8 year old children squabbling in the playground. They carry their seemingly inherent, flawed traits from the Playground to the Presidential Podium. No doubt, there are occasions when they're justified in directing blame at their predecessors. After all, even if they're of different Political Parties, they're all Politicians, and all Politicians are incompetent.

Do you find it unbelievably infuriating when, as our lives are suffering as a result of their gutless ineptitude, the Politicians don't even have the decency to either admit they're wrong or give a straight answer to a question? A Consolidist agrees with your straight & swift answer to that easy question.

Politicians seem to think that by using this lily-livered, evasive tactic, they dodge the bullet. In reality, it makes them look worse than if they'd just accepted blame and admitted they were at fault. This actually serves as a perfect illustration of the appalling judgement of a Politician. We know they've done something wrong. They know they've made a mistake. They know that we know, but, they don't have the integrity to admit it. It almost seems as though they can't help doing it. It's inherent, automatic, in the blood of this creature, the animal that is a Politician. While you're houses are being burgled. While the elderly are huddled under blankets in their homes, not being able to afford the cost of switching their heating on, a Politician is sat in a cosy TV Studio playing a game of "Yes & No Dodge" with a red-faced interviewer. Even more red-faced are the electorate sat at home watching. Some of us in our rundown homes. Homes we don't have the money to redecorate because our taxes and the cost of living are too high. Unfortunately, the electorate, the proletariat, we, have had no option but to vote for these imbeciles. Thus far, on the ballot paper, they've all been Politicians. No option, until now.

★★★

Let's take a minute to dissect one of the activities Politicians partake in during their campaign to become the person who ensures your misery continues for another term of Government. The election debate. Let's look from a different angle, read between the lines and identify what is really going on during one of these 'Shows'. Take for example the 3 way debates, as were held in the UK's 2010 General Election. Three Politicians from three different parties. Gordon Brown, the incumbent Labour Prime-Minister, Nick Clegg, Leader of the Liberal Democrats & David Cameron, Leader of the Conservative Party.

We all now know who won. With all the promises David Cameron made during that campaign, the UK Public must be enjoying great riches by now. Are you UK? Back to Business. The candidates spent a solid hour making claim and counterclaim against each other on a whole range of issues that they badly needed, and still need, to get to grips with for the sake of their citizens. In every claim and counterclaim about how the current Government has fouled up on this issue due to this set of published figures, and how someone is on record as having said that, one of them is lying. There can only be one right answer. One truth. The Simplest of Maths. All 3 of them differ in their official stance and opinion on the majority of issues. With that in mind, it means that on most issues & points raised where figures or quotations are touted, two of them are lying. A modest estimate would be that perhaps they discussed and made claims and counterclaims about 20 different sets of figures or pieces of information during the course of the debate. That means that between them, these 3 people who are putting themselves forward as candidates to run your country, your society and your lives.

These people who are putting themselves forward as honest & trustworthy. People we can put our faith in. People we can put our lives in the hands of. Between them, they've just spouted approximately 40 bare faced lies on live television. Forty lies rammed down your throat. Forty lies with the single purpose of advancing and elevating their position in life. And this is a conservative estimate. Each topic usually results in many sub-claims, sub-counterclaims and subsequent lies emanating from their shameful faces. On and on the claims and counterclaims keep coming. There's never any final definitive outcome to any of the discussed issues. Nothing is ever resolved. Identifying who indeed was right, who was lying, thus giving the country a concrete answer on what the facts of the matter are. They spend a few minutes accusing each other of incompetence, lying and lack of vision in their policy, then move onto the next subject. Nothing is ever resolved in debates, so is it surprising that once one of them slithers their way into power, no problem is ever resolved in your community, in your lives?

This is not just evident in debates but also in the debate chambers where our Governments waste vast amounts of time and money childishly squabbling over our country's affairs. They wouldn't admit it, obviously, but their stances on issues are most often driven first and foremost by self-gain, acquiring a feeling of self-worth & securing the position of greater importance over and above their opposition. Those are their number one goals in their minds. In their minds, that is what their aim is. They have one agenda inside, but externalise another, because if they didn't, they couldn't attain the position of power they so badly crave.

When it comes to election debates, a Consolidist would propose that, after the debate, the people deserve to have of every statement scrutinised by entirely arbitrary persons. Hard evidence should be obtained of who was right and who was wrong on their 'facts' and figures. One week on, the Politicians could return to appear in a live broadcast where they're statements are replayed, then the evidence presented to expose the lies. If this was done, do you think a Politician would admit they were lying or wrong or would they still try to squirm out of accepting blame? Exactly. The Consolidist party would be more than happy to take part in debates like this, because the Consolidist representative at the debate would not be a devious, egotistical snake. If this follow-up broadcast was proposed to a Politician by an interviewer, do you think they'd agree to do it, or else the viewing public would think they have something to hide? Then after they've agreed to do it, behind the scenes, employ whatever sly tactics are needed to be able to say "It's not feasibile"? Exactly. What would this leave us thinking? That they have something to hide. Which they do. They lie and do whatever it takes to hold onto their positions of power.

At any time, in a debate or not, if a Consolidist Societician doesn't know something, she or he will say they don't know and will have to check the actual facts. They won't blag. It's not possible to know all the facts about everything and have hundred mile per hour conversations about the serious issues in our lives. The fact that currently the Politicians conduct themselves in such a way, pretending they have all the answers instantly to keep up the facade of electability, means we in society conduct ourselves in this way.

Whether we realise it or not. Whether we like it or not, with subtleties of behaviour such as this, the way we conduct ourselves is dependent on how they conduct themselves. They can't possibly know everything instantly. We can't possibly know everything instantly. How many times have you heard a Politician say "I don't know the answer to that"? Never? They choose instead to blag and waffle, to the detriment of the resolution of our problems. In our everyday lives, when people are unnecessarily rushed and pushed for hard and fast answers, they end up waffling. Not sticking to efficiently discussing and planning solutions to problems. And when somebody is rushed into saying something, even if it is wrong, the majority of the time, they can't admit to being wrong for fear of loss of face, the equivalent of damaging your electability as a Politician. The result is non-identification, non-resolution of our problems and stifled societies. It's not just this that's resulting in our problems.

The style of communication and sharing of information amongst humans is very ineffective and filled with uncertainty, leaving us all open to suggestion, 'mind control' and mistakes. Consider how you witness scientists talk arrogantly about the 'facts' on the subject of stars billions of light years from Earth. As though what they're saying is unquestionably correct. Not only is that arrogant, and unquestionably some of the 'facts' are erroneous, we across the other side of the world, live our lives repeating these 'facts' verbatim. Over the past 2000 years of human history and scientific endeavour, how many times have scientists disproved the theories of those who have gone before them? Thousands of times. In 2012, are we at the pinnacle of human knowledge? With everything we state in relation to science being 100% correct? Absolutely not. Many of the arrogant scientific theories of today will be disproved in years to come. At which time, we'll start reciting the new theories verbatim.

When we talk amongst ourselves about how certain foods are 'definitely' good for our health. How can we know if we're not Biologists or Scientists? We can't is the answer. What 'facts' do you know about snowflakes and human fingerprints? Every single one is different? Have you put every snowflake that's ever fallen under a microscope and analysed them? Then how can you make the claim? There are many more snowflakes to fall, so we couldn't possibly say that they're all different. Have you analysed the fingerprints of every human who's ever existed to be able to state this 'fact' 100%? Exactly.

In a Court, when presented with the fact that DNA of the accused was found on the victim, can you be sure of this? Having never studied DNA theory or even looked under a microscope before? It's not possible to be "Beyond any Reasonable Doubt" that the evidence is there. Therefore, as per the current system, the accused has to be let go. Or should we be able to trust unquestionably the authorities and the evidence they present to us in our Courts of Law? Yes? Just like we can trust our Presidents. "I did not have sexual relations with that woman". Seven months later. "I did have a relationship with Miss Lewinsky that was not appropriate". Can we trust the authorities? The answer is no, because they're controlled by Politicians.

Can you see how flawed human communication and life is?

How easily those in the right positions can use misinformation to control us and achieve their selfish goals? We have no choice but to make the best of most of the above described, because there are certain things we can't change, such as depending on 'knowledge' gathered by people across the other side of the world, but, what we can do to make our lives better is ensure we don't continue to allow the Politicians to abuse their positions through lies and misinformation, and spend their time waffling to keep up a facade which subsequently ruins our existences.

The Politician is the perfect example of this defective communication. The majority of what leaves their mouths is piffle & tosh, off the subject waffle that doesn't help anybody. Would you agree that you never see a Politician talking clearly about precise measures they're going to take? They're always talking generally and vaguely. This is one of the reasons they never improve anything in our lives. We all need to slow down when considering important issues in our communities, call everything down the line as it is, without any worrying about PC, Phony Human Rights or loss of face.

We should never be afraid of saying "I got that wrong" or "I don't know the answer to that". It's a fact that we will all get things wrong in our lives. It's a fact that we can't and don't have the answers to everything instantly. We need to shed the facade that we all have to be right all the time and know everything all the time. If we do this, and stick to the subject in hand, without any waffling or complicating of issues, we can all live better lives. For this to become the way society operates, we need people in Government who are willing to say "I've got that wrong" or "I don't have the answer to that right now" or "Let's slow down and really think this issue through with 'Common Sense'". They set the benchmark. 'Everything' in our societies can be simplified, to our great gain, if we just adopt the right approach and think on the right wavelength. Politicians especially need to live by these rules, as they are the biggest culprits when it comes to breaking them all, but also, they play such an important role in our countries, as they make the laws and form the basis of the functioning of our societies.

If a Consolidist is in the wrong, a Consolidist will admit she or he is wrong. Is it too much to ask that the people running our countries, do so with honesty and integrity? From where you're sitting, do you associate the words honesty and integrity with Politicians? Precisely. As if the lies, blame dodging and relentless childlike accusations weren't enough, the Politicians top it off by proposing some of the most outrageous policies that could ever be dreamt up. It's obvious from a vast distance that their policies will not work, and their countries will simply descend deeper into chaos and poverty. The policies have never worked before, but they're still proposing the continuation of very similar, if not identical ones. Surely it's obvious that a drastic change is necessary in the way we run our countries? But no, they just bumble along, getting rich and planning a plush retirement. Meanwhile you're left worrying about how you survive on a measly pension fund, while billions is being spent on foreign persons, whether it be benefits within your own country, Post Unnecessary-War Redevelopment or Foreign Aid.

During an election debate, or any debate or interview involving Politicians for that matter, have you ever seen a Politician make a statement, have a counterclaim fired back at them, then say "Actually, you're right on that point. We've got that wrong"? Why haven't we been doing it that way? I will be looking into that as soon as this debate has finished. If it turns out to be feasible, we will implement the change immediately, thus improving the lives of millions of our families"? Because you can 100% guarantee, the scenario has arisen where one of them should have said that. In a trillion years they couldn't bring themselves to say something of that nature. Why? Because they're deceitful and they feel it would harm their electability.

Wouldn't it be refreshing to see such an occurrence? Would you have some more respect for them if it happened just a few times? Of course it wouldn't look good for them, and could perhaps result in some voter's minds being swayed away from their party, but, they should be telling the truth and calling things down the line whatever the ramifications. If it happened alot, then of course you'd have to start thinking that they're not the right Person or Party for the job. But, finally seeing some total honesty from a Politician, whatever effect their words will have, would be so incredibly refreshing. Because if they don't start to call things down the line, we will all continue to suffer. Truth. Truth. Truth. Truth and Honesty brings Prosperity. That is how the Consolidist Party views it. But the honesty won't be forthcoming. What do you think? Instead of doing the decent thing, when we can all see they've bungled something, they back themselves into a corner, claiming they're completely correct and everybody else is totally wrong. It has to be said that it's an absolute joke.

A perfect indicator as to how false the business of politics is, and also how very sad it is that up to now, we've had no alternative option to the Politician, is the fact that, in the UK, after the multitude of disagreements David Cameron and Nick Clegg have had on a wide range of issues since they've held their positions as party leaders. When they get the chance to latch their tentacles onto power, they suddenly drop the facade and say "We'll work together, our differences are not such a problem". There's no conclusion one can draw from that, other than the disagreements were simply a facade. An act. Why the act? If they agreed with each other, only one of them could be the Leader of that Party. But they both badly crave the power and financial gain that come with being a Political Party Leader. As soon as they get the chance at power, they drop the act. It may not be what Nick Clegg wanted, but, it was either Deputy Prime Minister or nothing. When faced with this choice, the greed in his bones took over. One week they're at each other's throats, the next week they're shaking hands and exchanging blushing smiles on the lawn at 10 Downing Street. Do you think that exposes the truth about the 'business' that is Politics? It just shows that a Politician's policies will be whatever they need to be to get them into a position of power. It's got nothing to do with improving people's lives. Coalition Governments are a preposterous concept, and the Consolidist Party thinks a referendum should be held, asking the people of the UK if they want to change the way elections are conducted, change the structure of the Political system such that they never have to suffer the embarrassment of a Coalition Government again.

Let the Consolidist Party ask you this question. In the UK, is it just coincidence that the Labour Party disagrees with 99% of the Conservative Party's policies? Of course not. It's by design. They have to disagree, or else one of them would be out of their jobs as a Party Leader. Many of them agree with many of the policies of the opposition party, but they can't allow a breakdown of the facade or else they won't get a chance to win absolute power themselves. All these shenanigans & antics that fill the lives of a Politician, result in your lives being of a lower standard than they could be. In the USA, the Republicans stand shoulder to shoulder with their fellow party members, pointing their guns towards the Democrats, until, 'Presidential Nominee' time rolls around. All of a sudden they re-aim, now glaring down their barrels at each other. Can you see that the above scenarios are so incredibly false it's beyond belief? It's all about the acquisition of power and money.

★★★

Consider this scenario that the Politicians of the UK Government allowed to play out. In 2011, Cornwall Bed & Breakfast owners Peter & Hazelmary Bull were ordered by the courts to pay a gay male couple £3,600 in damages due to the fact they refused to let them stay at their house if they were going to sleep in the same bed. To a Consolidist, who views issues with a hefty dose of 'Common Sense', that is totally absurd. What would you say? This couple have the right to refuse anybody they want the right to enter their home. Just as a nation has the right to refuse anybody entry to their country. A Consolidist Government would have never let that case go to court. 'Genuine' Human Right's Abuses, Yes. Non-Existent Human Right's Abuses, Absolutely Not. The Government could have stepped in and prevented this joke from ever occurring. Wasting people's time, money and effort. Wasting the world's finite resources on this non-issue. We have real problems we need to be solving in our communities. In the year 2012, we are living in societies that allow people to be sued for refusing somebody the right to sleep in their home. This makes perfect sense to Politicians. How on earth can it be so? And with the Politicians still in power, we're still living in this 'Present Insane Reality'. Hundreds of similar examples could be dredged up from the history of Politics and Politicians, but, there is just no time to dwell on their idiocy. We have to get on with our duty of improving 'everybody's' lives.

The Justice system should be processing Car Thieves, not Bed & Breakfast owners who have done absolutely no wrong. There's nothing at all wrong with being Gay, but if somebody doesn't want to allow a Gay person into their home, that's entirely up to them. Politicians have the power to stop ridiculousness like this before it even starts, so why aren't they doing so? They're too busy practicing to become the quickest liars in the West. Then they can wriggle and slither their way into positions of power and subsequent wealth. They're too busy practising waffling speeches which never actually mention any concrete measures which have been, are being or will be taken to improve your lives. On that note, let's consider a speech that a President or Prime Minister may make:

"Due to the policies of the last Government, the healthcare system is not providing people with the quality of service they deserve. We intend to fix it. Firstly, we have to reduce the current multi-tiered management structures down to ones which are simplified and streamlined. Instead of focusing on bureaucracy and the excessive administrative procedures, we need to focus directly on frontline patient care". How many times have you heard speeches by Politicians containing that kind of formless drivel?

Speeches like that can have no effect but the electorate not being clear on what you're doing for them. Is that how you feel? Worse still, the reason they drivel in this way is because they often haven't got the concrete ideas in their minds about what needs to be done. They either lack the intelligence or are too scared to enact the necessary radical change. But they have to say something to keep hold of power, so they just have a speech writer throw something together that they 'think' sounds good.

Do you think it sounds good when a Politician speaks? Are you impressed, crystal clear on what they're doing for you and your family? The result of their drivel, as you and the Consolidist Party are well aware of? No progress for the better, whatsoever, made in our communities and lives. If the speech isn't simple and clear, the strategies won't be simple and clear. If the strategies aren't simple and clear, positive results will not materialise. Let's consider an excerpt from what would be a typical UK Consolidist Societician's speech:

"I'm in the beautifully regenerated city of Manchester today, so I thought I'd take a few minutes to talk about the imminent projects we have planned to ensure British people in the community have access to good quality healthcare. The football matches at the 2 big clubs of the city, you know who they are, generated £10 million of funds during the month of April this year. The funds were used straight away to employ Engineers and Architects who commenced design work on two new GP Surgeries, one on Mosley Street and one on King Street. The plans are available on the Manchester City Council's website if you'd like to take a look. Construction, by a local construction company, will commence 1 week from today. Construction shall take 9 months to complete, after which time there will be 24 more doctors and 12 more medical staff available to you, ensuring any health worries you may have are quickly seen to. Thanks to not allowing 'Catatonic Currency' to exist in our country, we are able to create jobs and improve your healthcare system at the same time. Consolidism is working for you".

'Catatonic Currency' and how the £10 million was generated will be explained in later chapters. But does that sound more like the speech you'd like to hear from the people who are running your country? That's a speech which is moving us towards a functioning and prosperous society.

Here's an example of an actual Politician's speech, when in September 2011, a new Metropolitan Police Commissioner was appointed in the UK. Right on call, the typically vague Politician's speeches followed. To quote the then Home Secretary, Theresa May, "The Government's reforms are transforming the Police in this country and Bernard Hogan-Howe has the skills and experience needed to ensure the nation's biggest force is at the forefront of this change". Vague drivel? Here's what a Consolidist Societician's speech would sound like:

"We welcome Bernard Hogan-Howe into his new position. Due to the £60 million raised from your money that 'you' spent at Sainsbury's Supermarkets in London in the first 3 months of 2010, we were able to train 2,000 extra Police officers. They'll be on the beat from this Monday onward. Bernard Hogan-Howe will no doubt get the best out of these newly employed officers. We thank him and them especially for the brave work they carry out, protecting us and keeping our streets safe. The training of these new officers cost £10 million. The remaining £50 million, along with other funds we have at our disposal due to the avoidance of "Catatonic Currency", will be used to boost the salaries of all our Police officers significantly. Under the Politicians, a Police officer would have had a starting salary of £26,109. Under a Consolidist Government, our officers will have starting salaries of £101,059. We believe it is these people who we should be rewarding in our society, not Popstars and Basketball Players. Similar increases in Police numbers are being implemented across the country. Please check your local council's website for detailed information on the increases in your area, or visit your local community centre where a member of staff will tell you everything you need to know. We welcome any suggestions you may have for improvement, and have funds available to make your good ideas become a reality. Check your Council's Website for Contact Details or call in to the Town Hall to submit your suggestions." Does that sound better than Theresa May's balderdash? How the £60 million was raised will be discussed in future chapters.

Would you agree with some of the hypotheses put forward in this chapter? Or do you think Politicians are honest, forthright people with integrity and great moral fibre? Do you think Politicians are people who always make decisions based on 'Common Sense'? People who make decisions with your well-being at the forefront of their minds? For their actions, should we embrace them, or consign Politicians and Politics to the history books, starting afresh with Socieiticians & Societies? If you think we should, the Consolidist Party would like to throw its hat into ring.

Let's just end this diatribe of the creatures we've labelled Politicians by analysing one last time, their inanely illogical minds. Let's digest one last face crumplingly bitter pill that they're imminently intending to ram down our gullets, before we move on and explain how Consoldism can greatly improve your lives. In an effort to grow the UK economy by a few hundred million pounds a year, the creatures in charge of running the UK are proposing a possible elevation of the speed limit on Motorways from 70mph to 80mph. The then Secretary of State for Transport, the 'Right Honourable' Philip Hammond has appeared on television touting this proposal and explaining how he and his Government buddies believe it's a delightful sticky bun of a policy, which the people of the UK couldn't possibly disagree with. As a finishing topping to the sticky bun, a generous hoik of phlegm, he advises that the raising of the speed limit will result in more deaths on Britain's roads.

Without another word being written or spoken, is this 'Common Sense'? Taking it further though, having been catapulted inexorably towards a riposte when a Politician puts forth such a preposterous proposition. He's got no problem with the speed limit being raised because the odds of him or any of his family dying as a result are long indeed. Somebody will die though. Somebody's loved one will perish as a result of his sticky bun policy, if it's implemented. To him and his spluttering miscreants of colleagues, it may be a lovely sticky bun, but to the people who die or have loved ones die, it's ridiculously insulting. It's just so typical of the blithering idiot that is the Politician. Not only is it a ridiculous policy in itself, but it wastes time that could be spent talking about or implementing sensible policies. Perhaps the raised speed limit will never come into effect, but still they've wasted part of your life talking about this absurd proposal.

Here's a paragraph detailing Consolidism's proposals for improving the UK Economy. Bring your entire armed forces home from the deserts of the Middle East. Use the billions of pounds saved to invest in the UK becoming the world's leading manufacturer of Renewable Energy Technologies. First and absolutely foremost, this would avert the tragedy of our innocent soldiers dying when clearly there's no need for them to be. Secondly, the investment of 'your' money will create tens of thousands of jobs. Adopting this strategy, instead of raising the speed limit, as proposed by the Politicians, will eliminate the possibility of more of your family members dying on Britain's roads. Development of Renewable Energy Technologies will reduce Carbon Dioxide Emissions of the UK, thus reducing the negative effect on Mother Earth. The UK itself could make use of the renewable energy technologies, sold cheaper to its own people. This will result in a reduction of every household's energy bills and more money in more people's pockets. Pockets which already have more money in them due to more people working in the Renewable Energy Technology Factories and Workshops. More money in people's pockets, means more money spent and a stimulated economy. Does that sound a better strategy than raising the speed limit? Perhaps you might suggest that the UK won't be safe if they pull their troops out of the Middle East? If we do this, it will allow terrorists to recruit, train and plan attacks there? Read on, the chapters "Terrorism" and "Defence" will set your mind at ease.

Is Consolidism already sounding infinitely better than your current system? Can anything be worse than allowing the Politicians to continue their degradation of your lives?

The current systems, implemented by Politicians, pander to the Lazy, Dishonest, Foreign Persons and especially the Mega-rich 1% as you're all correctly identifying in the protests and demonstrations currently sweeping the world. Why do the Politicians continue to pander to the Mega-rich? It's because many of them are in the pockets of the Mega-rich. They're becoming rich with the systems the way they are. So would they really want to change them? We've all seen for ourselves the scandalous stories which surface over the years about Corrupt Politicians. That's undoubtedly a drop in the ocean. If we as a people could know 'absolutely everything' that goes on in the Politician's Dens, it would physically nauseate us. The amount of decisions and policies formed, with self-gain the catalyst? It would make our eyes water. All the while they leave us, the 99%, to continue the uphill slog we have no choice but to call life. As millionaires and billionaires sit on fortunes. Fortunes which came from the pockets of the 99%, You. All the while, the Politicians see fit to cut your Public Services to try and claw back the deficit. If you in your home were heavily in debt, but a family member had funds to alleviate the situation, would you all think it sensible to use that money? Would your family member probably be willing to use the money to improve your lives?

Consolidism and its Societicians will put You the 99% first. Being intimidated by no challenge, person or unwritten rule. By any means necessary, without any hesitation, it will achieve its goal. To promptly improve your lives. The goal, and path to it, should be as easily identifiable and simply laid out as that. With Consolidism it is.

CHAPTER 2

The Current State of Human Consciousness

With Politicians discontinued & extinct, the next obstacle to surmount is our collective consciousness as a Civilisation. The way in which we view and form the world around us. As a race, as human beings, where is our attention focused in our daily lives? Do we spend our time thinking about and dealing with issues which are important to us and others around us, like helping the sick and old, or do we focus our attentions on issues which are not even in the slightest important, like glossy magazines and their stories about 'famous' people's haircuts?

This is the next step on the path towards creating countries in which we can live, not just exist. We've already identified that we have to:

- Reject Politics & Politicians.
- Adopt 'Common Sense'.
- Be entirely open and honest about the world around us. Identifying and discussing any problems that we feel are negatively affecting our societies. Absolutely whatever they may be. Calling them right down the line and not creasing to PC or PHR.

A Consolidist Government would fiercely protect genuine Human Rights, but, they have to matter, in the vast majority of cases to its own citizens, and be worth the outlay of time, money & effort. There are instances where we should protect the human rights of citizens of other countries, though the execution of this protection should be conducted only in a certain fashion. This will be discussed in the chapter 'Defence'. Was the 'Bed & Breakfast' episode a case of "Phony Human Rights"? A complete waste of everybody's time? What do you really think? Being 100% honest. Saying what you're thinking in your mind. Answering without worrying about how society would view you. Without being put upon by your current society's farcical unwritten laws. Without worrying one ounce of what people will think about you if you are of a certain 'Mental' or 'Verbal' opinion.

Readjusting our consciousness will drive us, The 99%, forward on our quest to obtain a significantly betters lives. One where we're held aloft as most important by our Consolidist Government, not foreign persons. Who comes first in your lives, your children or the children from the family across the street? It will be a life where, when people grow old, society's millions will be spent on making sure everybody receives a tremendous quality of care, instead of having some of those millions sitting in the bank account of a talentless person who contributes nothing to society. Perhaps somebody who chases a leather blob around a grassy pitch for a 'living'. In society nowadays, this is known as "Soccer".

This next step involves what will at first seem to be a massive fundamental change of consciousness. Although it is actually just 'Common Sense', if we view things from a different angle. An angle we should all have been viewing the world from all along. If we are to live, we have no choice but to change how we view the world, how we view our countries. This will in turn effect and affect how we run our countries. The simple small act of viewing things with 'Common Sense' would have dramatic effect on improving all our lives. As a Consolidist Government, as people of our countries of the world, we all have a responsibility to focus our attention on what matters, and to reward those who concern themselves with what matters. We should all ensure that those within our societies who deserve the recognition and financial reward, receive it. A Consolidist believes that those people who contribute most to society, should be rewarded the most, and those who contribute the least, are rewarded the least. Would you say that is an incredibly simple, non-convoluted proposition? Additionally, would you agree with it? What you get out of society & life should be proportional to what you put in. Is that a maxim instilled within you by your hardworking parents? Is it one you raise your children by?

Consolidism believes we should strive to live clean, healthy, respectable, respectful lives that are considerate and highly conscious of everything which is genuinely important within our interactive societies. We all have a duty towards each other to do this. A duty towards our families, friends, neighbours, community, fellow citizens and world community, in that order of importance. If we don't live by these rules, it has negative effects, on not only ourselves, but those around us. If people want to live lives whereby they have negative effects on themselves, that's their right in a free society, but, we cannot allow the negativity of some to affect others. It is 'Common Sense' to suggest that this is unfair. Would you agree? Do you think it's important to live respectful, considerate lives? Do you think there are millions out there who don't? Do you think it's fair that other people's irresponsible ways are detrimentally affecting the lives of you and your children? A Consolidist Government doesn't think that's fair at all, and would right the wrongs.

Let's analyse the position at which human consciousness currently finds itself. To do this effectively, it's going to require that you analyse those around you, yes, but also yourself, from the 'Outer Body Angle'. Literally, close your eyes and look back on yourself as you sit reading this book. Can you see yourself sitting in the room? This is how you will have to analyse your life, your goals, your hobbies and where your attention is focused, as this chapter progresses. You'll need to constantly disect and assess the discussions which are to be had. How do you currently view the world's 'issues'? What's your involvement in them being a reality in today's world? How 'should' you be viewing the issues? How do you view the issues after looking from the 'Outer Body Angle'? It is a certainty that some of the craziness in the world around you that's about to be described, is aided by us and the alignment of our consciousness'. Will this statement turn out to be correct?

It would be ideal if you, we, could all completely realign our minds, but in reality, it probably won't happen. What we can do though, is partially realign, then have a Government that ensures, even with the remaining misalignment, the ensuing negative effects are kept to a minimum. How this can be done will be discussed in this and following chapters. Viewing from the 'Outer Body Angle' is one thing, but, the wavelength Consolidism proposes we should all be thinking on, will at first seem bizarre in the extreme, but that's because our minds have been literally programmed to think in a certain way, due to what we see around us in our every day societies. In reality, the proposed wavelength is 'Common Sense', and the existing wavelength is bizarre in the extreme. On large, the way the world works just seems normal to us, when in fact what's happening immediately around you every day is total insanity. As you're about to learn, human consciousness is a long way down the wrong path. Though it wouldn't take long to recover our bearings and point most of our minds in the mostly the right direction.

Close your eyes and picture yourself sitting in your home watching television. All night long. Sitting, staring, zombie-like into this electronic device. Is this normal behaviour? Yes? No? Would your time not be better doing volunteer charity work? Why as humans have we not got this inherent desire to help others? It's because of the way our societies have been allowed to form by the Politicians. It's normal to play video games all night, and abnormal to seek out those in need in your community. If you had been brought up in a society which was the opposite, you'd think the opposite. From a neutral point of view, which is the best? A desire to play video games or a desire to help your fellow humans? It's not that a Consolidist Government would ban video games. It would just reward greatly those who were active in the betterment of their community. Video Games.

Mobile Devices of all shapes, sizes and types. They weren't around 50 years ago. Did the world function without them? Absolutely. In a far better state than it's functioning right now. We should be developing technologies to make our lives better. The majority of what's developed is not only not needed, it's taking us backward as we waste our time using it. There are people out there spending thousands of hours developing Apps that are totally pointless. Time, money, energy and effort totally wasted. We all spend our days with our heads in our Mobile Phones. Texting and Tweeting. What good is it doing? Does it advance us as beings? Is it time well spent? All these 'technologies' we are almost forced to create because we have to provide jobs for an ever-growing population. The way we're currently living our lives is totally flawed. Population numbers is a serious issue and will be discussed in the chapter 'Consolidation'.

Try this one. From the "Outer Body Angle", imagine yourself and your family at a soccer match on a frosty January night. You're in the stands of a giant, brightly lit stadium, along with 50,000 of your fellow citizens. Twenty miles above you, an alien spacecraft and its crew have just stumbled upon planet Earth. They are about to witness human beings and their behaviour for the first time. With their technologically futuristic equipment, they're able to zoom in for close up shots, see through roofs and walls, and access our computer networks, instantly acquiring any information they desire.

So, after travelling millions of light years across the incomprehensibly vast molecular ocean that is the universe. Upon arriving at planet Earth, the home of the Human Being, Woman and Mankind, what's the first thing these galactic mariners see? Fifty thousand human beings focusing all their attention, and some of their money, towards 22 grown men chasing a leather blob around a grassy pitch. Four of those human beings are you and your family. Screaming, shouting and hollering as the blob is propelled around the grass with the human men's feet. What do you think would be going through the alien's minds? From the 'Outer Body Angle', what do you now think about it? When there's so much suffering in the world, why would anybody be so interested in a ball game? Is that a question you're asking yourself? If it is, you've tuned into the wavelength. It's that easy.

Have you ever heard the saying, "You get out of a situation, what you put in"? If we're all focusing time and money on ball games, how can we expect the issues that are genuinely important to us, to improve. The issues that we're all up in arms about across the world right now. The Economy, Healthcare, Poverty, Public Services. We can't is the answer. It's plain to see. Little time and money invested, means no improvement, or often backward movement and subsequent suffering. We should all set time aside to enjoy ourselves, but, we should also all engage in some 'charitable' activities. This is in an ideal world. Which we don't live in. Yet. Nobody should stop people from going to watch ball games, if that's what they really want to do with their time, but, a Government should ensure that billions upon billions of 'Catatonic Currency' doesn't occur because of these ball games. And a Consolidist Government would ensure that.

Not 500 yards away from the stadium, huddled beneath a bridge, the aliens see 5 homeless people. Dirt-caked clothes, blankets, and cardboard are all they have to shield themselves from the biting wind. They're not in that position because they're substance addicts, or are bad people in any way. They find themselves in trouble because their parents weren't responsible people, living clean, respectable lives. This resulted in them being poorly raised within dysfunctional homes, not being able to gain a good education and subsequently get a good job. As a result of this, they became mentally unstable, and down the line, now find themselves homeless and dependent on the State for benefits.

A quarter mile from the homeless people, the aliens see a middle aged woman laying on a stretcher in the Accident & Emergency department of the local hospital. In agony with her broken ankle, she waits far longer to be seen than she should. Why? There are too many people to be attended to, and not enough Doctors and Nurses. A crippling imbalance in the country's Public Services. Population? Just down the road, an 80 year old woman sits shivering under a blanket in her house. With her paltry pension, she can't afford the cost of switching the heating on. Do the Politicians care? With all the billions of 'Catatonic Currency' in society that they could use to help this woman and others, they leave them to suffer, and in some cases die. There's that term again, 'Catatonic Currency'.

Across the road from the old lady, what the humans call a bank. The aliens tap into the computer system and discover that the man on the grassy pitch wearing the number 10 shiny green jersey, who's just used his head to deposit the leather blob into a net, has £20 million pounds in his bank account. The aliens see you and your family going wild due to the leather blob having come into contact with the net. Viewing from the "Outer Body Angle", is this right? Truthfully, is it? What would you say is running through the alien's minds right now? Perhaps they have the following questions?

Why when there is so much suffering and need in their world, are these human beings concentrating their attentions on a ball game? Why do these human beings pour adulation and financial reward upon somebody who plays a virtually skill-less ball game, when there are doctors and nurses in a building close by saving lives and healing people? Should it not be the doctors and nurses who are the people within the human's society who deserve attention and adulation? Should the doctors and nurses not receive significantly more financial reward than people who play ball games for a living? Why does a soccer player, who contributes nothing of any worth towards society, have so much money sitting in their bank account? Would it not be a good idea to use this money to help the people who are suffering in their society? Why would 50,000 people pay so much money to watch a talentless ball game, when they know the majority of the money they're handing over will die. 'Dead Money'. 'Catatonic Currency'. Wallowing in the soccer player's bank account forevermore? When the soccer player gets old and dies, the money will be handed down to the next generation, but still, most of it will remain in a bank account, not ever seeing the light of day again, as the same thing happens when it's passed down to the next generation after that. This money could be used to create a functioning, prosperous, fair, safe, compassionate society.

A Consolidist Government wouldn't ban soccer, or any sport. What it would make sure of though, is that sportspeople receive what they deserve in terms of remuneration. There is not a soccer player, manager or anybody involved in the game that deserves to earn more than, in the UK where soccer is bizarrely so popular, £300 per week plus their expenses. Why? Soccer, Baseball, Sport, contributes virtually nothing towards society. The only real good Sport does, is encourage some children, women and men to live clean, healthy lives. Does that warrant paying a soccer player £150,000 per week in the UK? Exactly. The people involved in soccer and sport should be rewarded according to what positive effect they have on the issues that matter in society. The real salient issues, not what's currently believed to be important. Real issues like the homeless and tackling dysfunctional families, such that the next generation doesn't turn out to be a drain on society. Issues like taking care of the sick, injured and old. Don't be fooled by people who say that sports like soccer do alot for charity. The people who say this are the people who benefit financially from soccer. Obviously, they want to protect their finances. In reality, some of the money generated from soccer goes to charity, but the vast majority of it, that comes from your pockets, goes directly into the players, managers & agents bank accounts and sits there, dead, out of society forever. There are those who would argue that limiting soccer players' salaries would result in the 'best' players and associated revenues going to other countries. But where does this billions of revenue go, when it is coming into your country? A miniscule percentage goes to stadium stewards, hospitality employees, etc. The vast vast majority sits dead in players', agents' and managers' bank accounts. Conclusion? The 'best' players can go abroad. Soccer will survive just fine without them. The purpose of soccer should be to give everybody involved, a 'good, sensible' wage to live on. It doesn't matter that the extra billions aren't coming into a country. They'd be rendered dead upon arrival anyway.

If we want to prosper, this cannot be allowed to happen. With a Consolidist Government, if £1 million pounds is made from the ticket sales of a soccer game, or any 'game', the vast majority of this would be re-invested into society, Your society. Bettering the lives of You and Your children. This way everybody wins. Taking the UK as an example, the soccer "star" would receive a few hundred pounds a week as a wage. They get to play in fantastic stadiums, adored by thousands, if society still chooses to adore them. You get to watch your soccer game for entertainment, if of course you so choose to do so, instead perhaps looking around you in the community to see if there's an old & lonely person you could spend the evening with.

Using the "Outer Body Angle" would this be a better way for a human being to spend their time? Can you sense the wavelength? Do you think this use of time would make more sense to the aliens? Exactly. With a Consolidist Government, the nearly £1 million pounds would be used to provide more Carers in our Care Homes for the Elderly. This will have two effects. Creating jobs in what's currently, thanks to the Politicians, a lacklustre job's market, and, it would provide a better quality of life for the elderly among us. The soccer player won't mind receiving the few hundred pounds per week wages instead of £150,000. They'll have no choice but to admit it was ridiculous they were receiving that kind of money for having no use to society. That's if they call it down the line, as it is. Besides, it's all about the club they're playing for. That's what really matters, isn't it. This is evident when you see them kissing their badges after the leather blob has been deposited in the net. Or would they kiss any badge as long as they were receiving the enormous amount of money? Is it all an act? What do you think? Exactly.

The next day, the aliens visit another city on what's unfolding as a topsy-turvy planet. Here they witness a young girl being physically abused by her Alcoholic father. More Social Workers, better monitoring systems, better advertisement of helplines, could all possibly help this poor little girl. If society had the money and a manageable amount of people in terms of population numbers, see the chapter entitled 'Consolidation', it could tackle dysfunctional families and there's a good chance the father wouldn't be a violent Alcoholic. Just outside the girl's 'home', a gang of unruly youths run rampant, smashing windows, vandalising cars, terrorising the local community. The Police are called, but take too long to arrive, and the youths are long gone. They'll be running free again tomorrow, stealing cars and damaging people's property. They won't be stopped. The Government can't afford to put enough Police on the streets. Why? Because they're Politicians who continue to make shocking after poor decision.

Five miles away, 15,000 people are watching grown men hit little white balls around a huge expanse of grass. Their aim is to sink the balls into little holes in the ground. At this point in time on planet Earth, this game is known as 'Golf'. The man who's just achieved the depositing the ball in a hole, gets a rapturous round of applause. Why would anybody cheer a ball being deposited in a hole in the ground the aliens puzzle? What kind of creature is this human being? How much money has the man got in his bank account? The aliens investigate......$100 Million. Would this make sense to someone viewing our world with a fresh mind? Are these the people we should be pouring adulation upon in our societies? Or should we be exalting Doctors, Nurses, Soldiers, Police officers? Exactly. If it wouldn't make sense to someone viewing our world with a fresh, untainted mind, then it shouldn't make sense to us. And it doesn't, but we just haven't realised it, due to our minds having been programmed to think this setup is normal.

Being absolutely honest, now that it's been put a certain way, do you think the above discussed aspects of how our societies function are sensible and normal? Exactly. You're not alone though. A Consolidist doesn't either, and a Consolidist Government would ensure those who matter in society are recognised, rewarded and praised for what they do for us.

It takes money to right the wrongs in our society. It will take the 'Catatonic Currency' that's currently sitting in the bank accounts of those who contribute very little, if anything, towards our societies. It will take the 'surplus to requirements' billions that lay dormant in the bank accounts of the Mega-rich Businesspersons. A Consolidist Government would ensure the money, that comes continually from your pockets, is used continually, to make your lives better.

So having looked back at yourself, analysing all aspects of your life, not just perhaps a soccer match, do you think your time, attention and money is focused in the right direction? Would it make sense to have your money used to improve the lives of you, your children and your fellow citizens, instead of it dying a death in some sportsperson's bank account? How on earth did our consciousnesses get to the point where we idolise and focus our attention on people who play sports? The alien travellers have observed many different creatures on many different planets, but would have no hesitation in awarding us earthlings a trophy engraved "Embarrassment of the Universe". And you'd have to admit, they're right to do so. Not only are us humans stupid enough to pay all that money to watch a ball game when we know we're committing our money to death and our families to a sub-standard life. The Governments who run our countries haven't even got the sense to step in and say "Hold on, this is ridiculous, we can't allow 'Catatonic Currency' to be a reality, especially with regards to those who are useless to society. If we do, we'll never be able to rectify the problems in our societies".

Why would anybody want to watch a ball game, when there's so much work to be done out there ensuring people don't suffer in their lives? If it's not you suffering, you don't really care? Is that it? That's where human consciousness is. If you think this proposed new way of looking at things is unorthodox, that just reinforces the point of where our consciousness is. It's Broken. That's the best word for it. Broken. You can only see it when you view it from a different angle. Only then can you think on the different wavelength. If viewed from the normal angle, it looks normal. This may seem like a scathing attack on us and our minds, but it has to be said. A Consolidist believes in never shying away from issues which are negatively affecting its citizens. If we avoid and dodge issues, how can they ever be put right? If problem issues are not put right, they will always blight your lives.

Let's consider another scenario allowed by the Politicians. A Level One Corporal in the British Army earns £26,404 per year. This is a human being, woman or man, who's willing to fight and possibly die to defend their fellow citizens. On the other hand there's a certain kind of 'profession' in the UK, and the world, in which a person can earn as much as perhaps £10 million per year. So what could possibly be deserving of that much more money than being willing to give your life to protect your country? Being willing to spend 6 months on a Tour of Duty, away from your loved ones, and perhaps never return? What can it possibly be? The person who earns perhaps £10 million per year, does so by walking, sitting or standing in front of a camera whilst someone takes pictures of, or films them. That's not all though. Whilst doing the walking, sitting, standing, they're, wait for it……wearing clothes. Do you think that is deserving of millions of pounds? You may have heard of these 'professionals'. Our societies of today call them 'Models'. Can you hear yourself reading that last paragraph in your head? 'How on Earth' can we allow this insanity to be a reality?

You have the power to change it. How? Should we boycott everything that results in models making millions for contributing nothing towards society? Not really. It's good for an economy when people choose to buy things. There may be a few who wish to boycott in protest. That's their choice. There are many though, who will want to continue to indulge in the purchasing of luxury items. That too, is their choice. Consolidism believes in allowing its citizens the freedom to do whatever they want, as long as it doesn't negatively affect others. Therefore, people should be and would be allowed to buy luxury items. The problem is that our Governments are currently made up of a gaggle of idiotic Politicians who won't do anything about the highly damaging 'Catatonic Currency' that occurs following the billions spent on fashion and luxury. A Consolidist Government would do something about it. Guaranteed. And here's what it would do.

We have to inject 'Common Sense' into the situation. In an ideal world, you shouldn't spend too much money on luxury items, because as has been mentioned, there are many areas in society where you could spend or donate some of your money to help other people, after ensuring your own are well provided for of course. It should be noted that in a Consolidist Society, with all the measures discussed in this book having been taken, there would be very few people suffering and needing your monetary charity. Your money is yours though, and you can do what you want with it. A Consolidist Government then needs to ensure that the billions generated in e.g. the fashion industry doesn't sit dead in the bank accounts of fashion models, their managers, agents etc. We should give them all a wage that is proportional to what they put into society, i.e. not alot, perhaps $450 dollars per week, except for the companies owners, whose permitted fortune would be proportional to the amount of jobs they create. Following this, the rest would be invested back into society, precisely where it rang through the checkout.

Where does the billions of currency generated in the fashion industry come from? Exactly. Your pockets. Just as the million pounds in soccer game ticket sales came from your pockets. The pockets of the proletariat. All the fortunes laying dead in the bank accounts of the rich and famous all over the world today, came from your pockets. Will you ever see any good from that money again? Never? Unless. Together we implement Consolidism. When analysed, the difference in contribution to society between a soldier and a model is staggering, but not as staggering as the current difference in financial reward. A Consolidist Government would not let this happen.

The way in which Politicians are running our countries results in a sportsperson's Ferrari being paid for by the misery of the masses. The fortunes of all sportswomen and men comes directly from your pockets. Yes, granted some of it is re-circulated back into society when they buy their sports cars or mansions. Though most of their fortune sits dead in the bank and will never be used again. If this is allowed to continue, is it ever going to result in the creation of a fair, functioning, safe, prosperous society for you to live in? Exactly. This money. Your money. It has to be kept circulating in society. Creating jobs, regenerating our communities, providing great healthcare for you and your family. Funding deserving charities, which help those who are right now, regarded as the ordinary, average everyday nobodies. With a Consolidist Government, Your Government, 'You' would constantly get a say on 'Your' everyday issues through Non-Stop Referendums.

It won't just be a case of one vote for a Party Leader Candidate in an Election, then once in power, the Candidate or a couple of hundred Politicians do whatever tickles their fancy, or the fancy of the Mega-rich and currently influential, should we say. Why do so few, who are so detached from the reality of our lives, make such important decisions on our behalf. Billions of us. That's not Fair and it certainly isn't Democracy. With Consolidism, the 'average' people become the stars and focus within our societies. You will seize the influence and power.

We live in a world where a person can make millions from running competitively 100m down a track perhaps 15 times a year. Can you hear that as you read it? Is that really deserving of all that money? Should we accept this within our societies? Looking from the different angle, thinking on the different wavelength, it's total insanity. A person runs, puts one foot in front of the other very fast, and receives millions for doing it? They don't do anything skilful or talented before they start or finish running. They just run from A to B.

These kinds of people also get paid millions to endorse expensive sports clothing. Are the prices charged justified? A sweater with a 'tick' on it costs perhaps ten times that of one without a tick. Only the human mind could both propose, 'and', most importantly, 'dumbly', accept such ludicrousy. Similarly, we offer praise to a soccer player for "making a run off the ball". We are a creature who praises a person for running, placing one foot in front of another? These 'athletes' earn millions, whilst a person who teaches our children to read and write, might expect to receive $40,000 per year for their sacrifice. Is this Common Sense? When compared to an athlete, it's the teacher who's putting by far the greatest good into society, so it is they who should receive the praise and greater financial reward. If we don't allow 'Catatonic Currency' within our societies, we can use this money to raise the earnings of the important people in our society. That's You. If you're a hospital porter, a Civil Servant, a School Chef or a Librarian, you are vastly more important to society than an athlete, Popstar or Model, so you shall receive more praise and money. It's such a simple concept. One that makes absolute 'Common Sense'. Would you agree?

Consolidism would still allow all sports and entertainment, because it does create jobs, and also brings enjoyment into people's lives. They just need to be regulated, ensuring all your money isn't sucked out of your society. If we keep it alive, the money can be used to ensure that if your child becomes ill, they receive the best possible immediate healthcare money can buy. It's okay for the sportsperson's children, they can afford the private healthcare. They've got millions in the bank. But what about You and Your children? You who's more important to everybody around you in the job you do. You make the world tick. Not only would the money raised from sports events and industries such as fashion be used to improve your lives through greater investment in your public services and the creation of jobs. It would mean that you don't have to pay as much tax. As it is now, the Politicians tax you greatly and cut your public services, whilst allowing billions to lay dead in bank accounts. Is this Common Sense? Is this fair? With 'Catatonic Currency' a thing of the past, a Consolidist Government would lower your taxes, and, lower the cost of luxury and everyday living items.

It's important, especially due to the similarity in name, that Consolidism is not linked to Communism. Consolidism doesn't believe in a classless society where everybody earns the same wage. Consolidism believes you should be rewarded according to your contribution. For example, a garbage collector, who contributes to providing a clean environment in which you and your family can live, will earn more than a soccer player. Why? Because they are worth more to all of us. Communism, to a certain extent, does make sense, as you'll possibly now be appreciating. There are certain words which have been stigmatised within our societies, Communism being one. The Media and Politicians of the West have drummed into our minds that "Communism is Evil". Don't be fooled by them. Judge it for yourself, keeping in mind the imbalance of earnings for the worthless and worthwhile which have just been described.

A soldier in the UK earns just over £26,000 per year. A soccer player earns millions a year. Does Capitalism make sense? Is it really working for you as the Politicians try to tell you it is? Capitalism works for the rich, famous, and the Politicians themselves. To the hardworking proletariat, it's like a poison. If we are to prosper, we have to limit people's wealth. If you're an Architect, you can amass £500,000 through working hard all your life. There's nothing at all wrong with that. What we can't have is people being Architects, dabbling in property with their savings and ending up with £10 million in the bank. Nobody could ever 'actually need' £10 million pounds in their lives. We can't sustain our societies or planet when we allow people's consumer habits to reach those levels. There has to be a cut off point which ensures the money stays circulating within our societies.

If you're an entrepreneurial businesswoman or man who creates jobs within society, you will be allowed to amass more money for yourself. The more jobs you create, the more money you will be allowed to have. Millions. That's fine. But, again, there has to be a cut off point. You can't have £25 million pounds sitting in the bank forevermore. It makes no sense and is not conducive to a world that works. If you're a businessperson who's created thousands of jobs, would you really need more than £5 million to live on? Would having £5 million in the bank instead of £25 million be such a hard life? What do you think? Exactly. This limiting of fortunes will be set at a figure that ensures every person in a country lives as good a quality life as is possible.

The Politicians are lying when they try to tell us the reason our countries are in such great debt is largely because of the "Banking Crisis". The "Banking Crisis" was 'possibly' a minor contributor to the world's current economic woes. The second biggest contributor is 'Catatonic Currency'. If the "Banking Crisis" is real, and Politicians haven't fabricated the whole story to cover their mistakes, they were still incompetent in not regulating and monitoring the banks' activities. Yes their pure incompetence was a contributory factor to this, but, if countries adopted Consolidism and its most important policy, it would be so much easier to regulate and monitor such important institutions within our societies. Even the Politicians could have possibly averted the catastrophe. This most important policy will be discussed in the Chapter entitled 'Consolidation'. Let's suppose that the "Banking Crisis" is real. It is reported to have come about by banks making risky investments in an attempt to make more money.

If wealth was capped, as Consolidism proposes, would the "Banking Crisis" have happened? Exactly. There would be no point in banks making risky investments because the people who would benefit from them, should they be successful, are only allowed to be in possession of so much wealth. There would be no use in a company moving its operations abroad to maximise profit, because shareholders are only allowed to accumulate so much money. We've all seen how devastating it is for average people and their families, when rich business owners shutdown their livelihoods and move operations across to the other side of the world just to make 'more' profit. That's what it usually is, 'more' profit. Not just to keep a business afloat. Right now, with the Politicians in charge, the average person has no say or power in these matters.

With Consolidism, they would be the ones who call the shots. If the key policy of Consolidism, 'Consolidation', is implemented, rich or megarich business owners would also not have the need to make more profit in order to grow their business. Growth, as will be discussed in the chapter 'Consolidation', is a flawed strategy, and the absolute key reason why our children and grandchildren will live their sub-standard lives, buried beneath the deepest debts. Business owners will make handsome wage, proportional to the amount of jobs they create. They will also take enough money to pay for the upkeep of their existing business interests, thus ensuring 'average' people have the means to sustain themselves. Means that won't be taken away to make a rich person richer. Any 'surplus' profits will be returned to the 'People's Pot', thus ensuring their taxes are kept low and their public services are the best they possibly can be, as they deserve.

Businesses must only be allowed to grow, if population

numbers require it, or if employees are tempted away from competitors by improved salaries and/or benefits. And business growth due to growth of population will not be often, or involve any great numbers. 'Consolidation' is the key, as the 99% will let the Politicians be in no doubt about, when they get their say in Elections and Referendums asking them what they think. A refreshing change from the Politicians doing whatever they want.

So, it has been identified that we're rewarding and exalting entirely the wrong people in our societies. The obvious question. The obvious next discussion to have is "Why?". There's a simple answer to that. We are a being that is mesmerised by the electronic boxes that sit in our homes. We call them televisions here on Planet Earth. Have you ever heard someone say "It's true, I saw it on TV"? You've probably said it yourself. Just because something appears on the electronic box in your home, it becomes gospel, the undeniable, unquestionable truth. If the electronic box started to tell the world that bread was the cause of all cancer, nobody would ever eat bread again.

Not only that, for some reason, we think things that appear on the television are cool and amazing, when really there's nothing special about them. It's simply because they're on the television, being viewed by millions of others that somehow makes us think they have some kind of 'Wow' factor. Would your child desire a toy they saw in your 'local' toy shop, or would they not take a second look at it over a toy that appeared on the electronic box, flashing lights, music, and all the 'hypnotising' strategies companies use to make us part with our money? Since the birth of the television, we have made hundreds of thousands of talentless people rich and famous due to them, simply being on the television. The result has been billions upon billions sucked out of the world's economy, and laying dead in their bank accounts.

What is it about something appearing on the television that makes it so alluring? From the different angle, think about the statement that makes on the kind of beings we are. Of how are lives are easily controlled and manipulated by the television and media. Of how 'dumbed' the human being on planet Earth in the 21st Century really is. As with the electronic box, the same can be said when we see something printed in a newspaper. It's considered unequivocally correct if it's printed in a publication that many will read. When in reality, it's just the opinion or version of events from another human being or group of human beings. Either an opinion or a lie. If it's a lie, it's probably come from a Politician or a rich person who's looking to dumb you down and hold onto to their power and fortune.

On planet Earth in the 21st Century, the world works in such a way that you don't need to have any talents that society will benefit from to be highly regarded. All you need to do is appear on the electronic box in people's homes across the world. If you do that, you can become rich and famous. That's all it takes. What does that say about us as beings? What would the galactic mariners think about this? Exactly.

Take a certain person called Simon Cowell. He is absolutely talentless, with not a musical bone in his body, but, just because he appears on our electronic boxes, humans seem to think he's some kind of authority on music. He knows zilch about music. He's famous for speaking his mind, and being blunt and obnoxious toward people. Should we really allow people like him to amass wealth or should it go to the Police who put themselves in harm's way everyday so that we can be safe on the streets and in our homes? What is wrong with the people of this planet whereby we raise someone like Simon Cowell to celebrity status? Being obnoxious and honest is easy. What's hard is going to work every day, looking after people dying of cancer. What Simon Cowell does do constructively, to his bank balance, is identify people he can turn into stars in today's societies. People who he can dress up in shiny clothes, put make up on, and have them appear on the electronic box in your homes as they shout into microphones. When they appear on the electronic box shouting into a microphone, the public for some reason want to part with their money. These people who shout into microphones are currently known on planet Earth as Popstars. This money goes straight into the bank accounts of the Popstars and talentless people like Simon Cowell. Most of it will never be seen again. Does this make sense to you? Is shouting into a microphone really a talent? If you think it is, is it a talent that contributes toward communities and society? These people are stars for no other reason than the fact that they appear on television.

Think of your favourite 'Musician' or Popstar. If it just so happened they never made it onto the television, or radio, but instead you saw them performing on the street every day as you made your way to work, would you be so enamoured? Would you be so infatuated that you'd want their autograph and buy t-shirts displaying their names? No. Of course you wouldn't. Them appearing on television, performing in arenas and stadiums, wearing the music video costumes. This is what hypnotises you into being such a "huge fan".

When these Popstars are created by people like Simon Cowell, what's the real thought in the minds of the 'Music' industry executives? Is it to promote great Musicians? After watching television's music channels for a few minutes, it's easy to answer that question with a resounding "No". All it actually is, is a way to relieve you of your money and get rich. That is what it's all about. That is the goal. Behind the scenes in the music industry, the rich music label owners conduct meeting after meeting strategising about how they can extract the most money possible out of your lives and invest it into theirs. Why can't we all see this? Until we look at it from this different angle, it just seems normal for the 'music' industry to churn out empty, talentless money-makers, and for us to buy what they're trying to pass off as 'Their' 'Music'. One of the reasons we part with our money so easily and cheaply, making the talentless rich, is because of the very way Politicians run our countries. They've made the 'average' middle class person's life so sad and hard, that we'll part with our money in a desperate attempt to alleviate the boredom and pain. Take 'The Cheeky Girls' for example. These are "Musicians" that Simon Cowell feels passionately about the talents of. What do you think about the calibre of their 'Musicianship'? Exactly. It's a joke. They're a joke. They too, do not have a musical bone in their bodies. Is it right that they're in the 'Music' business? Is it right that they've made alot of money from the 'Music' they've made? It's all come from your pockets. They're created to take your money away from you and society. That's it. That's their only purpose.

This leads us on to the position 'Music' finds itself at in the year 2012. Think about the word, without just simply saying it. This is the problem with today's world. Our minds are not thinking for themselves. Their programmed to accept the insanity. Music, by definition, cannot be created without the playing of instruments. Not computer generated drumbeats, but human beings actually playing musical instruments. Nowadays, to be called a 'Musician', you don't even need to be able to play a musical instrument.

In the world today, people are turned into 'musicians' when a pretty teenage girl says "Daddy, I want to be a Popstar". Perhaps a 'star' is born via one of the many hollow, shallow singing competition television programmes. Or when a cute little boy with half a singing voice, grows a floppy fringe. Or maybe when a Soap Opera Star or Actress suddenly decides they want to be a Popstar. What happens in the latter scenario is actually that a music industry executive realises the Soap Opera Star, if transformed into a Popstar and aired on television, could make us put our hands in our pockets and part with our hard earned money. When you see this transformation happening, it alone serves as a perfect demonstration of how shallow and hollow the music business, and the world, really is. They come into the music business as a business decision. To make money. It's not because they've practised all their lives to develop their skills on a musical instrument and are able to write good songs. They put on some sparkly clothes, dance around, and the public swoons, "Here take my money. I saw you on television. You were amazing".

All a Popstar needs is half a singing voice. If they've got that, they can be rich and famous, if, the music industry executive manages to have them appear on the electronic box in your homes. There are millions of people out there who could be turned into Popstars. They just need to be in the right place at the right time, chosen and put on television. That too serves as a perfect indicator of how ridiculous the music business and society's acceptance of it is. Forget about actually playing musical instruments. As long as the make-up, the fashion, the dancing, the effects and the video are good, they'll be big stars. In the business nowadays, the element that gets the least consideration is the music, and that's the business they're supposed to be in. But why do people idolise these Popstars? It's all because they've appeared on the electronic box. What kind of being are we when we go giddy if we're standing next to another human being who has appeared on our electronic boxes alot? They may have no talent at all, but just because they've appeared on the electronic box, they're rich and famous and we're amazed by them.

To take it further, in nowadays 'Music', you don't even need half a singing voice to rob the millions of their money. What we currently call Rappers, bounce around on a video set like primates and 'mumble' into a microphone. Snoop Dog, Eminem, Jay Z, and many more. That's all it takes to separate the human being from their cash in the year 2012 on planet Earth. Not only 'Music', but all the arts, film & television for example, in the materialistically cheap world of 2012. Are they of a high quality? Comparing 'Gone with the Wind – 1939' to 'Maid in Manhattan – 2002', there's no other conclusion that can be drawn, other than the massive diminishment of quality. How would you compare the two? This entire book could be filled with a list comparing high quality, worthwhile classics from yesteryear, to artistically cheap, tawdry, contemporary efforts.

Music and Film especially have run their course as art forms. There's only so much that can be done with an art form before it starts to become repetitive and degraded in quality. Should the wannabe artists of today now be looking to create their own art forms? In the future of the planet, there will be other art forms. Just because music and film have been created, it doesn't mean they should or will be around forever. They are the art forms that belong to yesterday's generations. Should today's generation, and future generations, come up with their own instead of sullying the creative, worthwhile work of those who have gone before them? Why do the current crop of 'artistes' remake film after film after film from the days when filmmaking was still fresh and of a good quality? Is it because they don't have any good, bright, new ideas themselves? Do they not have good, bright, new ideas because everything has already been done, many times, with every idea having been completely exhausted?

Analyse the rich and famous yourselves. Right across the board, it's insane what people get paid a fortune for. Some are paid millions for driving a car around a track 70 times in a day, 20 times a year. This is known as 'Formula One', or any of the other variations of car racing. Is that where society's money should be going? Is it of use languishing in a Formula One 'Star's' bank account? We need to be pouring adulation and money in the direction of our soldiers and nurses, not people who dance and shout into microphones. We should be talking about the paramedics who save people's lives, not people who twang metal strings attached to a piece of wood, also known as guitarists. No doubt, there is talent involved in playing the guitar, but is it a talent that deserves millions as a reward?

At the moment, the world is backwards, upside-down, totally retarded in its operation and structure. Not only do we need to start identifying talent in this world, we need to identify talent that adds to the value of our communities and countries. This is the 'talent' that we should be rewarding. This is the definition of 'talent', not somebody strutting along a catwalk whilst wearing clothes.

***

Taking a closer look at the 50,000 people in the soccer stadium, what else do the aliens see? People knowingly ingesting substances that are bad for their health. Cigarettes, Alcohol, Burgers, Doughnuts. Do you know of any other creature on the planet that consumes substances that are bad for it? No, it's only humans. Do Ants have the desire to lay about getting drunk, or do they prefer to devote all their time to living purely for the good of their community and fellow Ants? Virtually everything about the way the world works right now, is resulting in dysfunctional humans and subsequently dysfunctional, broken and broke societies.

Consolidism wouldn't outlaw Beer, Cigarettes and Burgers, quite the contrary, as you will read in the 'Healthcare' chapter. What a Consolidist Government would do though is remind the population more of how bad these things are for them. In electronic box documentaries of jungle dwelling tribespeople, how many of them have you seen that are obese? None. Because they live, pure, clean, healthy lives, consuming minimal, natural foods. In developed countries, we've totally lost sight of how disgustingly gluttonous we are. At present, it seems so normal for electronic box advertisements to promote poisons for us to ingest. That's what Alcohol is. A pure poison.

We're living to eat, when we should be eating to live. Instead of adverts for poisonous liquids and artery hardening foods, should we not be broadcasting messages that identify the important issues in our societies and communities that require attention, such as sick people requiring organ donors or bullying helplines? Or perhaps health awareness messages showing what happens to a set of lungs if you smoke Cigarettes? If kids see these adverts at a young impressionable age, they'll be much more inclined to steer clear of cigarettes. Some may say that's too extreme, but unless we start taking some serious measures, nothing will ever change. We live in a world where we sell these things called cigarettes in shops, knowing how damaging they are to one's health. Then when somebody smokes all their life and becomes ill, we spend thousands of currency treating them. Who's paying for it? You are. There's no accountability or responsibility in the world whatsoever. A Consolidist Government wouldn't ban cigarettes, but it would make you pay for your healthcare if you start to need medical attention as a side effect of having smoked all your life. Sound unfair? Then how fair is it that you pay for it, when you have never smoked and don't even know this person living across the other side of the country? Exactly.

Think about the products that we see on supermarket shelves. A fair percentage of it is total junk. Not only food, but the world is full of junk an unnecessary items and pastimes. Eating this junk over decades it has terrible negative consequences on our health. Though, a Consolidist Government wouldn't ban junk food, but instead educate people more, and also propose making junk food more expensive and healthy food cheaper. Alcohol & Junk Food is made to look so glamorous or funny on the hypnotising electronic box. How can people of any age resist it? It doesn't matter though, if you drink alcohol all your life, then suck tens of thousands out of the healthcare system when your liver fails. We'll all pick up the tab. No problem, you go ahead and carry on. It's backward and unworkable, as no doubt you're seeing with the debt your country is probably in.

We live on a planet where the rap songs make it cool to shoot someone, not embrace them and ask how they're feeling. Where the main theme of most video games is killing. The fact that people would want to play video games instead of having the inner desire to perhaps help a disabled neighbour in some way is bad enough. But these games then promote the excitement involved in the taking of lives. Helping others and improving our communities. These should be the kinds of inherent inner desires our bodies hold dear, but, the shallow, glamorous, materialistic world we live in results in us having selfish, diseased desires, detrimental to ourselves and all around us. We live in a world where a person can hoard tens of millions in a bank account just for walking, talking, sitting, standing on our electronic boxes. We call these people Actresses and Actors. What would you think if you had never known any of this before and arrived at planet Earth for the first time? Insanity could be the only reaction. We'd rather watch certain singing competition television shows that make talentless people stars, than go and help the needy or aged in our community. These talentless people on the electronic box contribute nothing towards creating a prosperous society, but still we hold them in such high regard and reward them with millions.

One of the downfalls of the human being is that we're all individuals, with different needs and desires. Remember the Ants? Working as one functioning unit, with one single purpose. Most would say that individuality is a wonderful thing. It is to a certain extent, but it just needs to be curtailed. If it isn't, the result is what you see around you today. A mess. We can't allow our individual desires to get in the way of the bigger picture. Society.

There's an inherent desire within the human mind to disagree with anothers' viewpoint. Look for it when you go about your day. It's everywhere. Mostly in the most innocent and trivial of conversations, but it's there. And when Governments start to disagree, that can have major ramifications on its citizens, and possibly even lead to war. If you don't disagree, you're agreeing with somebody else. If they made the point first, they are elevated above you as the 'leader and most important' on the issue you are discussing. When there are others looking on, everybody wants to be 'leader and most important'. The trapings of llife don't go to 'followers and "the least important"'. Not at present anyway.

The antagonistic, individualistic state of the human mind can be perfectly illustrated by analysing and identifying what is present in every television programme, film, play and book that will ever be. Do you know what it is? It's conflict. Ask any Hollywood Film Director, Actress or Actor. Any Author. If you haven't got conflict in your story or film, you've got nothing. No human's interest would ever be raised if conflict wasn't present. Think back about every film, book, programme or even situation that you've ever had interest in. You're mind is only engaged due to the conflict. Whether it be between people, animals and people, the environment and people. There is always a protagonist and challenging them in some way, an antagonist. If there is no conflict in a film, you would not enjoy it. What does that say about the position of human consciousness in the year 2012?

The damage individuality does amongst us today is exacerbated by the electronic boxes within our homes. What we see on the electronic box, instils within us a desire to be the richest, the coolest, the most important, the sexiest, the most powerful. This makes for an avaricious society, inhabited by greedy Politicians and Businesspeople looking to siphon off the Proletariat's wealth and claim it as their own. No doubt, we too hold some of these desires, but never get the chance to amass any kind of wealth. What should be the case is that nobody is allowed to amass an absolute fortune, while the rest of the population lives in relative or absolute poverty.

The electronic box infects us with lust & greed. These emotions being the precursors to disease and conflict. There are many out there who are devious and two-faced in their quest for fame and/or fortune. We have to change it and focus on what really matters to us. Our families, friends and fellow humans. We're always looking to solidify our own status in social circles as the most important, knowledgeable person. If you manage to do this, it will bring you wealth. To do this, we lie and have one opinion externally whilst another exists inside our heads. Truthfully, how many times have you been of one opinion in your mind but externalised another in order to avoid loss of face or perhaps gain wealth or possessions? We all need to take a close look at ourselves and start calling things straight down the line, truthfully, whilst always keeping in mind the real important issues we should be pursuing. If we limit wealth and start to reward those who deserve reward, we can all start to move towards a better world.

Actresses and Actors are some of the highest paid people in the world today. What do they do? What's their contribution to society? They walk, talk, sit, stand, laugh, cry. All in front of an electronic filming device. We all walk, talk, sit, stand etc every day of our lives. Why is it considered a talent which deserves tens of millions of dollars in financial reward when it's done in front of an electronic filming device? Can you hear that, they get paid tens of millions for walking, talking, sitting, standing. What is wrong with this world? And don't be fooled by the thespians who "do alot of work for charity". Yes they do some token work for charity, but if a cause concerns them so much, why don't they donate $100 million of their $105 million dollar fortune? Why? Because they're greedy, false human beings. They give a pittance of their massive fortune to a charity, visit the needy for a couple of days, then return to their mansions and throbbing bank accounts. Why do they get involved in the charity work? It results in the Proletariat liking them and paying to watch their films. The more people who watch their films, the more money they can hoard.

We live in a world where someone walks straight past a person collecting for charity, on their way to spend $100 to get their fingernails painted. Can you hear that? Money is being focused towards painting fingernails. This is the point to which 'everyday normal human life' has brought human consciousness. Why do we not have the unwavering desire within us to help others? We're all throwing our money in the wrong direction, towards Popstars who can't play instruments and don't even write their own songs. We have people in the 'music' business that can't play an instrument and don't even write their own songs. Welcome to planet Earth. Even the very few who do play instruments, only have the most basic of 'skills', but still that's enough to make millions.

When one of these Popstars is interviewed, what about asking them, "What instrument did you play on your new album?". The reply "I don't play any instrument". "Which of the songs did you write the lyrics for?". The reply "I didn't write any of them". "Which of the songs did you help to arrange and co-ordinate the instruments on?" The reply "I didn't do any of that". This would be a reality for hundreds of Popstars if an interviewer was to ask such questions. But no, we all play into the charade. If faced with this, the next thing to come out of the interviewer's mouth, should be something like, "You have to be joking. You don't play or arrange any instruments. You don't write any lyrics. All you do is turn up and shout into a microphone? Why is your name on this album? Why are you pretending to be a musician in the music business when you're obviously talentless when it comes to music?". Worse still is the fact that not only do a large percentage of Popstars & Rappers not play instruments, there are many albums made today which don't feature any musical instruments at all. It's all computer generated. It's beyond belief that we encourage this by purchasing their 'music'.

All the 'Dead Money' lying in bank accounts around the world has come from your pockets. The pockets of the Proletariat. There is no other way of making a fortune. That's why you deserve to benefit from the wealth that you generate. Some may say "What about the many luxury markets that only the rich can afford to buy in?". Fortunes are made from those markets. How did those rich people become rich and able to dabble in the luxury markets? On the money from your pockets. The working class' pockets are the target of every Popstar, Soccer Player and Fat Cat Businessperson on the planet. When handing your money over at the checkout. Whether you're buying Chewing Gum, Soap or a Sofa. At the end of the line is a single person or very small group of people sitting on a fortune.

Behind the glamour and glitz of a Popstar, are teams of people developing new strategies to maximise the amount of money they're able to take from you. Ironically, they're the targets too, but they're just trying to make a living. The Popstars and record company executives must be laughing uncontrollably behind the scenes. "I can't believe everybody's falling for this. All you do is dance around and shout into a microphone and they're giving us millions!". Even the most talented of musicians. Are they deserving of millions for what they do? Or should it go to people who work in homes for handicapped children? A serious redirection of funds is required within our societies. One which only Consolidism will deliver. The question we have to ask ourselves is, "Do we want the money to sit in the bank accounts of the rich and famous, or do we want it to stay circulating in the community, creating jobs and improving our lives?". It's not really a hard question to give an emphatic answer to. A Consolidist Government would still allow people to be stars, but it would ensure they are rewarded accordingly. The rest of the money is kept alive.

★★★

It's not only a case of throwing our money in the wrong direction. In a world where energy is at a premium, we waste it, for example, on making and viewing electronic box dancing competition programs which may involve the amazingly talented, clothes wearing geniuses we call Models. Not only energy, but people's time could be better spent setting right the range of problems present in our communities. Anti-Social Behaviour, Crime, Poverty. These are problems we'll all need help to solve, but, this help will not come from any Politician, as it never has. It would however be forthcoming if a Consolidist Government was running a country. Anti-Social Behaviour & Crime can be tackled if we put more Police on the streets and educate kids when they're young about what their lives will be like if they choose to act inconsiderately and irresponsibly. This could be done using the money we're currently spending making reality television programmes. If we don't waste that money, we can employ more Police, put hard-hitting adverts on television, and implement programs in schools where kids are effectively educated about respect and how to act in society. Would that make sense? Not to a Politician, and even some of us. We prefer to see money and effort poured into producing glossy magazines that discuss what 'celebrities' eat for breakfast. To a being that hadn't been 'materialised' and brainwashed, it wouldn't be interesting to find out what Jesus ate for breakfast, nevermind a talentless nobody who's being encouraged to contribute nothing to society.

Reality television stars don't do anything. They just are. Here we are on planet Earth in the year 2012, where hundreds of millions of human beings out there, are willing to part with their money to find out about the affair a leather blob kicking man has been having. Who is making the decision that there is the need to print and sell such magazines? The answer is obvious. It's the person who's making millions, from us being readily willing to put our hand in our pockets and actually pay money for this tat.

★★★

The US Presidential elections. Billions of dollars spent over the period of the 4 years. Not millions, but billions. Countless Kilowatt-Hours of Energy. They start talking about the next election and the possible candidates immediately after a new President has taken office. They don't stop until the next election rolls around 4 years later. Then the process starts again. There are more important things to talk about in the world. Some may say that the money spent creates jobs? The fact is that the money, time, effort and energy spent on talking about the elections could have been put to good use, perhaps repairing the country's roads and bridges, ironically just as the candidates are promising to do if they win power. This creates worthwhile jobs.

Is it better for somebody to be paid for repairing roads, or pay them and use up the world's resources to make campaign banners or flags? America, do your Politicians solve your problems, or is it more of the same whoever wins office? Surely, a month of solid television debates between all candidates is enough time and coverage to choose a leader? Let's then use the time and money saved to actually put some of our problems right. The amount of energy and fuel used up during the election campaigns must be staggering. There's only so much Gas and Oil on the planet. Shouldn't we use 'Common Sense' to conserve it? As fantastic a country as the United States of America is. Middle Class People with morals and values. It sure is bizarre in many ways. Bizarre in ways that highlight perfectly the kind of flawed, 'susceptible to suggestion' creature the human being is. An example, 'Child Preachers'. There are Americans in the year 2012 who think an 8 year old boy has the power to miraculously heal them simply by touch alone. Welcome to Planet Earth.

We now have access to hundreds of television channels. Many, if not most of them, are wasting time, money, energy and resources on discussing ball games, a celebrity's shoes or perhaps a funny dog that whines when her owner plays the piano. These channels could be used to discuss social problems. A Consolidist Government wouldn't ban all reality television, glossy magazines etc, but it would simply remind everybody of what's important to us as nations, as people, and ensure societies function without 'Dead Money' existing in the accounts of talentless reality television stars. Some of the measures and wavelengths of thinking that have been discussed in this chapter may sound bizarre and draconian to you, but they're really not. They're just necessary if we want to live in functioning, fair societies. If we're not brave enough to start thinking differently and changing our ways, we'll be talking about the same problems in another 20 years. Only then they'll be 10 times worse. Ten times worse, unless, we adopt the most important policy of 'Consolidism', which will be discussed in the next chapter.

We're wasting all our time and resources on nothingness. How many thousands of sportspeople have you seen interviewed on your electronic boxes? They may aswell record one "Before" and one "After" game speech and just replay it for each game. They're always virtually identical. What do we expect the sportsperson to say? It's obvious it's going to be the same. "It was a hard game, they are a great team. We never gave up but just couldn't get the goal we needed". Is that news? Is that worthy of using time, money and energy to play on our electronic boxes? Wouldn't it be nice to hear a sportsperson say, "There are people all over the world who need help and you're here focusing your attention on a ball game? Is my answer to "Are you upset to have drawn and not won the title?" really going to be that interesting? Of course I'd rather we won the game, but no I'm not really upset to have drawn. I earn £150,000 per week for kicking a leather blob around a pitch, when there are doctors out there who work 80 hours a week for £50,000 per year. And you're asking me if I'm upset? Are you for real? Our manager was sacked last month after our losing streak. Not the players, who's influence on a game is approximately 90%, with 10% being due to the team selection and tactics chosen by the manager. The manager was sacked. And you don't flag that up as being ridiculous? How can you be so idiotic?".

Time, effort, money and energy is being used to interview somebody who gets paid £150,000 per week for hoofing a leather blob around a field. Everybody knows what he's going to say, because he and countless others have said exactly the same thing before, and will say exactly the same thing next time, and the time after that. And in this 90 minute game of soccer that's just taken place, there wasn't even 1 single scoring event. Can this be really happening the aliens think to themselves? So much money and attention invested in such a talentless game which involved not 1 scoring event? Are these beings some kind of sick joke?

★★★

We have to get out of the mindset of wanting to be the greatest, coolest, richest, sexiest, making more and more money, and start to focus on what's important. This greedy, diseased mindset is costing this planet and our race dearly. A Consolidist Government wouldn't want to stop all fun, but we have to ask questions of ourselves about the way our race behaves. Why don't we find it fun to do constructive things within our community? Because that's how our Societies have been allowed to form by the Politicians. Should helping others not be what we get a kick out of? What other creatures on this planet indulge in substances that they know are damaging to their bodies? What other creatures on this planet are interested in glossy magazines or have the concept of celebrities? None. They're all focused on the purity of life and their community around them. The human consciousness is so far down the wrong road, as much as one may try, it can't be put into words.

Consider the following as an example of gullible and flawed we human beings are. If a work colleague of yours was to come into work tomorrow, take you to one side and say, "I had an amazing experience last night. God actually talked to me. It talked to me all night long, telling me how we should all live our lives. What God said was brilliant. It really is the way we should live. I'm going to write a book detailing everything God said to me". What would you think or say? Exactly. You'd think they've gone crazy. Totally loopy. Well. This is how the religion of Islam came about hundreds of years ago. The people of the village in which the Prophet Mohammed lived, believed his story about God speaking to him.

Not just Islam. The Bible. All religious books for that matter. Fact of Fiction? Nobody will ever know, but if we're all totally honest. Totally, totally honest with each other, there's a much greater chance that they're all fictional. What are the odds that events happened 100% to the letter of what's printed in the religious books of today? Absolute zero are the odds. So if there's doubt about even just 1% of what's written in the bible, there has to be doubt about the whole book. We can't possibly know 100% correctly what happened thousands of years ago. So why would us humans take these books as gospel? Because we're gullible, flawed and misguided.

The level of personal interpretation and 'Chinese Whispers' that have taken place down the years in the writing of the religious texts, has undoubtedly had the effect of changing them vastly from what 'allegedly' truly happened. It goes without saying that this has occurred. But still they're accepted as the absolute truthful version of events. Did Jesus really exist? It's unlikely. Did a person called Jesus exist, who had the magical powers described in the bible? There's absolutely no chance that a person like this existed? It's just a story. We can all see that this is by far the most likely reality. If a person called Jesus did exist and was written about, the story has been blown way out of proportion, but, humans believe it. We need to get a grip on reality and where our attentions, beliefs and minds should be focused in the world.

Let Consolidism leave you with one final example of how material, tacky, cheap, shallow and misguided the world is today. A final indicator of the direction we're heading in. In museums around the world, we can view unearthed artefacts from ancient civilizations. Perhaps a Bronze Goddess statue, a Roman Sword or an intricately detailed Stone Carving. One thousand years from now, serving as an indicator of what life was like in the early part of the 21st Century, somebody will unearth...... the plastic figure of a World Wrestling Entertainment 'Superstar'. The WWE. One of millions of money-making machines that does nothing for the good of society, but, rather, serves only the purpose of sucking money out of it. Is there any wonder that Quantitative Easing is currently regularly required to reinvigorate our economies?

PART 2

A WORLD THAT MAKES SENSE

CHAPTER 1

Consolidation

Consolidation is the most important, central policy of Consolidism. Consolidation is the absolute key, not only to the prosperity of the human race, but its survival. To best convey the importance of Consolidation, the "Home Analogy" will be used. Our villages, towns, cities, countries are analogous to houses. They are our homes, where our family live. They have finite spaces and finite resources. Is it sensible to allow your family to grow in numbers indefinitely? Is it sensible to leave the world's population to grow unchecked? To leave it grow from now until the end of time? What would life on Planet Earth be like for its inhabitants if there were 100 Billion of us? Ordered, Enjoyable, Plentiful? Total Chaos would be a better description. It would not be even remotely practicable.

If this is the case, then it's easy to realise, if we can't let the population grow forevermore, there must be a point at which we have to put a cap on the numbers. There is nothing in this dimension that can grow forever. Not a person, a plant, a business, a celestial star. The scientists will tell you that not even the universe itself is going to grow forever. Is that 'fact' accurate? That's a different question. So why would we be under the impression that the number of human beings living on earth can grow forever? Why on Earth aren't the Politicians making this statement and taking action accordingly?

The population on planet earth currently stands at just over 7 billion. Would you say we're overcrowded now, with suffering as a direct result of the numbers of people? Precisely. With 100 Billion people on earth, Disease, Famine & War would be rampant. These would be everyday issues for everybody on the planet. We can't successfully feed 7 Billion people. Fish stocks in the ocean are already at seriously low levels. What about 200 Billion? The humans who are alive, if and when this becomes a reality, would be living in a never-ending nightmare. Like some kind of biblical apocalypse. But it won't be fictional. The scariest thing is that we don't have to come anywhere near to 100 or 200 billion for this nightmare to become a reality. It's pretty bad now, but, with just double the number of people, we'd all be suffering on an unimaginable scale. What effect would twice the people and cars have on your commute to and from your place of work? We don't need the Earth's population to double for that to happen. Populations within cities grow at a much faster rate than the overall world population. And the more a population grows, the more the rate of growth accelerates. We won't be able to move in our cities in the coming decades.

Take Tokyo's subway system, that deals with 8.7 million passengers a day. The stations' dispatchers have to physically ram and crush passengers into the trains before they're able to pull away. It's an incredible sight. Google it for yourselves. Imagine the scene with 20 times as many people? An unfeasible, impossibility. Just the fact that we're having to build underground and raised platform transportation systems should serve as major warnings that we're headed in the wrong direction. But we just don't see it.

Day in day out, on news channels across the world, do you hear talk of how Governments are striving to grow economies, and how there's a big concern when they're not growing? What's the reason the economies need to grow? It's so that a growing population have jobs to sustain themselves. No growth means the growing population have no jobs and no means to feed themselves. For this reason alone, it's immediately and startlingly obvious that it would be sensible to stop the populations of countries, of the planet, growing? That way, the extra jobs are not needed. If you Consolidate on the population numbers, you don't need to grow the economy. You cannot keep growing and growing and growing. It just isn't possible. Nothing, absolutely nothing, can grow indefinitely. Not only to ensure we don't have to provide jobs for an ever burgeoning population, it's plain to see that from a space, resources and environmental viewpoint, we can't continue to grow in numbers. We may in the future be able to harness renewable technologies, solving the problem of our dependency on Oil and Gas. Even if we did, which we probably won't, as will be explained, we still live on a planet with finite surface area. Much of which, up to now, we've all been striving to keep free of urbanisation, thus maintaining its natural beauty. That we know of, with woman and mankind's rapid growth, approximately 85 species of birds, animals and reptiles have become extinct in the past 500 years. Many of these extinctions can be directly linked to the growth of human populations and their gradual spread across the world. Imagine how many more will become extinct by the time there are 200 billion people on the planet. There won't be a single place of natural beauty left on the face of the Earth. The only jungles will be concrete ones that have Wars raging within them. Global warming and pollution has been a major topic of discussion over the past few decades. What will pollution be like with 200 billion people to cater for? The air will be toxically unbreathable.

Another major reason why we can't continue to grow? The more you grow, the harder it is to grow. Using another analogy, to be referred to as the "Diner Analogy", do you think it would be easier from a logistics and management point of view, to run a Diner with 2 tables or 2,000 tables? Which one of those scenarios offers the biggest headache in terms of running a smooth operation? The concept and the maths are not difficult in the slightest.

The bigger an operation, the harder it is to run the operation. Whether it be a Diner, a Financial Services Company or a Planet.

For a couple of decades now, Governments and industries have strived to develop green, renewable technologies. We've managed it to a certain extent, but have not made the significant strides we so desperately need to have made. What's the reason for this? If a country is aiming for the goal of becoming totally sustainable, with 100% of its energy coming from renewable sources, it's plain to see that there will have to be alot of Research & Development conducted. This R&D requires investment of Capital, Time and Resources. A country's chances of achieving its goal of energy independence are far greater if there isn't the distraction of having too many people in the country. The more people there are in a country, the more people there are that need to be taken care of, with their individual needs requiring attention. Some absolutely justified, others not so. The more people there are, the more time and money needs to be spent on infrastructure to allow society to operate successfully. There will be more people who are a burden on society, such as criminals. The more people there are to cater for, the more money and time is required to do it, and the less time, money and resources there are to dedicate to the R&D of 'important' technologies. Add to this the billions of catatonic currency in private bank accounts, where investment of the currency is optional. It's completely impossible to develop in any significant strides as a society.

It's not only about the burdensome elements of society and infrastructure requirements. Just numbers alone will mean that mistakes will be made in Government. Money and time wasted trying to provide for the overpopulated country, analysing the rate of growth, strategising on how to cope with the additional demand the growth will put on its public services. Consider your own lives. Would you agree that the more tasks that are fired your way in work, the more your quality of work suffers, and the more befuddled your minds become as they're overloaded and stressed. It is exactly the same type of scenario, only on a different scale. If we let populations grow, we will spend all our time, as is evident all around the world right now, just trying to stay afloat, furiously treading water. When instead we should be advancing our countries and people into a position where they enjoy a better state of affairs, and a greater quality of life.

With the earth's numbers as they stand, how is life for people around the world? What do you witness on your electronic box every day? Of course there is some happiness. But, the big question is, do you see crime, disease, wars, starvation, poverty, misery, injustice, genocide, persecution? Exactly. These banes of our lives are rife. Like a wildfire flaming across the Earth's surface. One that we will not be nearly able to extinguish if we don't implement 'Consolidation'. If we Consolidate our population numbers and infrastructure within our societies, we will be able to control these afflictions which befall us to an infinitely better extent. What about the Floods, Earthquakes & Storms which pour gloom upon the world's population every year? Not the result of a growing population I hear you say? Well, the debate rages on about whether or not global warming, caused by overpopulation, allegedly, is accounting for the rise in natural disasters? As yet, that's inconclusive.

Let Consolidism ask you a question though. In the many future natural disasters that will strike our civilisation, would it be easier to provide humanitarian aid for 1,000 people or 1 million people? Good people of the United States of America. More than most Countries, you frequently suffer the crippling blows dealt by Storms, Hurricanes & Tornadoes. Hurricane Katrina, Hurricane Sandy, Hurricane Ike, and many more. Has your Government used 'all' the funds possible to help you back to your feet? Or, do large sections of your towns & cities still mimic apocalyptic wastelands? Of course they do, because Politicians are in charge of your 'recovery'. 1 Trillion has been spent in Iraq & Afghanistan. There are reportedly 425 Billionaires in your country. Is Capitalism working for you? Nothing more needs to be said. 'When' Famine or Drought blights an African nation, will a million currency worth of aid go further for 1,000 people or 10 million people? Exactly. The concept is so simple. We have to stop the growth of the world's population and eliminate 'Catatonic Currency'. That's absolutely undeniable and 100% conclusive.

Even as we stand, at 7 Billion human beings, it's totally impossible to care for everybody and ensure their health & wellbeing, as you witness all around you every single day of your lives. If God called you forth to the witness stand and asked you to describe to sum up life on planet Earth in 2012 in one word, the absolute best anybody would be able to do is 'Miserable'. When there's 200 Billion? 'Agonising'. 'Hell'. Even in just 39 years, the population is due to grow to 9.1 Billion. We humans can't seem to mobilise our minds to picture what it will be like. We can't appreciate and imagine that the population will grow by 'at least' this much and that it will be chaos even with that 'apparently' small increase. Many will be thinking that they won't be around then, and if they are, they won't be around for long. All this is typical of human thought patterns whereby we believe "It will never happen" or "It's not my problem". It may not be your problem, but it will be the problem of your children, grandchildren and all your future generations.

Revisiting the 'Home Analogy', imagine just your home with double the amount of people living in it. How would it be? Exactly. That's just the microcosm that is your home. Infinitely simpler to run than the whole world. But still, such an increase would bring about big difficulties. Is it more difficult for twice as many adults to find twice as many jobs? Yes? Then some of your home's inhabitants would quite probably be dependent on the others, meaning quality of life diminishes for everybody. Does it take more money and effort to feed twice as many mouths? Would there be more arguments over resources and amenities? Disputes lead to violence. On a countries and world scale, that means War. With there being less free space and air in the house, would it be easier to catch each other's bugs and germs? On a countries and world scale, that means Epidemics. If we leave the population unchecked, War, Disease & Famine is all that will ensue, on 'unimaginable' scales. Imagine letting the amount of people in your home quadruple, which will happen to the population on Earth if we don't cap it. Instantly, you can see it just wouldn't be possible to maintain order and quality of life for the population. Therefore, there must be a point at which we say "That's our maximum". It would be a ridiculous policy for a homeowner to just let their family numbers grow and grow. Why do you not just keep having children? Because there's a limit on the amount you can provide for in terms finances, resources and space. We have to treat Planet Earth the same. It's our big home, with finite finances, resources, food and space.

Imagine if you will, the traffic on the roads, or the crowds in a train station during a rush hour as you make your way to work. Now picture 3 times the amount of cars and people. It's just not going to be workable. Three times the amount of cars on the roads means 3 times the amount of oil used up. Are there already wars occurring over oil, making your own minds up, and not accepting the Politicians' lies? Will there be renewably powered cars by the time the population grows to 3 times its current level? Maybe, maybe not? Scientists and Engineers have been attempting to develop the technology, and, make it affordable to the penniless Proletariat for many years. They still haven't come up with any viable, affordable, large scale solutions of any real worth. And the more people there are, the more difficult it will be to focus money, time and attention on the task.

Even with the current population, our countries are buried in debt because of the difficulties involved in trying to run massive operations. There are also other contributory factors, which have already been discussed, and more which will be discussed. The bigger a population becomes, the more difficult it will be to run. The more money, time and attention will have to be pulled from advancing ourselves and redirected towards just staying afloat.

What's the arch-enemy of the road user on their way to or home from work? Roadworks. Three times the amount of cars on the road, means roads wear out quicker and roadworks will be required more frequently. If you're thinking "We build more roads for the larger population". Is that the simple way the world works around you? Is it that easy in our societies? "We need more roads, so abracadabra, there are some more roads". Exactly. Why isn't it this easy? Because there are too many people for us to get our act together. Besides, there are only so many roads you can build in cities. It's not physically possible to build more roads as the population grows. So not only are there 3 times the cars, which increases your commute time, there are also roadworks blighting your lives at a much greater frequency than you've ever encountered before. This is just a singular snapshot element of how life absolutely will be.

Have you ever been in the following situation, or one similar? The end of a long day in work. Your train home is cancelled, eventually, after having already spent 30 minutes waiting on the platform. People pacing, mumbling, losing their tempers with staff as they try to find out what's going on. Eventually, everybody's led away. A bus is to be provided. People remain relatively orderly, but you're all scurrying quickly to make sure you get on that bus. You have to get on that bus at all costs. Can you feel how chaotic and stressful it was? Just that 1 minor inconvenience for 50 people. Imagine that all over the world involving hundreds of thousands of different inconveniences and billions of people. There will be arguing and fighting all over our towns and cities, all day, every day. This will happen, unless we cap the population numbers. If numbers grow, the wear and tear on the world and its infrastructure will result in situations like the above on a massive scale.

Think back to when you've been stood in a queue at the supermarket. Five people in front of you. A problem at the checkout. The operator has to call a colleague in to help. You look either side. The checkouts have more people than the one you're at. Five minutes passes. Can you feel the stress and frustration involved in this tiny 5 minute problem? Don't forget, this is with the current population. Multiply it by 3. Multiply the hustle and bustle and queues of the whole supermarket on its busiest day by 3. You look at your watch. You've got to be home in 15 minutes. Someone's coming to fix your broken gas boiler. Incidentally, with 3 times as many people on the planet, how much gas is left in the world? Not much, if any. Ten minutes later, you eventually get checked out, load your car up and you're on your way. Until you hit… Traffic Jams & Roadworks. Can you feel the knot in your stomach through this whole episode? That's just you. Tiny little you, finding yourself in this tiny, insignificant, inconvenient situation. When this is happening all over the world though, in every aspect of everybody's everyday life, it will whip up huge civil disarray.

We all need to wake up, Politicians first and foremost, and realise that we are headed for meltdown. As we're all too aware though, the Politicians will not do anything to avert this problem heading our way. Imagine the traffic jam you've been sitting in for 30 minutes on your way home from the supermarket. Two people get so frustrated and angry, they get out of their cars and a fight breaks out. Someone else gets out of their car to try and break it up. They end up getting involved too. A three way melee. One combatant is badly beaten, later ending up in hospital requiring medical attention. This medical attention costs money, which results in your taxes remaining high. Somebody in the traffic jam called the Police as the arguments raged, but, they never arrived in time because they couldn't get through the jams all across the city's roads. The person who was beaten up knows their attacker. In the following days and weeks, revenge attacks are carried out. More Police time. More hospital visits. More court cases. More prisoners. Full prisons. Society able to incarcerate less offenders. More criminals on the streets. More money poured into the losing battle against crime. Less money spent on your other equally important public services. We all need to strive hard to envisage this, and realise it will happen. Because it absolutely will.

What about 15 times the amount of people in the supermarket? You wouldn't be able to move. This is just one isolated example. All across society, the chaos and disorder would steadily rise with the population. Yes, there would 'eventually' be more supermarkets built, but still, in each one, the numbers of shoppers would grow. The more a population grows, the harder it is to keep up with providing for it, because it grows at a higher rate. We all know life on planet Earth isn't as easy as "We need another supermarket. There you go. There's another supermarket". Far from it.

What about the resources needed to run a supermarket? Electricity, Gas, Oil. By the time there are, say 21 Billion people in the world, they will be such highly valuable commodities, countries will be willing, and having to go to war to get them. The reality is that, ironically, supermarkets wouldn't need the energy resources, because, due to the wars raging, supermarkets won't be part of society. Rations will be handed out on street corners, with the backdrop being bombed out buildings from the wars which are occurring all around the world. This can't be allowed to happen. We can't allow our children to suffer this fate. If the Politicians remain in power, with their constant talk of growth, there can be no other future.

As you observe the world now. Is it a place where we're all able to manage to provide food, medicine, shelter, energy and a good standard of living for all? Is starvation widespread in Africa? Is crime rampant in every country across the globe? Are we able, via the virtue of a world where everybody and their minds are not overrun with tasks, are we able to provide every human being with good quality healthcare? Or are there millions dying each year of diseases which are easily treatable? Does every human have access to clean drinking water or do thousands of children die each day from drinking dirty water? The proof is there to see. Unless we embrace Consolidism, it's only going to get worse. We're so far from a fair, functioning world, if there is a God, she or he must never cease shaking her or his head. What's the key reason for all the suffering? Overpopulation. Is it easier to feed 10 starving children or 10 million starving children?

Across the world, Politicians often talk of how we need to help the people of Africa gain access to clean water, food and medicine. Or perhaps how we need to fight AIDS on the African Continent. The question that immediately jumps out is "Why haven't you mentioned, the first item on the 'Things to Do' list, should be tackling contraception and reproduction". Every time you see one of the poor, perhaps ill, African Mothers on your electronic box, the correspondent invariably mentions in the report that she's got 10 children. She can only afford one bowl of rice a day. Would this go further in feeding 1 child or 10 children? The first discussion topic on the agenda for helping the poor and starving of Africa should be how they need to help themselves by not having any more children? The international community can then help them when it sees they've made a conscious effort to help themselves. This as opposed to them just continuing to create tens of millions of children they can't provide for, and becoming a drain on the world as they ask for help. It may sound harsh, but it has to described exactly as it is if they're ever to remove themselves from their predicament. If the reality of the situation is dodged due to it being 'Insensitive' or 'Politically Incorrect', their suffering will continue. If they reduced their population, they'd be able to 'focus' their resources, which will by then outweigh the amount of people, on curing and feeding their sick and starving. If other countries did have the money to give, they could initially help them on their way towards better lives, but, the people receiving the help would need to stop procreating for a period of time as they're attempting to steady their ship. Once they're on their feet, they wouldn't need any charity. In the name of rectifying problems and achieving goals, if something must be said or identified, then it's said or identified and something is done about it. This is a key belief of a Consolidist.

It must be noted though. In this, and all other scenarios within our countries, people are responsible for their actions, and should only be afforded help if they're seen to be first helping themselves in every possible way they can. Aiding the irresponsible only engenders and encourages irresponsibility, thus ensuring the world's problems will endure forevermore.

★★★

The time is now. It's been overlooked for far too long by the Politicians. A Consolidist Government believes the world needs to reduce its population to approximately 66% of what it is at present. That's approximately 4.5 Billion people. The reduction in numbers of each country should be proportional to the current population of each country. If you are a country with under 10 million people, you should be exempt from the reductions. Immediately, the human mind would buck against a Government telling them they have to stop having so many children. It would be an automatic reaction, but, when carefully considered, looking from a different angle, thinking on a different wavelength, it's plain to see that reducing the population numbers will be directly and specifically beneficial to the children that people do bring into the world. There would also be the ever-present, unavoidable arguments between countries, this time on how much of a reduction there should be within each country. Humans just cannot seem to co-exist at all. We all need to cast aside the 'Political Machinations' and 'Greed', and do this for the benefit of our children and grandchildren, because that's who it would be for.

Where does the 'Greed' come into the equation? Reducing population numbers will result in reduced armies. Reduced armies are weaker armies, which leave countries without the influence and muscle to gain access to the resources their people need in the world. Some will be necessities such as food or energy, of course, but countries also strive for excessive wealth and power, not just acquiring what they need to get by. They want to be the most powerful. Or perhaps we should put it, the Politician's at the helm want to be the most powerful. That is where the Greed will come into the equation. Security is also a reason countries will not want to reduce their population and armies. They wouldn't be able to protect their natural resources as other countries invade in an attempt to lay claim to them. Why are countries needing to invade foreign lands to acquire natural resources? Because they need to provide for their growing populations. If we implemented Consolidation and all had the common decency and responsibility to live modestly within our means, there would be peace on Earth. Until we live in this fashion, there will never be peace on Earth.

As we go about our daily lives, simply allowing the population to keep growing and allowing Politicians to mess up our time on Earth, we're ensuring the generations that follow us will suffer greatly. You're children will suffer. Your flesh and blood. Look into their eyes. How on Earth can we do this to them? We're all too worried about soccer players and film stars to notice that we are in the process of creating a hell on earth quagmire for our children. So far, there have been 2 World Wars. If we don't change direction and head towards Consolidism, starting right now, our children will live in a "World of War". It will never stop. We have to start making big changes to improve. We can't afford to, as we have been doing, 'try' to make changes for the better, but just ending up bumbling along due to the Politicians, 'Catatonic Currency' and the confusion induced by the already overpopulation of our countries and the planet. We have to achieve the change, now.

So, how do we do this? Firstly, we all need to start taking responsibility. If you can't really afford to have a child, you don't have one. It's that simple. Why can't we keep things simple? Although it must be said, that with a Consolidist Government in power, subsidising salaries with what used to be 'Catatonic Currency', all Proletarians will be able to afford to start a family. For those who do have children, we have to limit every woman to having 2 children in their lifetime. Following this, she must have a hysterectomy. So too, a man must have a Vasectomy once he has procreated 2 offspring. Are you thinking this sounds like an oppressive, totalitarian dictatorship? Let us not forget who will suffer if we don't take these measures. It's the very children you're bringing into the world. You must always keep in mind that a Consolidist 'Government', is not really a Government at all. They are the people, working for the people. Genuinely. History would be the empty words of the Politicians who you've no doubt heard say this on countless occassions as they attempt to deflect your attention from their riches and plush lifestyle. The measures are to protect and ensure the quality of life for all the wonderful little Muslim, Black, White, Chinese and Mexican humans born 'in their countries' from now until the end of time.

If people don't start taking responsibility for their actions, and do have more than 2 children, there have to be consequences in place, otherwise what's to stop them from keeping the world in the mess it's in now due to overpopulation? If we all continue to have more than 2 children, we're all ruining each other's lives. If a woman has more than 2 children, she, her children and the man she had the children with, will be limited in the lives they can lead. Immediately, the sentence for the man would be 10 years in a 'Consolidist Prison', which will be described in the chapter 'Crime & Punishment'. All the other 'earned' benefits and subsidies that the responsible people of society enjoy, would not be available to the family, ever. They and their family would not get any free healthcare. Their earnings would be capped at a very low level, just enough for the family to survive.

Before a couple want to procreate, they have to come to the Government, who represent the people and the very child that the couple wants to bring into the world, and register their intentions. If they're eligible, of course, they will be allowed to go ahead with their plans. This strategy will eliminate the eventuality of a man saying, "I didn't know she already had 2 children". This may sound a difficult process to implement, but if we can bring the population numbers down, it will become entirely manageable, as will all processes within our societies. It also obviously requires that people act responsibly, which really isn't too much to ask. Do you act responsibly in every way in your lives that affects those around you? If you do, you will benefit massively from Consolidism. The above-mentioned measures may sound harsh, oppressive even, but if we don't do it, your children will pay the penalty. The growth of debts would be the least of their worries. Epidemics and Foreign Invasions would be what they'd have to focus their minds on every morning they wake. They certainly won't be worrying about whether or not their soccer team are going to win that day. Soccer will be no more in an Apocalyptic World. If any of us want anything to function properly, be it an electronic device, a machine or a system, it has to be maintained and proper rules have to be followed when operating it. You don't expect a DVD Player to operate underwater. Just like you can't expect debts, diseases, wars & rapidly diminishing resources not to escalate, if the population is left to escalate. They're proportional. They go hand in hand.

It is extremely sad that they have to be present in our societies, but abortions absolutely do, 'unless', people act responsibly. Will everybody though? Exactly. In a horrible, contradiction in terms, we have no choice but to identify the fact that abortion will ensure good lives for our children. It is the truth, so it must be spoken. Again though, no abortions would occur if everybody acted responsibly. None. A Consolidist Government would help in every way it can in terms of contraception and educating its citizens. Abortions would be optional for any 3rd, 4th etc child a woman bears, dependent on whether or not the family wants to live a sub-standard life due to their irresponsibility. If people continue to have more than 2 children, everybody across the globe will have to continue enduring great hardship. If a man creates his third child with a woman who has not yet become a mother, or is a mother of 1, he is imprisoned for 10 years, as he is for every additional child he creates. There must be consequences. Mothers do not go to prison, but instead will be subject to penalties rendering their lives far more difficult than those who choose to consider what effect they're having on the world around them. If Mothers went to prison, the state would have to take care of the children. This costs money. The taxes of the hard-working, law-abiding amongst us. This money should be used to better people's lives, not deal with the consequences of people's irresponsible actions.

With Consolidism implemented, Governments will need to monitor population numbers. If they start to creep higher than desired, an additional measure would have to be enforced. In a country whose population is exceeding the maximum, it would be illegal to have children, for example in the year of 2015. Of course, prior warning would have to be given, and it would be, 11 months in advance. Anybody who has a child in that year would be subject to the previously mentioned penalties. This way, the population numbers are brought down due to the number of people who sadly pass away in that year. Dependent on numbers, it may be necessary to enforce this law for 2 or even 3 years at a time. In order to ensure a bright, peaceful future for your children, would that be such a major problem, waiting 3 years to have a child? Are we really that selfish toward our own children? The minds of a nation may buck against this, but unless we do it, your children will feel great pain, in a world that's a hundred times worse than that which we're witnessing today. We all have to start taking responsibility for our place in the world. Do you run your household successfully by making irresponsible decisions? By having more children than you can afford to cater for? Are you thinking not allowing women to bear any children for one year will, for example, leave gaps in school years? If no children are born in a year, there will come a time when the first year of schools across the country are empty? There will be some who break the law. That will result in some children being present in that school year. The remainder of a country's teaching resources could be used to offer education to those older persons who wish to improve their skills. This Consolidates the population's skills and improves society. It's insane to propose that, for whatever the reasons people may come up with, we have to continue to have children born every year. If you're thirsty, do you cut off your foot just so that you can drink some blood? No. There are alternative ways to find a drink without continuing to damage ourselves in the way that we are. We can put a man on the moon, so any minor, initial issues we face if we change our course for the better, will be easily surmountable. Overpopulation is the biggest problem we're faced with as a planet, and we have to do whatever it takes to avert the chaos that will befall us as a result of it.

Consolidating the population numbers allows you to Consolidate and improve every aspect of society. Providing better healthcare and public services for all. Providing good quality education for the children of tomorrow. Providing a reliable, but more importantly, safe transportation infrastructure. It's estimated that if Air Travel increases at current rates, there will be at least one Air Accident Per Week somewhere in the World. When will that be? 2050, 2075? No. 2015. Air Travel Numbers increase as Population numbers increase. Why more Accidents? One reason is just by sheer virtue of the Numbers. The probability of accidents happening, increases with each additional aircraft we put into the air. The other reason though, is that people within the Aviation Industry will become Overworked & Overstressed as they have to process and transport more passengers. Accidents will follow in greater numbers, guaranteed. The bigger an operation, the more difficult it is to run. We have to Consolidate. If we do, we can focus all our minds and efforts far better.

If we did Consolidate, we could 'focus' on manageable economies, ensuring people have jobs to go to. Roads wouldn't need resurfacing so often. There wouldn't be such a large demand for fuels, and the subsequent pollution. Less Air Travel. Travel of any kind for that matter. It will be safer. Less people needing to Travel, means the world's Resources will last longer. Absolutely everything is improved if Consolidation & Consolidism is set to work. Instead of having to go through the incredibly difficult process of building new bigger infrastructure, such as a hospital, in order to cater for a larger population, we can simply adopt the strategy of refurbishing the existing hospitals, or any infrastructure, for a longer period of time. This still creates construction jobs, but doesn't take nearly as much time, thus ensuring good healthcare is in place quicker for those who are badly in need. When a hospital has fewer patients to process, its staff are not overstressed, and there's less wear and tear, thus providing a better service for longer.

If we don't Consolidate, we will continue to be blinded and handicapped by the numbers. With Consolidation and Consolidism, the otherwise muddied waters of our societies would clear, with the way forward appearing plainly identifiable before us. If we put a cap on population numbers, and look after our own, everything will fall into place. From having ample housing, to good roads, to no wars with other countries over resources. If we don't cap the numbers, the 'Diner' becomes a 200 table Diner and everybody spends their days running around with their head in a whirl, never actually achieving anything to move us forward as beings, as a planet. What happens in large busy Diners or Restaurants? Delayed orders, incorrect orders, orders arriving cold. That wouldn't happen in a 2 Table Diner. The first people to announce that they're rejecting Politics, adopting Consolidism and taking the so far discussed steps, will be rewarding their country with the honor of having enacted the biggest, most important change in humankind's history. That would be quite an accolade to hold as a country, as a people. Without Consolidism, we won't have a history to look back on. The history books will quite literally go up in the flames of the conflicts which lay ahead.

★★★

In addition to controlling population numbers, it's also vital that we eliminate 'Dead Money' or 'Catatonic Currency'. Currently, the Politicians think it's a good idea to let millions of people across the world sit on fortunes in their bank accounts. In the USA in 2007, 1% of the population owned 34.6% of the country's total wealth. It would take a Consolidist Government approximately a Nano-Second to identify this as being not only detrimental to society, but being positively and unmistakably unviable as a strategy for creating a prosperous and fair society. How can the 99% good citizens of a country be provided for bountifully, both by themselves and their Government, when so much wealth is being hoarded by so few. They can't is the answer. The Maths is simple and unmistakable. Millions receiving Food Stamps, i.e. your taxes, whilst a Hollywood Executive sits on hundreds of millions of dollars. Crazy to the extreme, and beyond. It would take a Pico-Second for a Consolidist Government to decide that it was going to act to put right this craziness that's been allowed by the Politicians for so long.

Businesspeople will not be allowed to hoard millions, or even sometimes billions for themselves. Why should some people's salaries be thousands of times greater than others? Have you ever wondered that? There's only so much a person and a pair of hands can do. As the world is now, if a Businessperson has a $100 Million fortune, they may spend $30 Million of that over their lifetimes, but the rest wallows in the bank, Dead. When they die, what happens to the fortune, that has come from the pockets of the Proletariat, You? The money gets handed down to their children, and the same happens again. The money is Dead. Out of society forever. Although, some Mega-Rich Businesspersons do spend a lot more than $30 Million. What about the Mega-Rich who spend $500 Million on Mega Yachts? Acceptable when hundreds of millions across the globe don't have clean water to drink? Good for the Economy? Gives people jobs? Wouldn't it be better if the Mega-Rich Businessperson's Fortune was capped, at still a very generous level, then the rest of the money used to create 'Society-Bettering Jobs', such as Cancer Research Scientists or vast teams dedicated to seeking out Child Abuse. This instead of creating jobs making 100ft Jacuzzis to be installed on the Mega-Yacht. That is Common Sense that would improve all our lives. Allowing the Mega-Yachts and Jacuzzis is insanity. A Consolidist Government realises this and would cap the amount that everybody is allowed to have in their bank accounts. For somebody of great use to society, such as a Firefighter, the limit would be, for example, in the UK, £1 Million. If it is somebody who is totally useless to society, such as a soccer player, it would be capped at £50,000. Anybody who decides to try and somehow hide money from society, dodge the much reduced taxes or play the system, will have all their money taken from them, and feel the full punishment of a Consolidist Prison, with their sentence dependent on how much they've tried to hide.

The mega-rich might try to play the system by 'spending' millions quickly, or 'give money away' in underhand transactions, thus allowing them to bank more of the multi-million currency profits at the end of the month. With Consolidation making the operation more manageable, and the end of Catatonic Currency resulting in teams dedicated to auditing businesses and their profits. This 'playing' will be easily exposed and even more easily punished, as their entire operations are shut down and handed for free to a patriotic, compassionate person to run and benefit from. This only following 'warning' sanctions which cap their spending each month, albeit at an extremely generous level. Perhaps $250,000 per month for a businessperson whose permitted fortune is $5 million. This is a thousand times more than us 99% have to spend each month, 'currently'.

For Businesswomen & Men and Entrepreneurs, many of which in today's world are filthy rich, the fortune you are allowed to have ownership of, should be proportional to how many people you employ. This with the previously mentioned maximum of $5 Million, or the equivalent of whichever country the person resides in. Anything more is just not necessary and excessive. Also, somebody earning maybe hundreds of thousands of currency a year, doesn't need bonuses the size of which the Politicians currently allow. A Consolidst Government would see that bonuses are limited to a maximum of $2,000, or the equivalent, should the public vote for it. Will You? We all know it's a 100% guarantee. For years, You the 99% have expressed your disgust at gluttonous bonuses. Have the politicians listened to you? Not a chance. They never listen to the 99%. There are currently hardworking people out there who are forced by the Politicians to get by on $20,000 a year. So why when a rich businessperson earns say $300,000 a year, would they need a bonus of any more than $2,000? It's just not 'Common Sense' and a Consolidist Government would not allow it to happen.

It may be said that if we start capping fortunes, Businesspersons and their money will move abroad, resulting in the loss of jobs. The first thing to say is if we all adopt Consolidism, that will not occur. Will this happen? To be entirely honest, it's unlikely. Therefore, the next statement to make is that, as previously mentioned, we need the mindset of people to switch from greed and themselves, to generosity and those around them. Currently, in the vast majority of cases, the human mind is a long way from this wavelength frequency of thought. What is most important to keep in mind is that all the fortunes sitting in every bank account of the rich and famous across the world come from one place, your pockets. The pockets of the Proletariat. There is no other way to make a fortune in the world. There is no other way to make money in the world. As long as a country has its Proletariat masses, it can survive. The wealth is in the Proleteriat. The world's economy is fuelled by you, and a Consoldist Government realises this.

If the greedy choose to move to Non-Consolidist countries, a Consolidist Government would invest in installing patriotic, compassionate people in their place to run exactly the same type of business. Using the same infrastructure and resources that are currently in place. The type of person our countries need, is someone who's selfless, not focusing solely on taking as much money as possible away from the hard-working Proletarian. The Consolidist Government would help ensure the patriot has everything they need to continue the business. No doubt, money will be needed to implement this policy, but, the millions generated around the country every week from not allowing sportspersons and other "useless" people to earn fortunes and render it "Dead" in their bank accounts, can be used to reinvest into producing a society where everybody gets a fair crack of the whip. Those who mean more to us, will receive more. Those millions generated every week, where do they come from? Your pockets. Would you stand up and say "Yes, I'll run this company for 200,000 currency a year, first & foremost with the people in mind, not wealth & power"? If the company employs a lot of people, that is the kind of salary which can be expected. There are many capable people out there who are very capable of taking opportunities like this, and a Consolidst Government would give them all the help they need.

If we cap the amount of money business owners and shareholders make, this could jeopardize investment from outside a country? A Consoldist Government realises this too, and would give special concessions, 'if' the economic climate requires it, relaxing the rules to attract investment and create jobs. What would have been 'Catatonic Currency', could be used to subsidise foreign businesses, making a country an attractive investment, again, 'if' the economic climate requires it, which it may well not due to the implementation of 'Consolidation' and the elimination of 'Catatonic Currency'. For example, a Consolidist Government would subsidise the workforce's wages. This would both have the effect of, 'first and foremost', ensuring the people receive good salaries, but also resulting in the owners of the business not having to use so much of their turnover to pay their employees. Consolidism would also subsidise businesses, both domestic and foreign, in such a way that it makes the products cheaper for its own citizens, subsequently leaving more money in your pockets. All this good the 'Catatonic Currency' can be used for, but the Politicians are not willing to make the change.

★★★

At the moment, away from the cameras, there are Soccer Players, Popstars, Filmstars and rich Businesspeople around the world, laughing at the Proletariat and their Governments for being so gullible and stupid, allowing them to earn so much money, while the masses hover around the breadline. They have to be laughing, because it is an absolute joke. A Consolidist Government taking office, signals the end of this clandestine giggle culture. This practice of accepting millions for giving no "service" whatsoever to justify it, is sanctioned by the Politicians. It's crazy. What you put in, is what you get out. A Consolidist believes we must start living by that. A Consolidist Government would cap wealth and the rest of the money would be poured back into society. The turnover from a sport's game, the money that has come from your pockets, would be available for all to see on the relevant website. Be it a soccer club or perhaps a tennis venue such as Wimbledon. The total would then be broken down as to how it's going to be 'used'. How much is to be paid to players and the staff needed for the 'game' to go ahead. And by far the biggest figure, how much is going to be fed back into society, creating jobs and bettering the community local to the sports venue. Of course, not all areas of every country have sports venues, therefore some of the money will be 'used' to invest in other areas of that country. As can be seen by the total mess many countries are in around the world, we can't kill the money off that's taken from your pockets. We have to keep it alive. If it dies, so too does your quality of life and prosperity.

Again people might say that for example, the best soccer players will leave the country, which means the fans will lose out. They might well move abroad, but this will give other players a chance to play. Players who haven't quite made it, due to the fact that there can only be so many players competing at the 'highest level'. We will give those a chance to play on television, in the big stadiums. We're all completely kidding ourselves if we think that the current crop of professional footballers really are the best in the world by far, and there are no other players who even come close. There are tens of thousands of people around the world who can play the virtually skill-less game of soccer equally as good, if not better than the current players.

The current players are in the position they're in right now, just because they were in the right place at the right time. As opposed to those who haven't made it, because they weren't quite in the right place at the right time. When a soccer club sends scouts out to watch games and search for young 'talent', there's only so many games and players they can watch. Also, people sometimes have bad games. If they have a bad game when a scout comes to watch, they're obviously not going to impress. All this means that there will be some equally 'talented' players who do not get seen or do not get seen playing well. Those who do make it then become the massive, idolised stars, because humans are mesmerized by seeing them on television, playing in the big stadiums, wearing their shiny shirts, under the bright lights.

If you have a decent level of 'skill' and you are the one chosen to play on television for the big clubs, you will become the star. It's not the case that you become the star because you really are better than virtually anybody else in the world who's playing the game. How many times have you heard about extremely 'talented' people who never make it to the top? If they happened to have been watched by the scout, and the player who's made it hadn't been, they would become the star. With this in mind, a Consolidist Government would allow those who want to, to become famous, but not rich. You can't become rich for playing a ball game. It makes absolutely no sense at all that you could put virtually nothing into society and get so much out, as Politicians are currently allowing.

You get to play a ball game for a living, wearing the shiny shirt, in the big stadium, adored by the fans. That's your reward.

There are people out there who have to undertake hard, physical labour everyday to earn their money. If you get the chance to play a ball game you enjoy for £300 per week, you can't not count yourself extremely lucky. When talking about the game of soccer, the word 'talent' must be placed in inverted commas due to the fact that a soccer player has a miniscule amount of talent. Soccer is a game with an extremely low level of skill. It's not a case of making unnecessary derogatory comments about soccer players. It's just a fact. A fact that needs to be identified, because it is just plain wrong that these are the people within our societies who are rewarded the most. We have to put this right, together, for the sake of you and your children. It's not just soccer. It's the case with any Sports Star, Popstar, TV Chat Show Host or any of the 'Celebrities' that our current societies create from nothing. If you're in the right place at the right time, and are chosen to appear on television, you will become the star. You don't need any of what society currently regards as talent.

Not only do we need to realize actual talent, and not just 'Television Talent', where people fall under the spell of seeing someone on their electronic box, somehow believing their talented. We have to realize talent that makes a contribution to society. Dancing, a.k.a. throwing your body, arms and legs around, is not a talent. Shouting into a microphone, a.k.a. singing, involves no talent. Not even the greatest voice that's ever been, constitutes talent. You can either shout into a microphone in a way that, for some reason, humans in the year 2012 think is amazing, or you can't. There is virtually zero development of skill in singing. You've either got it or you haven't. Even if it did take decades of painstaking training and practice, it contributes nothing to society.

Bouncing around and mumbling into a microphone, a.k.a. Rapping, not only involves no talent, it's actually the antithesis of talent. Walking, talking, laughing, crying, sitting, standing, a.k.a.

acting, involves no talent. Walking, sitting, lying down and pouting, all whilst wearing clothes, a.k.a. modeling, involves no talent. Kicking a leather blob around a grassy pitch, a.k.a. soccer, involves no talent. There are sports that do involve talent. Snooker & Golf for example are games with relatively high levels of skill. But as a people, as a being, as a civilization, for the sake of our survival, we need to realize that even though they involve talent and skill, they make no contribution to a fair and functioning society, and therefore should be rewarded as such. Soldiers, Police, Firefighters, Medics. These professions involve talent that contributes vastly to society, and it is these professions that should be rewarded as such. A Consolidist Government would make sure your money both stays in society and goes to the people who deserve it.

Not only are we all mesmerized by ball games instead of important issues such as Child or Animal abuse. The television channels use up so much of their time, and the planet's energy, talking about ball games and other sports. There are some channels dedicated solely to this purpose. When there are so many important issues in the world that we need to concentrate on, the news channels spend alot, if not all of their time, discussing Tennis, Basketball or whatever sport. A Consolidist Government wouldn't ban these channels, or ban them from discussing sports, but, it would propose that we limit it. Planet Earth's resources are finite. There's only so much of them we can sensibly afford to waste on 'Games'.

Currently, reality television programmes elevate people from nothing to musical superstar status. These people have half a singing voice, can't play an instrument, don't write their own songs and don't have a musical bone in their bodies. In just a couple of hundred years, the evolution of our race, has taken music from Ludwig Van Beethoven to Leona Lewis. This is a perfect illustration of how far down the wrong path the human race is. Not only are these non-musical, "musical" superstars talentless. They're judged by people who also have no musical skills. Yet we take what they say seriously. We're all falling for this charade. A charade which has one aim. To take your money from you. The 'business' of being talentless in a 'profession', and being judged by talentless people, is hoarding hundreds of billions of your currency. Why do we fall for it? Because it all takes place on the electronic box. Behind the scenes they must be rolling around with laughter "I can't believe they're all so stupid to fall for this. She shouts into a microphone, I say it's great. That's all it takes for us to get rich. They're such gullible idiots". A Consolidist Government would still allow reality television programmes, but, it would make sure people don't make hundreds of billions of currency from them. Even if you are, for example, a fantastically skilled guitar player, who's practiced hard since you were a young girl or boy. You can't become filthy rich for such a non-contribution to society.

We mustn't be under the misapprehension that Consolidism would rule with an iron fist. Some of the measures laid out in the manifesto so far, may at first seem draconian. The reason for this is that we've all had our minds numbed to the ideas, opinions and totally ineffective policies of Politicians over the years. Initially, change always seems ominous, whatever it may be that you plan to change. These will be changes for the better. If you're a law abiding, hardworking, contributing citizen, such as a supermarket checkout attendant, somebody who makes the world tick, a Consolidist Government would make your lives immeasurably better. All around, it's plain to see that Politicians and their money-making baby, Capitalism, don't work. In 2012, the UK's debt stands at £1 Trillion. In 2012, the USA's debt stands at $15 Trillion. This is the position your Politicians and their Capitalist ideology have put you in. In simple terms, and in ascending order, the Consolidist Party would like to lay out in clear terms, the 6 Main reasons for these debts.

- Allowing population numbers to grow unchecked, thus introducing unmanageable operations.
- Allowing 'Catatonic Currency', which is so incredibly

damaging to our Societies, it can't be put into words. Not allowing 'Catatonic Currency' has so many benefits, such as, among others that have already been discussed, the "Banking Crisis" would not and could not have occurred if 'Catatonic Currency' wasn't allowed to be a reality in our lives.

- Pandering to foreign persons, allowing them to freely enter your country and take advantage of your Politician-created PHR, PC & also State Benefits. As you can no doubt see, this results in your taxes being spent on the foreign persons, not You and Your family.

- Fighting Wars in foreign lands, when there is a simple solution, the only sensible solution, to the problem of Terrorism. This will be discussed in the chapter "Terrorism".

- Pandering to, and not putting any consequences in place for the criminals, dishonest, irresponsible and lazy within our societies.

- Taking Health & Safety, Phony Human Rights, Political Correctness & Bureaucracy to a level which is beyond a joke.

It is that simple. If we tackle the above, we will propser. Will the Politicians do it? Have they done it yet, with all the time and chances they've had? Do you feel like thanking them or throttling them for the position you find yourself in? Exactly. But, we can't do that. We can say what we want about them, and anybody for that matter, but, to physically harm, and negatively affect somebody, is wrong. We need to 'throttle' them at the ballot box. It's time to change your country for the better. Consolidism will do just that. Consolidism doesn't sit on the left or right. It sits on the side of 'Common Sense'. Saying and doing "Whatever it Takes" to improve the lives of its citizens. We have to drop the Politicians, the façade, the charade, nonsensical Health & Safety, PHR, PC, Bureaucracy, the inherent greed-fuelled desires within us, and get on with improving our world, for ourselves 'and' our fellow citizens. Everybody matters. Not just ourselves.

CONSOLIDATION

The world the Politicians have created for us is one of debt, suffering and injustice. Not only have 'they' got us into this debt, but they have the gall to try and blame it on the "the banks". We're not stupid though. We realize that the blame lies largely with them. For a long time, they've had the power to cross each of the points off the above list as having been eradicated or rectified. Due to the Politicians, we live in a world where change and improvement is always said to be on the horizon, but never ever arrives. We live in a world where the lazy, dishonest and criminal elements are not only not punished, but rewarded with free money. A world where foreign persons come before our own. A Consolidist Government would look them all straight in the eye and say "We cannot give you any of the hardworking people's taxes. Not a penny or dime".

The Politicians have you living in a world where you work hard to save money in a bank account ready for your hard-earned retirement. They then announce the banks have lost all your money, and, 'more' money will have to be removed from your lives in different ways, shapes and forms, Taxes, Public Services Cuts, just to be able to get the money back that you've worked all your life for. All this and the bank bosses still get million currency bonuses at the end of the year. Not with a Consolidist Government. Never. It would stop instantly, should you ask it to at the ballot box. What's the reason the irresponsibility of the banks went unchecked? The Government is trying to run too big an operation and missed the transgressions. Just as in your job, you will inevitably make more mistakes as your workload increases. The mistakes and mismanagements are proportional to the workload, in a job or a country. It's a simple concept.

We have to keep our lives and societies simple. Don't let the Politicians complicate matters. They've created their own little complicated world of waffling speeches and policies in which you can never identify any concrete substance. You can never put your finger on exactly what they're trying to say. Would you agree? They do this to mask their agenda of Self-gain, the gain of the Mega-rich

1%, or in an attempt to blind us to their mistakes and mismanagements. Adding insult to injury, some of them actually make up an element of the 1%. Everything can be boiled down and simplified, with the sole aim of making the 99%' lives better. With a Consolidist Government, we wouldn't be fighting unnecessary wars abroad. We would be providing for our citizens before foreign persons. Due to Consolidation, we would be effectively monitoring major institutions important to the functioning of a society. We would make the taxes of the banks, who 'You' had to bail out, higher. As is the Politician's way, a Consolidist Government wouldn't just talk about it, it would do it.

There are now ultra-rich businesspersons in certain countries indicating they would be willing to pay higher taxes. They're willing to give more of the tens of millions they earn, from your pockets, back to society. They realize that this is a 'Common Sense' approach that will produce a fair and bountiful society. This is highly commendable of them to care about the people of their country. To realise that the current system is flawed, where they pay the same rate of tax as someone who earns millions upon millions less than them. These are the type of people we need. This is the mental approach we should all adopt. We need to be people who care about our fellow citizens. People who are not just working to suck every penny we possibly can out of the system. The Consolidist Party applauds these emerging altruistic businesspersons greatly. This is the kind of patriotism that Consolidism calls for. And even though it would cap their earnings, albeit at a very generous level, proportional to the amount of jobs they've created, it would help them in every way to grow their business, if, the population numbers require growth.

Consolidism would implement a multi-tiered tax system based on how much you earn. Not just for example a 2 tiered tax system. In the UK, is it 'Common Sense' that somebody earning £150,000 per year pays the same tax as someone earning £40,000 per year? Exactly. The UK Politicians think so. With the elimination of 'Catatonic Currency', these taxes would be a lot lower than they currently are. Consolidism would cap the fortunes of everybody in society. This has to be done or nothing will ever improve. The people who make a contribution to society, will be able to have a greater fortune than those who do not. A soldier makes a major contribution to society. A Pest Controller makes a contribution to society. A Soccer player makes no contribution to society. Does keeping the money alive sound like 'Common Sense'? Or shall we continue with Politicians, who see fit to allow talentless reality television stars to hoard millions of your hard earned currency? All this while you sit in a roadwork riddled traffic jam on the way home from the 'important to society' job you earn 20,000 currency 'a year' doing. Is this really how the world should be functioning? Just as you lay down sensible rules in your house, we too have to lay down sensible rules in our countries.

★★★

Consolidism is a force of the people, for the people. A Consolidist Government, with the now abundant funds in society, would setup permanent Referendum stations right across its country. You and Your family would get a real say in all the important issues in Your lives. A say about the 'actual' important issues in your lives. That's what should occupy our consciousnesses every day of our lives. Not ball games & film stars. Do you ever wonder why it's the Politicians who make up the laws and implement their idiotic policies on your behalf? Just a hundred or so people deciding on laws for tens of millions. Is that Democracy? Should you not have a say much more often? These referendum stations would avert the immensely frustrating restrictions 'Partisan Politics' puts upon your country's prosperity.

Not only do the Politicians continually discuss the wrong issues and proposals. They either then have these time and money wasting proposals watered down or completely blocked by 'Partisan Politics'. Consolidism believes you should ask the people if they want to crack down severely hard on criminals. It should ask the people directly, if they want to stop the meg-rich sitting on billions, while they struggle along on next to nothing. Consolidism knows what the answer would be. Consolidism wants to hear what the people think. The people must be allowed to speak, and they must be listened to. A Consolidist Government would have many referendums every year, even every month and week, on the key issues in your lives. You'll be able to cast a vote online or call into the referendum station on your way home from work, with no traffic jams and very few roadworks, and push a button which gives You a say in 'Your' lives. You'll have a voice. A Consolidist Government will make sure of it.

With Consolidism, You, we as a collective, hold the power, not the smug, lying and cheating, issue-dodging Politicians. Would you prefer to see 50 million currency of your taxes, go to your children's education, or go towards the education of children halfway across the world? You'll get a say in it. In Your home, do Your children come first, or the children who live across the other side of the city? Even though we have duties to those across the other side of the city and world, it cannot be at the expense of our own. We all need to look after our own financially, and be respectful and responsible towards others in every other way. On a family level, looking after your own, means your children and close relatives. On a country level, a Consolidist Government would ensure it looks after all its citizens before those of other countries. 'If' the money is available, and a foreign cause is worthwhile, it would help, absolutely. But not at the expense of its own.

Consolidism will create a society, a world, where you wake up in the morning, look out of your window and say "Ahhhh" not "Arghhhhhhhhhhhh!". Where the real heroes and talented people are rewarded and lauded. Where people can do whatever they want with their lives. Chase your dreams by all means, but you will be rewarded appropriately. If you choose to be a criminal, we must punish you as is appropriate. If you choose to be a sportsperson, you will be rewarded accordingly. If you choose to be a Paramedic you will be rewarded greatly. It will be a world where the Politicians and Politics can no longer foul up your lives, with you being powerless to stop them. Where our inner cities are regenerated, community centres built and hospitals refurbished with regularity. Where Soldiers being kept in their jobs, is regarded as more important than looking after unwanted, unskilled foreign persons and asylum seekers. Where International Aid budgets are cut before Domestic Public Services spending. Would you give money to feed your neighbours child before your own? Is that 'Common Sense'? It would be a world where people are rewarded for doing good, not 'not doing bad'. Where Rappers sleep safe in their 1 bedroomed apartments due to the now many patrolling Police their 'songs' are so critical of.

Would it be 'Common Sense' to grow our businesses by first putting a cap on the population, then gradually training and sucking all the unemployed people out of the system? Or would it be 'Common Sense' to let the population grow, enabling your business to grow, but also having the amount of unemployed, lazy, criminals and immigrants grow from the numbers that are already sullying your existences? Exactly. There are certain benefits of 'Consolidation' that would no doubt take time to become apparent. It's not possible to reduce the world's population to two thirds overnight. There are though, certain things that can be done immediately, such as capping earnings and keeping money circulating in society, to yours and your children's great benefit. How are we supposed to run a tight ship when, firstly we have Politicians running the show, and secondly we have too many people to cater for on the planet? We can't is the answer. It's impossible. We have to change if we are to improve our lives. The way the world is currently set up does not work for 99% of the people. Would you agree? Should we change course is the next question? Whether you come from Mogadishu, Massachusetts, Manchester or a planet orbiting Betelgeuse, the only 'honest' answer you can scream is "Yes!".

We can either have totally non-consequential, open-door, dysfunctional societies and countries, where people can afford to be lazy or partake in criminal activities. Where foreign persons are allowed to prey on the hardworking people's taxes. Or we can stand up and say "We are not going to let this happen any longer. If you're a foreign person in need, for whatever reason, sorry, we feel for you, but at the moment we just don't have the money to help you. If through Consolidism we manage to work our way into a position where we're debt free and all our citizens are living good lives, we will consider helping you. If you're a citizen of this country, now that Consolidism has eliminated 'Catatonic Currency', your earnings will be far better and the cost of living cheaper, as every expense in our lives is subsidised by a Consolidist Government utilising what is right now 'Catatonic Currency'. Groceries, Fuel, Utilities. Everything 'can' be much cheaper than it is now, if the Politicians would just use some Common Sense. With this greater reward and incentive to work, you have to pull your weight like everybody else, otherwise you get nothing". We have to start being "Positively Harsh" towards each other, just as you are towards your children. How would your children grow up if you weren't this way towards them? It's for their own good, and Consolidism is for our own good. Consolidist Societics will put an end to 99% of the world's problems. Just by virtue of the creatures we are, and the way in which we co-exist, it will never be perfect, but it will be infinitely better than the state the Politicians have it in at the moment.

★★★

The Politicians try to scare, blind and confuse us every day. Deflecting our minds away from the fact that if they never existed, our problems would never have existed. They spend their days dreaming up and implementing measures which we all know will never work. All the while, they allow hundreds of billions of currency to lay dormant all around the world. Using this currency will go such a long way to solving our problems. It all boils down to the fact that the Politicians are running a devious, flawed operation, in which You are the ones who always lose out. If we keep things simple and take the steps laid out in this chapter, You will Win. Consolidism can change the world. Currently the taxes you pay are not going to resurfacing roads or building healthcare facilities. They're being used to make sure the bank bosses, whose incompetence has cost your countries massively, continue to receive million currency bonuses on top of their already multi-million currency salaries.

Has anybody ever actually been indicted in connection with the "Banking Crisis"? No. Why? Because the Politicians are in the pockets of the people who cost all of you a fortune. If you cost the taxpayers of your country billions of currency, would you expect to have the Police knocking at your door? If you act irresponsibly in running your household, will the Government bail you out? Would you expect them to bail you out and give you a million currency bonus? Exactly. This system is insanity. How difficult can it be? Take our money, keep it safe, don't gamble it away in any of the multitude of complicated investments or arrangements, and make sure it's there when we come and ask for it. Not a chance though, under the Politicians. They allow the Mega-rich Bankers to do what they want with our money in an attempt to become even richer than they already are. Somewhere, in some way, the Politicians make money from allowing the banking industry to conduct its business in the way it does. Whether it be from direct, unseen bribes or from secret 'society wealth-stripping' investments. This system, as far as the 99% are concerned, and many many other systems currently in our lives, needs to be stripped down and simplified if it is to become sustainable. If we don't simplify it, we will continue to encounter the problems we're currently experiencing. Simplifying this, and other systems in our lives, involves firstly implementing 'Consolidation' of population numbers. Only then we will be able to view and rectify our problems effectively. As is plain to see, the banking system is broken. But it's a system that you can change by adopting Consolidism.

A Consolidist believes that there are those in society who deserve to be championed and those who don't. It is the 99% who are most important within our societies, and it is the 99% who should be rewarded as such. No doubt, some Political blocs will attempt to identify Consolidism as supporting a "Redistribution of Wealth" and label it "Communist", but, the people who do this will be the Media Tycoons and Capitalist Government Politicians, both with their 'Political Agendas'. They've intentionally stigmatised the "Redistribution of Wealth" & "Communism" over the years. Why? Because of their desire to have the wealth and power for themselves.

How can they be the most important, most powerful and richest, if they are seen to be agreeing with systems that other people hold sway over? Especially when they're systems that won't allow them to hoard billions of the people's currency for themselves. Tony Blair would quite probably attempt to ignorantly dismiss Consolidism. Why? What is he worth now? Estimations are in the tens of millions range. How is he worth this? All the privileges and handshakes that came with being a Capitalist Politician. He wouldn't be able to amass the kind of wealth he's currently enjoying, if Consolidism was a reality. So why would he tout such a system?

Forget for a moment, the words Communism & Capitalism. Cleanse your minds of them. Is it 'Common Sense' that in the UK in the year 2012, a soccer player earns £150,000 per week, and a nurse earns £20,000 per year? Whatever Socio-Political persuasion anybody may be of, if they're totally honest, saying outwardly, exactly what they're thinking in their minds, they could not say that this is 'Common Sense' and that they're proud to live in a society where this is a reality. Consolidism supports a "Redistribution of Wealth" in our societies. It's not a bad thing, as the Capitalist Politicians will try and tell you. It's a good thing. Consolidism believes the wealth should go to those who deserve it, the 99%. Currently the wealth in our societies 'sits' in entirely the wrong places. Would you agree? Although supporting a "Redistribution of Wealth", Consolidism has many other theories and policies which have never been identified by any previous Political party. Consolidism is not Communism, or any of the other Socio-Political Ideologies demonised by the greedy Capitalist Politicians. Consolidists are a Party, Political Bloc and Societicians in their own right. A fresh, fair start for the beleaguered 99%.

A Consolidist wants to see a world where our children are thoughtful, community and career oriented. Not ones who are interested in being the coolest, baddest, meanest, richest, sexiest, toughest and most expensively dressed. These are the kinds of things that are important to the youth of today. It's down to us to a certain degree yes, but mostly it's the fault of the Politicians. Consolidism wants to see a young man interested in making old people's lives better, not extinguishing a young life with a knife or gun. Because one day they'll be old too, and will be greatly appreciative for any generosity that comes their way.

★★★

As the world population continues to grow, certain countries are having to build multi-billion currency nuclear power stations. Politician run Governments, due to decades of incompetence, simply don't have the money to be able to do this. Would it not make sense to stop the population growing, subsequently eliminating the need for the power stations? Politicians don't think so. Instead, they think it's 'Common Sense' to let the population grow, borrow the money to build the nuclear power station, but at the same time, allow a model to make millions on a reality television show which is using up the electricity generated by the power station the country couldn't afford. Can you hear that as you read it? Is it really happening? The borrowed money results in your taxes being raised and public spending being reduced to pay for the interest on the loan. All the while, what additional effect does the continual growth of populations have? More dishonest and State-Dependent people. A larger operation to try and run, resulting in more mistakes and wasted money.

A Consolidist Government wouldn't simply ban everything it sees as negative. Society would be free, but, if a television channel wants to show a pointless reality television program, instead of a program discussing how a community could be made better, there'll be an affordable premium to pay. There's only so much coal and gas in the world to generate electricity, and we're currently wasting alot of it on reality television shows and printing magazines which discuss what colour a talentless Popstar paints her toenails. When the coal & gas start to run out, World Wars will rage hard, and we'll all suffer. With the population growing unchecked, the carnage will come quicker. And all the while we're making television programs about low-intelligence models that spend the entirety of the program Cat-Fighting. Not everybody is highly intelligent, obviously. But persons who are of low intelligence should use their skills for the good of the community. Perhaps as Taxi-drivers or Supermarket Janitors. Under Consolidism, they'll be better rewarded if they do choose to do something that isn't totally useless to society. Is it 'Common Sense' to allow the wars to approach us with an ever-quickening fury? Who will pay via the currency of pain & misery if we don't act now? Your children and grandchildren. This is why we have to Consolidate and adopt the new Socio-Political Ideology that is 'Consolidism'.

Existing Governments and Politicians would no doubt, for reasons of self-interest, tell you that the ideas & policies of

CONSOLIDATION

Consolidism would be disastrous. Of course, we can all see straight through the fact that they're bound to say this. If you the people start to support Consolidism, they can no longer make their fortunes and hold onto the power they've craved all their lives. Let Consolidism ask you this? What kind of mess are we in at the moment, having given the Politicians their chances? Is Consolidism worth a try? Consolidism will absolutely work. Imagine one day, your electronic box breaks. You decide to try and fix it yourself, because money is so tight in your home. Why? The Politicians. First you attempt to remove the back cover with a screwdriver, but it doesn't quite fit the screw. What do you do? Wake up every day and try the same screwdriver? Or perhaps try a different one. We have to start doing things differently. The first stop, is consigning Politicians to the history books.

CHAPTER 2

Crime & Punishment

Do you hate to see how little respect many young people have for the elderly nowadays? How little manners and consideration they exhibit towards them? Some of the elderly were involved in wars which have ensured the young people enjoy their free lives today. Do you hate the fact that the Politicians keep releasing a life-time repeat offender criminal from prison, who then continues to be a drain on society? Let out to steal your car, again, or burglarise your home, again. You would no doubt feel frustration and anger on these subjects, but, is it as much frustration and anger as you feel towards the Politicians who always promise to reduce Anti-Social behaviour and crime significantly when they're trying to win power?

Not only during a campaign phase, but also when they're the incumbent, holding the power required to get tough. Do they ever manage to achieve any of the results they put their hands on their hearts and promise they'll deliver to you? You are deserving of a Government and Justice System that protects you by being severely harsh on criminals. The Consolidist Party would like to be given the chance to make a difference. And here's how it would be done.

Prisons are one of the absolute key elements to forming a solid Monolithic Block of a foundation on which a successful society can form. This cannot be overstated. A society can't fulfil its potential without prosecution and incarceration working in perfect synergy. A society needs to have the provision to put offenders in prison and keep them locked up for as long as they deserve to be there. This is something the current systems cannot achieve. We need to be able to appropriately punish offenders who consciously choose to commit crimes and negatively affect you, the fine, upstanding citizens who go to work every day, pay your taxes and would never dream of breaking the law. It's your taxes that pay for the prisons, and pay the Politicians to make the kinds of decisions that ensure you're protected from offenders, and they're 'punished' for their crimes.

In many countries around the world, prisons are stretched to breaking point, not able to accommodate those who continue to choose to break the law. What effect does this have? Offences go improperly punished. If offences are improperly or lightly punished, there's no real deterrent for potential lawbreakers. That's a very simple concept. Do the Politicians understand this and take the necessary steps to put it right? Exactly. This is the first reason why Politicians never ever achieve any significant reductions in crime, as they always promise to, whenever an election comes around. The second reason is that prisons are not punitive enough. Not even close.

Prisons need to be able to accommodate anybody who commits a crime of any significance with no problem whatsoever. They need to easily be able to hold, depending on the size of the city they're in, tens of thousands of prisoners. Once an offender is in prison, they need to be kept there for the duration that they deserve, under humane, but very unpleasant conditions. There are those who would say no matter how hellish a prison is, people will still break the law. Of course this is true, crime will never be totally eliminated. But what a Consolidist Government would make sure of is, if you break the law, you're removed from society for a duration that is deserving of your crime. During this period of incarceration, you can't negatively affect the lives of the honest and hard-working. As the Politicians currently have it, an offender may be given a suspended sentence or a fine for their crime, thus allowing them to offend again, and perhaps not be caught for the next crime they commit.

If in your life you choose to be a repeat offender, you will feel the biting punishment of a 'Consolidist Justice System'. If you make the conscious decision to one day leave your home and steal from a shop or business, you will be sentenced to 5 years in a 'Consolidist Prison', that is, if the people believe you should be, after they're asked their opinion through a referendum. Do you think people who steal cars or carry out similar crimes should be locked up for a long time? If when you're released, you make the conscious decision to burglarise a house, or commit a similarly rated crime which has a negative effect on those around you, you will be sentenced to 10 years in a 'Consolidist Prison', should the people support it. If when you're released, you make the conscious decision to commit a robbery, or similarly rated crime, you will spend the rest of your life in a 'Consolidist Prison'. After being arrested for committing a crime, a blood test will be conducted. If the person is found to have alcohol or any substance in their system, and are committing the crime to feed an addiction, the sentences for the first two crimes will be doubled.

Sentences are served in full in the 'Consolidist Justice System'. Five years means 5 years. Not a day more or less.

Life under the 'Consolidist Justice System' means Life. If a single crime committed has been particularly brutal, perhaps a murder, or you're a repeat offender as detailed above, a Consolidist Government would make sure you are never again able to negatively affect a member of our positive and prosperous societies. The construction style of a 'Consolidist Prison', which will be discussed at length in this chapter, would be such that it can accommodate absolutely everybody who breaks the law for as long as they deserve to be locked up.

In today's world, a Politician's incompetence, lack of intelligence, cowardice to exact change and the inability to think on a different wavelength to that which has gone before, has resulted in short sentences being handed down for serious offences, such as, perhaps 8 years for Rape. To a Consolidist this is an inappropriately short sentence for such a serious crime, if, the evidence strongly suggests that the Rape occurred. This is bad enough, but in addition, due to the inefficient and expensive method of imprisonment, the offender who has made the conscious decision to Rape someone, is released after 4 years for not misbehaving whilst in prison. Is this really happening? The Politicians think it a good idea to reward a Rapist for not misbehaving.

What rewards do the Politicians pour upon you for not misbehaving in your lives? Does it anger you when you hear of criminals being sentenced to life in prison, but instead serving perhaps 20 years? It certainly angers a Consolidist. To reward a criminal for not misbehaving is totally backward and typical of the way a Politician's mind works.

What's the reason for the policy of reduced sentences for good behaviour? To maintain order within the prisons? To encourage an offender to rehabilitate? These are the lies a Politician would give you. The real reason is that, due the Politicians being unable to come up with a more cost-effective style of prison, and having no money due to them bungling the running of your country, there isn't the space or money to keep people in prison for the duration of time that they deserve to be in there. Once again, the stupidity of the Politician is negatively affecting you. Not only does the person who stole your car get released early, but, while they are in prison, more of your taxes than should be, are being spent on keeping them there. Is that justice? Is that 'Common Sense'?

If you broke the law under a Consolidist Government, it would keep you in the punitively harsh environment of a 'Consolidist Prison' for the entirety of a sentence, deserving of the crime you have committed. The style of construction and efficiency of maintenance and upkeep of the prisons, means there is no problem at all in ensuring you behave whilst inside, and even less of a problem in having the funds available to keep you away from what a Consolidist Government treasures most, Society.

Would you say that a prison should rehabilitate people? If we keep prisoners in hellish conditions, they'll end up being released as worse human beings than when they entered? Let's consider some figures from a 1994 study that was carried out in the USA. Within 3 years of their release from prison, 70.2% of Robbers were rearrested, 74% of Burglars were rearrested, 74.6% of Larcenists were rearrested & 78.8% of Motor Vehicle Thieves were rearrested. Is the current system working? If something clearly isn't working, is it a good idea to try a new strategy? Within 3 years of release, 1.2% of people incarcerated for homicide were rearrested for homicide. A Consolidist believes that if just 1 human is ever lost as a result of a Politician's policy of releasing convicted murderers, that's one too many. Would you agree? What if it was the family member sitting next to your right now who was murdered?

In 15 states across the USA, the 272,111 people discharged from prison in 1994, accumulated 4.1 million arrest charges before their most recent imprisonment, and a further 744,000 charges in the 3 years following their release. Conclusion? The only possible conclusion? The system is not working. The Politicians are releasing criminals who should be permanently incarcerated. Not only will Politicians allow people to be released after serving too little time, but, prisons are an absolute dawdle for the criminals, especially the hardened. So where's the deterrent? There isn't one.

Prisons are at worst an inconvenience for criminals, and at best, from the criminal's hardened viewpoint, they're like hotels. So the person who decides to break into your home and steal your LCD Television is sentenced to 1 year in prison. They serve 6 months in hotel-like conditions, and are then released to burglarise your home again before Christmas. Welcome to a Politician's mind. Come on in. They don't care though. It's not their home that will be burglarised. They live in low crime areas, and have close Police protection. The worst aspect of this hasn't yet been identified. An offender will probably only go to prison for say, stealing your car, if it's not the first one they've stolen. If it's the first, they'll more than likely receive a suspended sentence, fine, a period of probation, or perhaps community service. This is the dangerous world the Politician's mind has created. But it's your dangerous world, not theirs.

Many prisons across the world have the following, and it's unbelievable to think that the Politicians have allowed a society to form, where this ink can be printed on this paper, and be true in what it's saying. Prisons have Exercise Yards, Pool Tables, Free Good Quality Food, Soft Beds & Blankets, sometimes in their own private cell, Gyms, Libraries, Televisions, Games Consoles. Do they sound like the kinds of provisions society should be making for the people who are a negative, sometimes violent drain upon it? Not only do they get all the above, you're paying for it! Instead of the money being invested in your children's schools, the Politicians think it should instead be used to give murderers books to read. Do you think that's Common Sense? Then, under the Phony Human Rights Laws created and allowed by the Politicians, these prisoners could make a case for suing the Government if they feel they're not getting enough protein in their prison diet. If the prisoner wins, it's your money that will be used to compensate them. That may seem like an unlikely scenario, but as you will know, there are cases like that occurring within our prison systems. These people who've quite possibly broken into a war veteran's home, are allowed to sue the state, you, and further negatively affect society in the most ridiculous black comedy-like situations. Does that sound like Common Sense? The reason the Politicians can't put criminals away as long as they deserve to be, is because too much 'hotel' type space is provided, and too many 'hotel' type provisions are made for the prisoners. They're too luxurious and too expensive to build and maintain.

The drain and scourge on society that are criminals, should be locked up in 'Consolidist Prisons'. Locked up for as long as they deserve, in an environment they will be highly keen to ever avoid returning to. And if they do return, the next time they come back, they'll stay for alot longer, thus taking them off the streets away from Society for longer. As a 'Consolidist Prison' is described, you may well be thinking it's too harsh. This is a key reason why countries are in such a mess. Why the world is in such a mess. There's too much PHR, PC, H&S & Red-Tape. Too much pandering to those who are a drain on society. The societies we live in, which have been formed by the Politicians, have us all crawling up our behinds concerning ourselves with things that don't really matter. If we don't, seemingly at first, 'drastically' change our mindset, how can we ever expect to effect a 'drastic' betterment in our quality of lives? What every Politician is either failing to realise, or shying away from, is that our societies are fundamentally and completely flawed. We are flawed as a civilization, as beings. The people in Government should either realise this, or, if they do realise it, front up and 'lead' us to improving ourselves and our societies, but, they're Politicians, who either don't have the sense or gumption. Either way, it's you who's going to continue to suffer unless we actually take measures that will actually have results, like a 'Consolidist Prison' and the 'Consolidist Justice System'.

Before we make an effective plan for how we as societies incarcerate people, we'd obviously like to not have to do it at all. If we could prevent, that would be far better than attempting to implement the costly cure. The Consolidist Societician's cure being far cheaper than the Politician's cure, it must be said. Probably the most effective prevention we can implement is catching the kids early. A personality, the way a person conducts themselves and acts within society, is all formed and shaped when their minds are young. It's all down to the type of people their parents are, their education, the type of people they see around them, and learn from in society. Is it easier to ensure all of the above is conducive to producing a good citizen, if we have 100 people living in a town or 100,000? It's a simple concept. Wouldn't you agree? If we implement Consolidism & Consolidation, we will be able to improve every aspect of our societies, thus ensuring that the next generation coming through are respectable, law-abiding citizens. The implementation of Consolidation results in every aspect of our societies being easier to improve. It is the cement that will grip everything, and hold us together as strong units.

Do you remember how certain things you saw when you were a child, left a lasting effect on you. Like perhaps a scary film. This is when our minds are most impressionable. We have a duty as a society to use this time wisely in our collective quest to produce decent citizens. Instead of showing adverts which peddle the poison that is Alcohol, and pointless reality television programmes about 'nothing', a Consolidist Government proposes that we air adverts and programmes showing how horrible a 'Consolidist Prison' is, and how this is what awaits bad people who have no regard for society around them. These airings will show the absolute full brutal realities of life behind bars. They will show actual footage of prison assaults and attacks. There are some who will say this is too extreme, but, if we don't start to take measures like these, which at first seem extreme, but actually aren't, nothing will ever change for the better.

We need to make an impression on children and 'absolutely deter' them from a life of crime. Of course, making it not so harsh a measure as it first seems, the parents will be with the children to comfort, educate and reinforce as they watch the transmissions. It just makes no sense at all to hide all the negatives that would befall a child, if, they do later choose a life of crime. If we shy away from letting them know exactly what will happen to them, where's the deterrent? There isn't one. Simply saying "Be Good" has, on the whole, never worked, and never will.

A Consolidist Government would arrange for trips to schools by former inmates, under Police supervision. They could describe the horrors, amongst others, of how they couldn't rest for a second because they didn't know if they were going to be attacked. To have the inmate there in front of the children, would leave such an impression on many, if not all the children. Most effective though, Non-Mandatory school trips to the prisons would be arranged and conducted. The children's safety of course would be paramount, with parents and many Police officers accompanying them. These trips will be made easily possible due to the style of construction of a 'Consolidist Prison', as will be discussed, and they will leave a massive impression on the children.

Do you think it would be too much, to show adverts which dissuade children from lives of crime and Alcohol? To show adverts and television programmes of, for example, a drunk person fighting with Police in an arrest cell. Just 1 hour prior to the fight, they were caught Burglarising someone's home to pay for their Alcohol addiction. Next, the advert would show the person the following day, suffering the pain of Alcohol withdrawal in the brutal environment of a 'Consolidist Prison'. This person started to take Alcohol, couldn't drink responsibly, and turned to crime to pay for their habit. This is now where their life is. Do you want this kids? We have to give them the full, shocking story. How can we ever expect the vast majority of our children to steer clear of a life of crime and Alcohol abuse, if we aren't totally truthful and proactively forthcoming about what will happen to them?

We can't keep giving them the diluted education currently peddled by the Politicians. A single, isolated advert on television with a 'Soap Opera' sketch, showing none of the painful realities of Alcohol and crime will not work. It's plainly obvious that this is the case. Children need to be responsibly 'scared' away from a life of crime and substance irresponsibility. It's the responsibility of the parents, the Consolidist Government and everybody in society to be totally open, thus giving our children every chance of avoiding a life of prison and misery. If we don't start enforcing serious measures, we'll still be talking about crime as a major problem in 100 years.

There are already a fair percentage of people in society who are good citizens. They and their children would never contemplate committing a crime. Then we have the element of society who are a drain on us all. The unruly, the disrespectful, the argumentative, the combative, the Alcohol abusers, the law breakers. It's a reality that causes major problems within our societies, therefore, as is the belief of a Consolidist, it must be spoken as it is, and tackled head on. The proposed hard-hitting education is aimed more at these people. We all have a responsibility towards each other in society. A responsibility to be respectful, productive and thoughtful. Is that the way you would bring your children up? If it is, then you are the productive members of society who will be rewarded and protected massively by a Consolidist Government. A Consolidist Government would not allow those wrongdoers in society to continue to blight your lives. It would end.

It has to be said that there are those amongst us who are abusive, obnoxious, disrespectful, violent. Those who drink Alcohol all day and don't work. What is the Politician's deterrent to dissuade people from acting like this? In certain countries, they give them free money and housing. Another gem of an idea from the Politicians. These people's children are never educated about where Alcohol, unruliness and crime get you, because society is too PC timid. As they grow up, there are no deterrents, warnings or punishments in place to dissuade them from consciously choosing the same kind of life, which they're likely to due to their lack of exposure to hard-hitting education, and having a natural tendency to follow their parents. We have to break the cycle. Who decides that Political Correctness is vital within our societies, thus having us all carefully treading on eggshells about anything and everything we say, and resulting in the identification of problem people being deemed Politically Incorrect? Who decides on the 'punishments', 'warnings' and 'deterrents' that are supposed to be averting society's problems? It's the Politicians.

When one of these problem people or their children does steal their third car, they'll eventually be sent to prison, where they've got their own bed, free good quality food, books, televisions, pool tables. When this is the case, there's going to be no other outcome than the continuation of their crime upon release. Would you agree? It's an insane, never-ending cycle that will not cease unless we take action. With a Consolidist Government, all your young life, you'd be effectively educated about where crime gets you. If you still end up doing wrong, you face the harsh consequences. That's how a Consolidist sees it. Very simple. You do wrong, you're punished accordingly. Is this how you were brought up? That's a fundamental law that this planet should be operating on. Thanks to the Politicians, it's currently operating on the law of, "If you do wrong, you may not be punished at all, because we don't have the money or space to keep you in prison. If what you've done wrong is exceptionally bad, we'll have to somehow find a place in prison for you. We call it prison, really it's a holiday camp. What will happen then is, we'll slash the punishment in half for you not misbehaving further. Your victim? We don't care about them in all of this. The decisions we make are based on what the capacity our prison system allows. We know it offers no deterrent against crime, but we just cannot figure out how to get our system to a position where we're able to imprison criminals for as long as they deserve". Is this Common Sense?

Let's analyse the Non-Existent measures the Politicians deem to be deterrents within our Justice Systems. In 2007, 460 people were killed on the UK's roads as a result of drink-driving. Surely, with this in mind, the penalty for drink driving should be harsh indeed? Not at all, thinks a Politician. In the UK, they've decided that a driving ban and a fine of a few hundred pounds is appropriate. Prison is only considered if the offender is massively over the limit, more than 115 micrograms of Alcohol per 100ml of breath, or they've committed the offence more than once. A prison sentence for a first time drink-drive offender with no previous convictions, is very rare indeed, virtually non-existent. So with people being killed by this offence, where's the deterrent that's going to drastically reduce it? There isn't one. Why? For one, the UK can't afford and doesn't have the space to imprison people for drink-driving, and secondly, it's not the Politicians or any of their family members who are likely to be killed or injured as the result of a drink-driver. Why should they worry?

With a Consolidist Government, if you're caught driving under the influence of Alcohol, you go to a 'Consolidist Prison' for 2 years, should the people support it through a referendum asking them of their opinion. Not a day less, not a day more. If you're caught a second time, you serve 4 years. Every time after that, you're sentenced is doubled. This is a serious problem that requires a serious deterrent. People are losing family members because an irresponsible few, make the conscious decision to drink and drive. This problem must be drastically reduced, and those who still decide to drink and drive must be harshly punished for their crime against the society which they have duties towards. Does that sound sensible? Do you believe these measures to be harsh?

Imagine one of your closest loved ones is killed by a drink-driver? You've lost them forever and will never see them again. Is it harsh now? This is happening to people. We have to start appreciating that, and putting in place robust deterrents and punishments. There are those who would say, "No matter how big the deterrent, you'll never eliminate any crime". Of course this is undeniably true, but at least with a Consolidist Government, if someone does commit a crime, what was the deterrent, becomes a harsh punishment, taking them out of society so they can't do it again for a long time.

In the UK, the legal blood Alcohol limit for driving is 35 micrograms of Alcohol per 100ml of breath. Yet, if you're found to have 39 micrograms or less, you're not charged. Is that 'Common Sense'? Which is illegal, 35 or 40 micrograms? With a Consolidist Government, if you have precisely 35 micrograms or more, you serve a 2 year prison sentence, should the people support it. What society would actually be telling the irresponsible amongst us is,

"Don't even risk drinking any Alcohol at all if you're going to drive. If you're caught with 35 micrograms or more on your breath, you will go to prison for 2 years. Not a day more or less.

This is a serious problem that's killing people, and we will not stand for it any longer". Sound like 'Common Sense'? Is it too much to ask, in the name of saving lives, that we don't drink Alcohol before we drive? Would you ever consider driving a car whilst drunk? No? Why should those who do it, get away with soft 'punishments' when they're putting your valuable lives at risk. What the UK Politicians say to drink drivers is "You can have one drink, maybe two if you leave some time in-between them. If you're caught, we'll give you the second chance of only prosecuting if you're found to have 40 micrograms or more of Alcohol in your breath. If you are charged, it won't be anything you really need to fear. Just a driving ban and a fine". Is this what you would describe as an effective deterrent against drink-driving? The Politicians think so. If it was the Politician or a close member of their family that was to be killed by a drink-driver, do you think they'd want to put a much stronger deterrent in place to avoid it happening. Or a more of a punishment than a driving ban and fine? Exactly.

People using mobile phones whilst driving is also emerging as a big problem on our roads. This is injuring and killing people, irreparably ruining lives. What is the deterrent the Politicians in the UK are enforcing in an attempt to avoid these tragedies? A £60 fine and 3 penalty points on a person's license? Is that going to work? Do people really fear these repercussions, should they make this transgression? How would a Consolidist Government propose we deal with the offence? If you're caught using a mobile phone whilst driving, without a "Hands-Free Kit", you will serve 3 months in a 'Consolidist Prison', should the people support it. If you reoffend, the sentence is doubled, and so on and so forth. The offence must be filmed, either by a Police officer or a member of the public. With the elimination of 'Catatonic Currency', all Police officers will be provided with helmet and handheld cameras.

What we would saying as a society is "We all have a responsibility towards each other to not use mobile phones whilst driving. It is killing people. Be responsible and take measures to ensure you never use a mobile phone whilst driving. Place your phone in the trunk of your car. Write yourself reminder notes. Anything that will ensure you don't affect your concentration whilst operating a motor vehicle". Better than advertising Peanut Butter, television airtime would be used to broadcast public service messages detailing measures which can be taken to avoid a lapse of memory, and remind people of the consequences if they don't live up to their responsibilities. Does this sound too draconian? Perhaps you don't think it will be you or your family affected by this particular crime. But guaranteed, somewhere in the world, within the next 24 hours, someone will be killed by somebody not concentrating on the road because they're using a mobile phone. Imagine that's your child. Does the punishment and measures to try and prevent it happening sound harsh now?

We have to put an end 99% of situations where people's lives are negatively affected by other people's downright irresponsible behaviour. If we don't start taking robust measures, we'll still be talking about these problems in 50 years. Drink & Mobile Phone Driving are just two isolated examples of crimes which we have to start to reduce massively. Not just talk about it, as the Politicians do.

The Consolidist Party proposes that we need to educate the young minds who are our tomorrow. Educate them effectively, not half-heartedly. If you take watered down measures, you can expect nothing else but watered down results. You get out, what you put in. In your home, when you're child steps out of line, do you meekly ask them to stop what they're doing? No, of course you don't. If your child transgresses, you have to raise your voice, adjust your facial expression and, it has to be said, scare them into line. You take whatever measures are necessary to make sure they don't start to gain the upper hand in your relationship. As a society, we must do the same with the irresponsible amongst us. It's for the benefit of you, your children, your neighbours and everybody in society, that you and your children are responsible, productive members of society.

In addition to public service messages and effective deterrents, a Consolidist believes "Youth Service" is an excellent tool, and should be compulsory. Upon turning 16 years of age, every young girl and boy will attend a camp for 2 months where they'll learn about respect, hardwork, responsibility & clean, healthy living. This will reinforce what they've been taught by you the parent, and also the Consolidist Government through public service messages. A Government which has actually done something in an effort to help You and Your children lead better lives.

★★★

The lack of respect the youth of today show for themselves, their parents, the older generations, their peers or the authorities, is a major problem within our societies. Their attitudes, due largely to what they see on television and the internet, are Annihilatory and Fatilist. It's considered cool to be zany and crazy and not care about anything, including your own body. It's considered uncool to care about, and work to improve your community. They see Rappers objectifying women and 'Cop Hating', with their 'music' always having the theme of "I'm better than you. Screw you. You can't touch me". Being irresponsible and offensive is made to look hip and trendy. This culture must be changed if the future generations are to live in a world that's fair, responsible and prosperous. In the UK, Anti-Social behaviour is rife, with the Politicians constantly promising to wipe it out. Have they actually done anything about it UK? Exactly.

A Consolidist Government wouldn't ban any type of music or television programmes, but, it would put greater taxes upon them, and constantly reinforce through public messages and education that you can't bring the hating and crazy attitude into the real world. You cannot be allowed to disrespect and be abusive towards people because that's what happened in the Rap Video you saw on television last night. A Consolidist Government would, with great intensity, promote the message that you must be responsible and be responsible for your actions. To drastically reduce Youth Crime and Anti-Social Behaviour, a Consolidist Government would swiftly make the following measures a reality.

In every school, in every year from the ages of 7 to 16, 'Respect Teams' would be installed. These teams will comprise of 10 adults per school year/form. The members of the team will be sharply and smartly dressed. They will be confident, fit and healthy people with good attitudes towards life. It will be their job to be constantly present amongst the children, both in lessons and during break times. They will be the kind of impressive people that the children will look up to. Constantly interacting with the children, they'll instil within them, a sense of respect, pride and responsibility. They will educate the children on the negatives of arguing, fighting, swearing, drinking, smoking, and how these activities have a negative effect on all of us. If the children have these people amongst them, they won't be able to partake in all the negative activities they're currently susceptible to, and their minds won't become entrenched in this behaviour.

It is actually the job of the teachers to do this, but, a Consolidist Government realises that they have to be focused on educating academically within the classroom, and often do not have the time or numbers to be constantly around the children during break times and lunchtimes. The more people you have to help with a task, the more chance the task will be completed successfully.

With the implementation of 'Consolidation', there will be fewer children in schools, meaning the staff to children ratio will be greater, thus ensuring children can be effectively educated. The current system has not worked thus far, and the Consolidist Party realises we need to try something different. A compulsory lesson, in every school, for children of all ages would be 'Respect'. Members of the 'Respect Team' would give these lessons where the children are taught about their responsibility towards their parents, society and themselves. We need to constantly remind children, in an effective way, that we all have to toe the line. Would these 'Respect teams' be too expensive? They would, if we continue to allow 'Catatonic Currency'.

To deal with the youths and young adults who do still choose to cause trouble, be unruly and vandalise property in their communities, a Consolidist Government would create 'Police Diffuser Squads'. These would be teams of 12 women or men, dressed in Police uniforms and protective equipment. Many 'Police Diffuser Squads' would patrol the streets of all the towns and cities of a country in marked vehicles, ready to provide a quick and effective response to Anti-Social Behaviour. One of the main reasons the problem of Anti-Social Behaviour is not being solved by Politicians, is that it takes the Police too long to attend a scene where the trouble is occurring.

A Consolidist Government believes it owes it to you to be able to walk safely down your street at night, live securely in your houses and get a peaceful night's sleep ready for work the next day. Have the Politicians made this a reality? Have they constantly promised to, when they're on their knees begging for your vote? They pretend to care, but, they don't. Not one little bit. Why can't the Police get to a scene quick enough? There aren't enough of them. Why aren't there enough Police on our streets? It's all the issues that have already been mentioned many times. As yet, the Non-Implementation of "Consolidation", resulting in an unmanageable operation with too many people to cater for, and, where mistakes and wastage of time and money occurs. 'Catatonic Currency'. Pandering to foreign persons, the lazy and the criminals. Phony Human Rights, PC & Health & Safety, which pulls all your taxes away from what they should be being spent on. This is all the fault of the Politicians.

Are any of your relatives affected by Anti-Social Behaviour? With the 'Police Diffuser Squads' backing the Police up, they can be at the scene quickly, ready to alight and rundown the miscreants. It will be made clear to everybody in society, that if the Police or the 'Police Diffuser Squads' arrive on a scene and ask to speak to you, but you flee, this will be an offence punishable by 10 days in prison. The Second time it's 20 Days. Police and 'Police Diffuser Squads' will be fitted with helmet cameras so evidence of the offence is recorded. Do these 'Police Diffuser Squads' sound too extreme? Perhaps the punishment for fleeing is over and above? If you were politely asked to stop by the Police or a 'Police Diffuser Squad' Leader, so they could speak to you to investigate an offence, would you flee? Of course you wouldn't, because you've got nothing to hide. You will only feel the punishment of the 'people', if you're doing wrong. It will not be the punishment of a Consolidist Government. The punishment is there because the people want it. They want it after being fed up with decades of the Politicians talk, but no action. You only have something to fear if you're one of the irresponsible or disrespectful elements of our society. The good citizens are absolutely sick and tired of people misbehaving, draining their taxes and getting away with crimes. The Politicians will never stop it. A Consolidist Government will put an end to it.

Once they arrive on scene, it will be the job of the Police to lead the investigation of an incident. If after the investigation, there is no evidence for any arrests, the unruly will be asked to quiet themselves down and be on their way. Just the fact that these 'Police Diffuser Squads' are ready and waiting at a 'moment's' notice, will deter Anti-Social Behaviour. If the unruly are disrespectful by continuing to shout and swear in your respectable community, they will be filmed, arrested and imprisoned for 'Disorderly Conduct' for 10 days, should the people support this sentence. Every raising of their voice after the initial offence for which they are to spend 10 days in prison for, thus having a negative effect on the community, will be caught on camera and result in a small fine.

Every future offence after this day, will result in the sentence and fines being doubled.

If they are children, the parents will have to pay the fines. Their children are their responsibility. If their children are resulting in your taxes being spent to deal with their misbehaviour, there has to be some recompense. If they have no parents, the fine will be paid by any family member anywhere in the country. Does this sound too severe? Let's us not forget, they've chosen to be unruly and disorderly. Then when confronted by Police Officers & 'Police Diffuser Squads', they've chosen to be abusive and uncooperative. It's all a conscious choice, made by them. Would you in a million years run wild in the streets, swearing and shouting and vandalising people's property? Exactly. They should not be allowed to get away with it, and with a Consolidist Government, they wouldn't. Is it unfair that the parents or distant family members have to pay the fines? If that's unfair, how unfair is it that you, totally innocent, respectable people living over the other side of the country, have your taxes spent on this unruly element, before it's spent on bettering the lives of you and your children. Every time a youth or adult is apprehended for a minor offence such as criminal damage, where they have physically negatively affected somebody, they're sentenced to 1 month in a youth or adult 'Consolidist Prison', should the people support this sentence. Their next offence results in a 2 month imprisonment, and so on and so forth.

A 'Consolidist Prison' and Justice System has no problem accommodating criminals. None whatsoever. Currently, the Politicians allow your elderly family members to feel like prisoners in their own homes, as the Anti-Social run riot in the streets, vandalising at will, with no fear of any punishment from the Politicians. It has to stop. 'Police Diffuser Squads' all over the country. Cameras for every member of the 'Police Diffuser Squads' and every Police Officer. Does all this sound too expensive to implement? Not with the elimination of "Catatonic Currency".

In the UK for example, the £100 you pay for you and your

family to go and watch a soccer match on the weekend won't lay corpse-like in the bank accounts of the soccer players forevermore. They'll get what they deserve, £300 per week. The rest will go towards making your community a safer place to live. Your money used to improve your lives, and the lives of the soccer players for that matter. If you're streets are actually made safe, with you not just continually having to suffer the frustration of the Politician's empty promises, would you be more content to pay your taxes? Taxes, which with a Consolidist Government would be considerably less than they are now. You and your family get to watch a soccer match, the soccer players, managers and staff make a living, and your streets are secured. It's a system and society that actually works.

With the effective 'Respect & Responsibility' education the children will receive in their schools and through public service announcements, the level of Anti-Social Behaviour in a country would be minute anyway. The thought of actually making the conscious decision to run rowdily through housing estates, inconveniencing and disturbing other members of the community, would never cross a child's mind. The 'Respect Teams', 'Police Diffuser Squads' & extra Police Officers that countries could afford due to the elimination of "Catatonic Currency", would create jobs for people. Through and through, these are measures that will work for everybody involved. These measures would no doubt reduce crime. Would you agree?

It's not enough though. As societies, we owe it to our lonely, sick, aged, vulnerable, law-abiding to take the fight against crime to relentless lengths. What else would a Consolidist Government do to reduce crime figures to virtually zero? After all the education, public service announcements & extra law enforcement personnel. For those who do step out of line, be they an irresponsible parent setting a bad example for their children, a lazy thief, or wayward layabout that's the product of bad parents, we have to actually 'punish' them. They need to be put in an environment they will never ever want to go back to. A 'Consolidist Prison'.

The prisons of today are almost comical in terms of what they provide for criminals. You'd be excused for thinking that the Politicians are possibly playing a joke on us all. They're also flawed in their style of construction and layout. It costs 'you' a fortune to construct and maintain these prisons which provide criminals, privacy, nooks & crannies where they can carry out further crime such as assaults, extortion and production of Alcohol. After a burglar has broken into your house and stolen the possessions you've worked hard for, the Politicians think it a good idea to give them their own room with a comfortable bed? Is that Common Sense? Do you think that's a good idea? Is it supposed to be punishment or reward? The icing on the cake is that your taxes pay for this and many other privileges. A Consolidist believes that these are privileges which shouldn't be afforded to someone who's made the conscious decision to break the law. What do you think? Quite the opposite of providing them with privileges, a Consolidist Government believes everything possible should be taken away from them. One thing it believes would have a punishing effect, and serve as an effective deterrent, is to take away their privacy and personal space. This is how a "Consolidist Prison" would do that…..

On the outskirts of a city, an enormous circular concrete slab set into the ground, a third of a mile in diameter. 220,000m², ready, waiting and able to accommodate the criminals. The outer walls are five metre thick, steel reinforced concrete. Rising 8m up from the concrete slab, steel columns which support a meshed ceiling and walkways where armed guards patrol, looking down on the vast open expanse, seeing everything and anything that goes on. There are no individual cells or spaces provided for the criminals. The toilets and showers are within the open space. There are no cubicles or booths. The criminals will never have a second's privacy. Hundreds of CCTV Cameras capture their 'every' move. The lights are never switched off, only dimmed to a lower level at night. Five metres above the patrolling guards is the prison's roof, keeping the 20,000 prisoners warm and dry inside this simple construction facility.

Not deserving much more than that, they live side by side with the thousands of other criminals. Sleeping on plastic mattresses at night, they then store them around the perimeter of the facility every morning. The cheap construction and maintenance costs and massive capacity of these prisons, would make it possible to build more of them, thus ensuring if someone makes the conscious decision to negatively affect the lives of a hard-working, productive citizen in any way, they will spend time in prison. Separate, appropriately sized prisons would be built for women, men and youths.

Taking the UK as an example, there are currently approximately 97,000 people serving time in the Politician's prisons. If 12 Consolidist Prisons were constructed across the UK, and, Consolidation was implemented, this would mean society has ample capacity to punish those who choose to be a drain upon them. No Fines, Suspended Sentences or Probation, which the judges currently have no choice but to hand down because of the Politician's incompetence. Commit a crime and you go to prison. Not a prison with televisions and games consoles. A harsh, punishing prison. There will be no time deducted as a reward for not misbehaving. This Government has the money and strategy to keep you in prison for as long as you deserve. You're sentenced according to the severity of your crime, and you will serve every day of it.

This means a wannabe terrorist who's planning an atrocity to murder innocent people, can be imprisoned and never released. In prison, terrorists have a reputation almost as bad as paedophiles. A Consolidist Government is not spending any of your hard-earned taxes to protect them, or paedophiles, by separating them from the rest of the prison population. They'll be living side by side with the thousands of other prisoners. They'll not be able to rest for a second. Does it incense you when you hear of paedophiles being housed separately to the general population in prisons to protect them? Did they have any sympathy for their victims? Did they have sympathy for your defenceless children as they abused them?

With a Consolidist Government, they would not receive any special treatment. If they happen to get attacked, the guards will stop it, with their array of weapons, but that's what happens to you if you want to abuse children. They should have thought about it before they made the conscious decision to mentally scar a young child for life. Some may say there are mentally ill people out there who can't help committing a crime such as the above. That may be true in a miniscule amount of cases, but in the majority of cases, the person is playing at the total and utter softness of the system. Playing the stupidity of the Politicians. A Consolidist believes no extra time, money or effort should be wasted on people who've chosen to abuse children or plan or commit terrorist attacks. Would you agree?

Attacks of any kind, against prisoners of any kind, wouldn't be allowed, and would be punishable by the increasing of sentences. The guards would take action to stop the attacks, using rubber and mace bullets and other offensive weapons their provided with. Though, everybody is aware, this is what happens in prison. This is what our children will be taught and shown as they grow up. There are people in prisons who don't care about having their sentence lengthened or being fired upon with rubber bullets. They will still attack you. If you didn't want this to happen, you shouldn't have broken the law. This is the kind of message that would be broadcast within society. This is the kind of deterrent that needs to be provided to drastically reduce crime, and it is this level of deterrent that will be provided by a Consolidist Government.

If there are people out there thinking of planning and perpetrating terrorist attacks, with the implementation of Consolidation, resulting in a more manageable operation. With the elimination of "Catatonic Currency", resulting in far larger security forces. We will be watching you closely, and when you're caught trying to harm our citizens, imprisonment Consolidist style will be your destiny, for the rest of your lives.

Citizens of the UK. When watching the news on television, have you ever heard a report such as this? "MI5 say they are currently monitoring 2,000 terrorist plots in the UK". Can this be real? The Politicians are allowing this? If they have emails or recorded phonecalls which enable them to classify them as terrorist attacks in the planning stage, why, why, why, would they not immediately make arrests, try, then imprison the culprits? Do you think it's too severe to do this after perhaps just a few emails or phonecalls? How would the 7/7 & 9/11 victim's families answer that question? If Consolidist authorities collected just 3 pieces of correspondence from a potential terrorist attack, the people would be arrested and the evidence presented in court. We have to do this to protect our citizens. It serves as both a prevention and cure in a highly effective fashion. Of course 'Common Sense' must be adopted in every case. If it's a 13 year old Caucasian boy writing a joke email to his friend, the authorities should step in and advise that this is not a subject to be joked about. If it's a 30 year old male who fits the profile of a terrorist, talking about explosive's materials on the phone to his friend, and who also fits the terrorist profile, then they must be arrested and tried, if, it's the third occasion they've conducted this type of conversation or sent a piece of correspondence discussing such subjects.

Continuing on the style of prison which awaits potential terrorists and other criminals. Around the perimeter of the circular edifice, Administration, Laundry, Kitchen and Healthcare blocks would be attached to the outside of the reinforced concrete walls. Riot-ready Prison Guards would only in an emergency situation enter the prison and walk amongst the prisoners. If a prisoner requires treatment, or is to be released, they would enter a serious of holding chambers, where steel gates are strategically opened and closed in front of and behind them.

The 'constantly' shackled Prisoners would receive 2 small bags of basic rations per day. Forming orderly queues, the bags would be dropped through hatches by the guards upon the mesh ceiling.

There is no commissary for prisoners. This is supposed to be a prison, not a holiday camp. The prisoners would receive 1 change of clothes and 1 shower per week. Getting the prisoners showered would involve thgem being unshackled through hatches, but, only so many prisoners are free of their shackles at any one time. Everything they require, such as soap and toothbrushes, is dropped through the hatches.

The prisoners would be responsible for keeping their environment clean. Trash such as empty food bags and toothpaste tubes would be collected by the prisoners and deposited through wall mounted chutes where it would then be collected on the safe side and disposed of. If the criminals make the conscious decision to riot, cause damage and a mess, which would be limited and unlikely due to their limited, shackled existence, and no personal possessions, they will live in the filth until they clean it up. That could be 20 days or 20 years. It's up to them. They're responsible for the mess, so they have to deal with the consequences. If the shower and toilet facilities require maintenance, the construction of the prison will be such that a giant steel gates can be rolled across, thus isolating these areas of the prison.

Upon the mesh ceiling, a tear gas delivery system would be installed ready to extinguish trouble should it begin. Perhaps an assault on a terrorist might occur. The patrolling guards would be provided with Gas Masks which they'll carry with them at all times. If tear gas does not diffuse a situation, the guards will use rubber bullets, and as a last resort, tranquiliser guns. Everything will be captured on CCTV and will be available for family members to view, letting them know their relative is being given chances, but is continuing to make the conscious decision to conduct themselves in a negative fashion. Do the above measures sound harsh, inhumane perhaps? If they do, this is the reason our societies are not only not improving, but getting worse.

Our minds have been dumbed down as we've witnessed the Politician's weak measures, pandering to those in society who are resulting in us living sub-standard lives. How many chances do we have to give people? In this situation being described, the criminals are already in prison for breaking the law. Imprisoned, they choose to continue to break the law and ignore the demands of society. There has to come a time when we as a society say "That's it. We're not giving you any more chances". Do you bring your children up giving them as many chances as they want and never punishing them for any misbehaviour? A country is analogous to a home. We're all a family and have to effectively enforce rules and boundaries which ensure we conduct ourselves with others in mind.

Non-contact, family visits through a glass screen will be allowed. Prisons are rife with contraband, and this will be stamped out by a Consolidist Government. Currently, the Politicians know full well about this problem, but do absolutely nothing to stop it. Substances are privileges which only law-abiding citizens should heave the pleasure of. With them not pandering to criminals, Consolidist Prisons will be far cheaper to construct and maintain, thus resulting in you paying less taxes and being able to spend your money on your lives and your family. A Consolidist believes law-abiding families should get first consideration, not criminals. A Politician appears to believe the opposite. Would you agree? To further reduce the burden on you the taxpayer, the families of an imprisoned offender make a payment for each week that the offender spends in prison.

Whether it be the Wife, Mother & Father or the Uncle across the other side of the country. Whether it be 1 week or 20 years. This payment shall pay for their food, electricity and toiletry provisions. Sound unfair? The system right now, as thought sensible by the Politician's, has you paying for not only their food and soap, but also the electricity for them to watch reality television programmes. With dwindling resources soon to create wars all over the globe, the Politicians think it's 'Common Sense' to allow electricity to be used by criminals to watch pointless reality television programmes. It also has you the total stranger to the criminal, living across the other side of the country, paying for ridiculously unnecessary provisions such as these. Is this really happening?

While you're in work one day, a criminal steals your car from your driveway. This person stole somebody else's car just last week, but the system the Politicians currently have in place, doesn't afford society the luxury of being able to put people like this in prison for their first offence. The taxes you're paying have to go towards the Police trying to catch the criminals still on the streets, when they could be spent on you and your families. When the Police catch them a second time, having now just stolen your car and driving it drunk endangering the lives of the people within your community, you have to pay for their food, laundry and electricity to play game's consoles while they're kept in prison for the duration of their light sentence, which is also cut in half as a reward for them not misbehaving. Can you hear that as you read it? Not only is that not 'Common Sense', it's totally Nonsensical!

Before any family members are made to pay for the prisoner's incarceration, the criminal's bank accounts and home are checked for funds. If they have the money, it will be used by society to pay for their stay in prison. If they have possessions, these can be sold to raise money to pay for their stay in prison. If they have enough money in their bank accounts to pay for their stay in prison, their offence was stealing a car, and they have a car, it will be seized by society, sold, and the funds passed on to the victim of their crime. Will they enjoy having their possessions taken away from them? If they have no funds, society will have no choice but to take money from the family members. Perhaps the family don't deserve to have this put upon them, but, you the total stranger certainly don't. This is another effective deterrent. Perhaps a parent will be inclined to bring their children up instilling morals and values, if any of their wrongdoings are going to negatively affect their lives. If a prisoner doesn't have any relatives or funds themselves, then we as society have no choice but to foot the bill for their stay in prison. Though, it will be a meagre existence, as has been described.

This is how a Consolidist Government would deal with criminality. This is the strong education & deterrent that would be put in place. Will as many people break the law with a Consolidist Government looking out for you? What do you think? Those who do, will be removed from society so they can't do it again. A Consolidist believes Prisons should be awful places to exist. If being in prison is like staying in your own bedroom, where's the deterrent? People have the choice to be rehabilitated before they enter prison. It's so simple and should be fundamental to every human. Don't steal. Don't fight. Don't rape. Don't murder. Do you make those decisions every day of your lives when you wake? They're not difficult choices to make, are they? With a Consolidist Government, the people who still break the law will have been educated and warned at great length about what awaits them. They will only have themselves to blame. Under the Politicians, how many chances must this "Sucker Society" give criminals and irresponsible people? We have to put humanity right, right now. Our Politician induced, sub-standard lives are passing us by.

Consolidist Prisons would be built close to military installations. With its style of construction, there is no chance of escape, but, if there is a mass problem within the facility, hundreds of soldiers could be on scene quickly, with automatic weapons and the license to kill. It has to be said that the prisoners are constantly shackled, so a 'mass problem' is highly unlikely. This brings us neatly on to the Military. What role should they play in deterring crime within our societies?

On top of the additional Police Officers and 'Police Diffuser Squads', Consolidism believes the military should be used to clean up our streets and provide safe communities in which we can bring up our children. Instead of having our armies sent to dusty desserts to fight and die in wars that would be totally unnecessary if the Politicians implemented 'Common Sense' policies such as those which will be discussed in the chapters "Immigration", "Terrorism" & "Defence", a Consolidist Government would have them patrolling the streets, playing a similar role to the 'Police Diffuser Squads'. Not only would they provide woman or manpower when situations require it, they will act as a major deterrent.

How much less crime do you think there would be in your city, if there were 1,000 troops patrolling? Would criminals feel as comfortable attempting to steal a car, rob people or vandalise property? Though, it is important to make sure our armed forces are trained and ready, just in case we have to justifiably ask them to fight for our national security. To ensure their skills are kept sharp, they will be rotated in and out of these city patrolling duties, spending periods in training and periods in our communities. The way Politicians are running our countries at the moment now, has your billions in taxes being spent on sending your troops to fight and die in countries where further billions are being spent on the almost impossible task of developing the country. It's an absolute joke. The troops and the money are needed at home. So that everybody feels safe in their communities. So that an old lady can walk out of her home at night and not feel threatened.

This is especially the case in America's crime-ridden cities. The billions and the troops are needed there Mr President. Not in Iraq or Afghanistan. Following the tragic murders at Sandy Hook Elementary School, Gun Control Debates have ignited. The US Government is considering new laws to prevent these all too common tragedies. Will they ask the people what they want done about it? They may 'sham-listen' to the public's suggestions, but, in the end, the Politicians will do what they want. And it is a guarantee that the eventual measures taken, if any, will not be effective at all. It's not their children being murdered due to the inaction. It's not the children of the minority die-hard gun supporter's children that are being killed. So why should either of them care. Point by Point, let Consolidism give a succinct and crisply clear outline on what it would propose, then ask the people to vote on:

- Bring any Troops home from the other side of the World. Put them on the streets and in schools in their thousands.
- Use what is now 'Catatonic Currency' to flood the streets with more Police Officers.
- Allow 1 Handgun only to be owned by a person or family. Nothing higher specification than a handgun. This handgun cannot be taken outside the home.
- Jail anybody who is caught on the streets with a gun for 10 years. If they have alcohol or drugs in their system, the sentence is 20 years.
- Advertise reminders on TV. "Do not carry a gun outside your home". Constantly remind people. Better this on TV than hundreds of Cookery Programs or advertisements for Perfume.
- Ban Violent Video Games and put harsh prison sentences in place for those who broke the rules that 'You' have voted for to try and keep You and Your children safe.
- Hold multiple Amnesty Days per year, resulting in the primary thought on a Communities mind, being to look at those around them and encourage everybody to hand guns into the authorities. Or even report suspected Gun-Carriers to Police. Is this a better issue to have on our minds than ball games?
- Before the law is changed banning guns carried outside homes, the plentiful Military & Police Officers would need to have been deployed. That way, you, the innocent person trying to live your life right, will not be preyed upon by the bad guys.

Those are measures. Real measures that will really effect a change in the Culture of the great country of the USA. Those are measures that will save lives in massive numbers. In the USA, we've all seen footage of Security Personnel as they carry out drills, running through schools with guns drawn. That's a sickening sight. It points to a sickening reality that the politicians have failed us in a big way.

Our societies are continually blighted by crime, with the Politicians taking no real effective strides to reduce it. 'The' major contributory factor to crime and disorder, is Alcohol. When you go out on a Friday night for a few drinks and a good time, do you get so blind drunk that you end up violent? No, of course you don't. You wouldn't dream of it. It's totally wrong, and people who do it should know that. If you don't do it, why should others be allowed to continue to do it? What measures are the Politicians taking to solve this problem? Exactly.

Taking the UK as an example, all across the country, there's major unrest in its towns and cities on Fridays and Saturdays due to Alcohol. More than half of all violent crime in the UK is perpetrated by people who are drunk. The UK Police have to deal with approximately 23,000 Alcohol related fights or incidents per week. Alcohol results in billions of pounds being sucked out of UK communities and being ploughed into policing Alcohol related incidents and providing healthcare for those injured due to Alcohol related aggression and accidents. What drastic and effective deterrents are the UK Politicians putting in place to tackle this massive problem? Somebody who's convicted of being drunk and disorderly in the UK, receives an £80 fine and 1 night in a cell, with a bed. Is this going to solve the problem? Is this an effective deterrent? With a Consolidist Government, any person caught, and filmed, being drunk and disorderly will be sentenced to 1 month in prison, should the people support this sentence in a Referendum. The next offence will attract a sentence of 2 months, and so on and so forth. The irresponsible among us will soon learn that it's not acceptable. And if they don't learn the lesson, they will be removed from society for a long time, and placed where they cannot be a drain on your taxes and lives. If you're a person who makes the conscious decision to go out and drink excessively, knowing you will not have the wherewithal to control your actions and behaviour, there's plenty of room and funds available to keep you in a 'Consolidist Prison'.

If this was any other drug, causing countries to be engulfed with this kind of behaviour every week, there would be absolute civil uproar against it. How can we allow Alcohol to be legal, but deem Marijuana or Cocaine illegal? It's totally hypocritical and typical of the warped mind of a Politician. A Consolidist Government would propose that all drugs are legalised, and would ask the people their opinion in a Referendum. Why should drugs be legalised? This would take the money away from the drug lords who currently run the drug's trades. That way the proceeds, that are coming from some of your pockets, are put back into your community. Non-Drug Users also will see massive benefits from the Turnover. Proceeds which will be used, amongst many other things, to flood the streets with Police, deterring and preventing crimes committed by those who are attempting to feed a habit they can't control, be it drugs or alcohol.

With the amount of money that exists in the drug trade. A trade that will be around forever, whether they're legal or illegal. We could massively improve all our societies and lives. As the Politicians currently have it, billions of funds are in the hands of the drug lords. Billions in currency is spent on incarcerating drug users who would never dream of breaking the law to feed their habit. All the while, Police Officer Numbers are being cut, that's livelihoods lost, or at the very best, numbers maintained, due to the current Austerity measures being taken by Politicians. Our Populations are growing. That means the number of Police and Security Personnel on our City Streets and in our Neighbourhoods needs to grow, or else the Safety & Security of our Children, Families and Friends will be compromised. But the Police Numbers aren't growing under the Politicians, because they don't know how to manage our finances to make sure there's enough money at our disposal.

Legalising Drugs would in itself create tens of thousands of very well paid jobs for the citizens of a country. 'Well paid' Jobs that nowadays are in short supply and great demand. There's hundreds of Billions of Currency available to us, if we just make some simple, bold and obvious decisions. The few police who are on our streets, spend all their time chasing the drugs instead of being in place, ready to deter and prevent burglaries or robberies.

Is the Politician's current strategy working? If something isn't working, after many decades of trying, is it a good idea to take a different approach? Precisely. Quite the opposite of promoting and advertising the legalised drugs to increase revenue. Some of the proceeds will be used educate about how all drugs are extremely bad for your health, but, if you're going to take them, you should take them in moderation. If you don't exhibit Self-Control, as many out there do, you'll end up feeling the full force of the extremely well funded correctional system.

Legalising drugs would make them safer to use, as they'd be produced in professional Government laboratories. In the USA and across the world, how many people over the past decade have been killed or severely burned in Meth Lab Explosions? Lives lost, that could have been saved. If victims do survive explosions, it costs millions over a long period of time to treat their charred bodies. That's millions out of your lives. Time that could have been used to advance our lives, instead of just struggling to bring us back to an even keel. "Just don't attempt to produce Meth, and you won't get burned alive". Is that what some would say? That would be ideal. But as we all know, we don't live an ideal World. People will still attempt to produce Methamphetamine, and have accidents doing so, if it's illegal. 'Perhaps' there'll be a few random incidences where people still try, even if it is made legal. True, but, for every accident we prevent, that's millions extra in your pockets, and more Public Services Time invested in your lives. Just as is true in the finances of your household, in our countries, every little we can save, will improve our lives.

Alcohol is a far more dangerous, addictive and destructive drug than any other in our societies. Currently, society seems to be under the misapprehension that anybody who takes drugs is a non-productive addict curled up in a dark corner, but Alcohol has its responsible and irresponsible users. This is just plain wrong. It's an opinion which has been implanted in our minds by the Politicians.

The only reason most don't see alcohol as being as bad as drugs within our societies, is because that's the way they've known society all their lives. If they had been born into a world where 'drugs' were legal and alcohol was illegal, they'd view alcohol as the demon substance.

There are many among us who use 'drugs' and remain responsible, productive members of society. The word Drugs has such bad connotations, thanks to the Politicians demonising them. So too, many believe that just taking one pill or dab of powder can kill you, but a bottle of Alcohol can't have the same effect. This is true, but why? It's because drugs are produced underground, without the help of knowledgeable scientists. If Alcohol was produced underground, there'd be many thousands more deaths from the killer liquids created. Do you agree that drugs should be legalised? Have the Politicians been trying to solve the problem of drugs for decades? How are they doing? They should have the problem pretty much wrapped up by now, surely? Whether they're legal or illegal, drugs will be part of our societies forevermore. That's a 100% fact. An undeniable reality. The more revenue that's raised from legalised drugs, the more money that needs to be, and can be, invested in Police & Security Personnel. If the revenue falls, the Police & Security Personnel Numbers can be reduced. It's a self-regulating system that will look after itself.

Should we try a different screwdriver to that which the Politicians are using now? If we don't, we'll still be talking about the problem in 100 years, and, we'll still have the billions generated by drugs, in the pockets of druglords and warlords, and not in the pockets of you, the hard-working citizen who deserves a better service than the Politicians are currently providing you with. It's time to change. If we bring drugs out into the open, we can monitor those using them better. We can help them, instead of criminalising them and having them hide their problems because drugs are deemed Non-PC.

If you do get hooked on drugs, and start stealing to feed your habit, a 'Consolidist Prison' awaits. Your addiction could well be to Alcohol. Let's be under no mistake. Let's say it as it is. Many crimes are committed all over the world everyday to feed Alcohol addictions.

Let's break down the phony partition that separates "Drugs" & "Alcohol". Alcohol is not only a drug, it is by far the most expensive and destructive drug to our societies. It kills millions all across the world every year. As many as 75,000 people die every year in the USA from Alcohol related diseases. Each year, approximately 100 people die from taking Ecstasy in the USA. That number could have been drastically reduced if it was produced in controlled laboratories. Search this for yourselves. Professor David Nutt. Sacked as the UK Government's Drug Advisor in 2009, because his 'scientific' results pointed to the fact that Alcohol is the most damaging drug in society. That didn't fit in with what a few hundred stuffy politicians believed, so they got rid of him. The politicians didn't listen to him, and they don't listen to you. They don't listen to anybody or anything except their own 'brains'.

The facts are there and unavoidable. With a Consolidist Government, you can take as many drugs as you want, but, you have to pay for them yourself and you have to remain a responsible person after you've taken them. It is wrong to impose upon anybody who is having no negative effect on those around them. If someone wants to take drugs, they can take them, but, there'll be no free money for people to spend on drinking Alcohol or taking drugs all day every day. See the chapter on 'Housing & Benefits'. You won't be able to deal drugs because the Government are providing good quality, safe drugs for anybody who does choose to partake in drug-taking.

Intertwined with the presently underground drugs in our societies, is the use of weapons as a means to intimidate and control areas of drug distribution. The Politicians know this but still allow the drug's trade to be run by criminal elements. Legalising Drugs would 'drastically' reduce violent crime on our streets in an instant. Not only is violence, knives and guns used for this purpose, but people also, due to the position of human consciousness, feel or are seen as being cool amongst their peers if they carry a weapon. Would you carry a knife when you go out onto the streets, with the intention of stabbing another person to death? Is that really the kind of behaviour you would put upon your fellow citizens? Knife & Gun crime are major problems in our societies. The Politicians continually tell us they'll deal with it. The UK Government's penalty for carrying knives or guns is 5 years imprisonment. Not only do they not carry through with this threat because they can't afford to keep people in prison. If they did sentence someone to 5 years, that person could well be released in just half that time for not misbehaving.

With a Consolidist Government, through the capture of filmed evidence via every security personnel's helmet camera, anybody caught carrying a knife, a gun or any kind of weapon that is unnecessary, will be sentenced to 5 years in a 'Consolidist Prison'. You will serve 5 years, not a day less or more. Once released, the same offence repeated would earn you 10 years in a 'Consolidist Prison'. And so on and so forth, the sentence is doubled. Of course, in handing down such severe sentences, discretion and 'Common Sense' need to be adopted. We all know the profile of the types of people who are committing the knife crime. We know who we should be stopping and searching. Males between approximately 13 and 40, white or black, dressed and acting in a certain manner that has been glamorised by films and rap music videos.

★★★

The Consolidist Party believes that there are millions of people out there who are desperate for Governments that have the courage to take some of the steps mentioned in this chapter, to not only protect you and your families, but also to ensure your taxes don't get wasted on those who don't deserve them. It's not complicated. A Consolidist Government would always strive to avoid overcomplication in everything it provides for you. 'Common Sense' is the driving force in decision and Consolidist policy making.

Everything in society is intertwined and interconnected. If you solve problems and implement effective policies in one area, like crime, this will have the knock-on effect of ensuring less of the people's taxes are spent on tackling crime. This enables you to reduce taxes. More money in people's pockets, means more money spent, thus resulting in an ever-stimulated economy. If the money being spent isn't then allowed to wallow in the bank accounts of the Bourgeoisie, it can be used to ensure dedicated, robust Fraud squads are poised and ready to deliver speedy justice against those in our countries who try to strip people of their hard-earned money.

We all hear of these scam stories virtually every day. Has it ever happened to you? Or perhaps an elderly relative? A Consolidist Government would guarantee that this, and many other of the 'genuine' important issues in your lives, are given ample funding and top priority. These 'scams' are often sometimes 'legal'. Such as mobile phone companies charging exorbitantly high rates for 'lost phone' lines. Knowing full well you have no choice but to call.

We can use the money to provide Cancer Patients with expensive, life-prolonging medication. Medication that, for example, isn't available on the NHS in the UK. And no doubt isn't available to lower income families in the US and across the world. We can use the funds to ensure swift and good quality healthcare for our elderly generation. After being decent hard-working people all their lives, they deserve this. Would you agree? The Politicians think so little of these people who have put into society all their lives, they allow them to live on paltry pensions, while sportspersons worthless to society sit on millions that they'll never spend. To call a sportsperson worthless is not a term of abuse. It's simply stating the fact that their profession contributes nothing to society.

★★★

In the UK in August 2011, riots ignited in cities such as London, Birmingham & Manchester. Once the riots had subsided, the debate began about why they occurred. The type of flawed society we live in was all too evident as the UK saw the debates play out on television. There were news channels who actually interviewed some of the youths that took part in the riots. With their faces concealed beneath hoods and scarves, the reporter stood and talked to them, actually taking them seriously. These people, who just a few days earlier were burning people's houses down and looting businesses, said they did what they did because "The Police and Government don't respect them, and don't provide job opportunities for them". There is no decent, responsible, respectful human being who could accept this as a justifiable reason. The fact that a news channel gives these people a voice, and airs their absolutely ridiculous reasoning is incredulous. This is a perfect illustration of the joke of a society the Politicians have us living in. Firstly, there are hundreds of thousands of jobs' vacancies in the UK. Admittedly, the number of unemployed does outweigh the number of job vacancies. What's the answer to this? Try and grow the economy? That will never ever work. Never. You reduce the population numbers. It's the only answer.

Thanks to the Politicians, the types of unskilled jobs these youths would be able to do, don't pay very well and a Consolidist has sympathy in that respect. This would be put right by a Consolidist Government, as salaries are subsidised using the billions that the Politicians currently allow to lay dormant in the bank accounts of the Mega–rich and talentless. Even with the current low-paid salaries of unskilled jobs, there are people who would be willing and thankful to work instead of having to claim benefits. Why would it be that the youths are unskilled and currently having to accept low salaries? Do you think they're the type of people who tried their hearts out when they were in school? Yes or No? Were these youths the type of children who were always polite to their teachers? Who were always attentive in the classroom? Who always completed their homework on time? Who always revised hard for their exams? Exactly. It's highly likely they were, and did, none of the above. It's highly likely they spent their days fooling around, thinking it was all a joke, listening to rap music, or skipping school altogether.

This is why they're in the position of being unskilled and unemployed. But instead of looking them in the eye, speaking the truth and telling them this is why you are where you are in life, the wavelength the Politicians have got our minds operating on, makes us actually think that we have all done something wrong. Do you think the parents of these youths brought them up well, or were they themselves dysfunctional, lazy, or both, to varying levels, dependent on the household? These youths sit on benefits, drinking and doing nothing with their lives through the conscious decisions they and their parents have made, and the conscious decisions they continue to make. It's that simple. Society has done nothing wrong by them.

There were a few within a London community who were justified in exhibiting anger towards the Police and Government. These were the family and friends of a young man named Mark Duggan, shot dead by Police just days earlier. A sad as it was, not even they would have been justified in burning innocent people's houses down and stealing property from innocent businesses? Would those kinds of violent and destructive actions ever gain anybody the kind of recompense they deserve and were looking for had such a tragedy occurred in their lives? That wasn't even the reason for the riots anyway. The family and friends of Mark Duggan would undoubtedly have more respect and dignity than to act in such a way. But it wasn't the family members who rioted, or probably even the close friends. It became a situation where people took advantage of the recent sad events to steal for their own gain. Not only steal, but simply be violent and damage property. With the contemporary music videos, computer games and television programmes, this is an inherent desire within many people these days.

The youths who were 'searching for recompense' due to the 'lack of respect and jobs provided by the Government'. Do you think these youths spend their days smartly dressed, knocking doors and handing out their resumés with a pleasant smile? Exactly. They spend their days hanging around street corners, wearing trousers 4 sizes too big for them, listening to rap music and doing nothing to improve their positions in life. That's why their unemployed and have no money. They were lazy in school and they're still lazy now. That's the truth that has to be spoken. What is wrong with society whereby we actually pander to the nonsense these youths are trying to pass off as they attempt to justify burning people's houses down and smashing windows? Politicians, that's what's wrong. The Politicians espouse insane behaviour amongst us that they call 'Political Correctness'. This is seriously stifling our societies and preventing us from solving our problems and advancing our lives. No matter what a person's gripe is, random destruction of other people's property is so obviously not the answer, and nor could anyone ever justify it. In a Consolidist Society, people who burn and vandalise other people's property get no voice at all. A voice and respect is earned, when you are seen to be respectful and considerate of society around you.

If a Consolidist Government had been in power for the duration of the lives of these youths, the riots would never have happened. They would have been educated all their lives about where misbehaviour gets them. About what's wrong and right. It would be in their schools and on the television. Their parents would also be responsible, teaching their children how to behave. This would happen due to them knowing that if their children turn out to have criminal tendencies and end up in prison, they will be paying for it. The tab won't simply be left for society to pick up. They'd bring their children up properly because the Consolidist Government would have the time and money to ensure programs and social workers are in place to encourage orderly and respectful environments in which children can grow up. The implementation of 'Consolidation' and the elimination of 'Catatonic Currency' would provide the time and money to make this a reality.

The youths would have received a quality education and upbringing due to the implementation of 'Consolidation'. The less people there are to provide for, the better you can provide for them, both in terms of education and jobs. It's simple Mathematics. Why are 'Special Needs' children placed in classes with fewer pupils? Simply because the less children there are in a class, the more time you can invest in each child, thus bettering their chances of succeeding in their education. If we implement 'Consolidation', there will be fewer children in all classes. Absolutely all of them will have the best chance of a great start in life. When they leave school, even if they're not of the highest intelligence, with 'Catatonic Currency' history, wages would be subsidised and it would be worthwhile for them to be working.

★★★

With a Consolidist Government, the deterrents against committing crimes would be infinitely harsher than those which are currently in place. There would be far more Police Officers, 'Police Diffuser Squads' and Military Personnel on the streets. More Security personnel per capita, thanks to 'Consolidation' and the Non-Existence of 'Catatonic Currency', gives the law-abiding citizens the upper hand in the fight against crime. Why would the criminal element riot if they know they will be quickly arrested and sent to prison? As it is now, thousands get away with their crimes, and those who don't are insufficiently punished.

Right across the spectrum, the policies of a Consolidist Government would drastically reduce crime. How does a Politician see it? Allow population numbers to swell unchecked. Allow millions of foreigners into the country, confusing issues and making the country harder to run. Shy away from effectively educating children about respect, responsibility and hard work. Don't put consequences and deterrents of any gravity in place for dysfunctional parents, thieves, violent people. If for example, riots do occur, deploy the few Police that they can afford due to the permitting of 'Catatonic Currency' and allowance of foreign persons to claim state benefits. Due to 'Phony Human Rights' & 'Political Correctness', instruct the Police use soft to no measures in an attempt to stop the looting and destruction of the community. When the trouble ends, and a few are caught, give the perpetrators 'punishments' that will be laughed at. Instead of taking all the money possible from the rioters and their families to pay for the damage done, allow the law-abiding tax-payer to pay for it. Due to this extra spending, cut certain public services for the respectable elements of the community, but continue to give the rioters unemployment benefits. And the final insult is to take the youths seriously when they try to say it's Society's fault. Is this Common Sense?

Do you think the Consolidist policies described in this chapter will have a far greater effect on reducing the crime that the Politicians have allowed to flourish in your communities?

CHAPTER 3

Immigration

It's plain to see that if we don't implement Consolidation, world affairs and the standard of living for every single human being will gradually worsen, until at some point in the not so distant future, it has descended into us encountering great hardship, misery, disease & death on a daily basis. It's equally as plain to see that 'Consolidation' can't be successful unless countries have clear, definitive, simple and strict Immigration policies.

Using the UK as the example to convey the importance of a robust Immigration Policy. The third biggest reason its people are in so much debt is because of the lax Immigration policies of its Politicians over the past 70 years. Citizens of the UK, let the Consolidist Party ask you this. Time after time, election after election, for decades, you've seen the Politicians of each party vying for your vote and subsequent power, pledging with everything they are to resolve the hardship brought upon you by the influx of foreign persons.

Have the Politicians ever kept their promises? Exactly. Once they win power, they spend the following 4 years periodically announcing that tough new immigration measures are imminent, without ever actually saying what they are. The tough measures never materialise. The subject isn't mentioned again until perhaps 1 year later when they again announce they're on the cusp of solving this huge problem. It's a joke, and the people of the UK, and every country around the world, deserve to have effective measures put in place so that they don't suffer, following their taxes having been directed towards foreign persons.

The unchecked flow of foreign persons into the UK has cost the British taxpayer hundreds of billions of pounds over the past 70 years. In the words of the Prime Minister of the UK, David Cameron in Feb 2011, "Multi-Culturalism has Failed". Has he followed up on those words and taken action? Not a chance. He's a Politician, and they never put any of our problems right. The allowance of free movement throughout Europe, of people from all over the world, skilled or not, to enter, live and work in the UK, is a major contributor to the mess the country finds itself in. It's a totally unworkable system, and unbelievable that anybody could have even contemplated, let alone implemented it. If we all allowed free movement into and out of our homes, could we run successful households? It would be impossible, if one month you had 20 total strangers marching into your home and setting up camp in your front room. You have to limit 'your family' to a certain number of people.

A country is exactly the same. Freedom of movement doesn't work. Across Europe, and in the UK especially, not only foreign persons from countries within Europe, but millions of foreign persons from all over the world have entered our countries, ballooned the population and resulted in unmanageable operations. When deciding on the policy of freedom of movement throughout Europe, did the Politicians ever consider that the vast majority of migration around Europe would involve the flood of immigrants to the UK, France and Germany? No. They didn't contemplate that for a second did they. That was always going to happen. How many Europeans are desperate to go and live in Slovakia or Romania? Not many at all. Especially given that you can easily take advantage of the UK, French & German Governments. They're all too willing to hand the country's taxes over to you. Did the Politicians not think that the Public Services provided to the citizens of the UK, France & Germany, should be the privileges of families who have paid taxes for generations, and not those who have just arrived and just started paying into the system? And nobody can say anything about these issues because of the Politician-Created, Insane PC climate in those countries.

Establishments and the politicians promote, no, force tolerance of other Nationalities, Races & Religions on their Citizens. It's wrong and totally unjust. Would the British Royal Family ever allow a Japanese Person to marry into the Royal Family? Would they let someone of Bangladeshi or Colombian Descent procreate a child which would one day sit on the Throne of England? Would they ever allow a Kenyan to stand on the Buckingham Palace Balcony, involved in a Family Photo? No answers needed for those questions. The Height of Hypocrisy. They externalise one belief, instructing that you 'have' to join them in liking and accepting foreign persons into your lives with open arms, but, internally have completely different beliefs which are kept well hidden, as once again the 99% have no choice but to suffer in silence.

Not only do the Politicians allow all foreign persons to handicap your societies and degrade your infrastructure, they also provide them with free money in the form of unemployment benefits, disability benefits, housing benefits, child benefits and free healthcare. Where does all this money come from? Your pockets.

This is not at all a racist viewpoint. It's not about being against Christians, Hindus, Mexicans or Chinese. It's about adopting 'Common Sense' so that everybody lives better lives. Consolidism is saying, for example, that the UK shouldn't let Somalians into the UK and Somalia shouldn't let British people into Somalia, unless, they satisfy one simple criteria. The Consolidist Party is not going to waste any time waffling like the Politicians do. It is going to lay out its simple, unambiguous policy on Immigration right now.

A foreign person is only allowed into a country if they are deemed to have skills that are useful to the citizens of that country. That's it. Seeking asylum or opportunity in another country, or whatever the 'reason' may be, is not 'reason' enough to have thousands or even millions of foreign persons stifle the systems and society of a country. Even letting its own population to continue to grow is having a negative effect on countries. To let foreign persons swell population numbers to even more unworkable levels is an absolutely flawed way to operate. The 'Diner Analogy' can be used to illustrate this. Is it easier to cater effectively for a country of 70 million or 7 million? First and foremost, it's for the good of the citizens of the home country absolutely, but, not allowing mass migration is also for the good of the migrants. It is both the citizens and the migrants who will have to live together in overstretched, sub-standard societies that don't have enough money to provide a good quality of life for any of them.

Of course, for example, an immigrant entering the UK and receiving all the free benefits the government is willing to shower them with, will be better off than they were back in their own country, but, if they stayed in their own country, rejected Politicians and adopted 'Consolidism', they'd live much better lives than they could in an overstretched UK. As countries, as a planet, we need definition in our existence. Well defined borders, boundaries and laws will enable us to prosper. After all, that's the reason we have different countries, separated by borders. If we break down those borders as we currently are doing, and allow free passage for anybody, anywhere in the world, we're all going to 'continue' to suffer the consequences.

The "Home Analogy" can be used well to illustrate the importance of this definition. Does your home have limited space, limited resources and limited funds? Do you have to look after your family in your house first before other members of society? Would you be able to afford to allow 20 dependent, foreign persons into your house to live permanently? Would that be sensible and feasible, or would it overstretch and confuse the functions and processes by which you and your family live in your home? A country is precisely like a home. Our countries, be they the USA, Pakistan, Thailand or Argentina, have finite space and finite resources. Allowing as many foreign persons as want to, to enter and live in our 'homes' will obviously have a negative effect on everybody, including the foreign persons. We all have a duty to each other to ensure we don't allow this to happen. We all have to concentrate on Consolidating our own infrastructure and citizens. We have to make sure our finances are kept strong so that we can feed, water, cloth and care for our deserving citizens. In our countries, we're all part of a big family. Allowing the operation to grow and become unmanageable will only have the result of degrading everybody's lives.

There are many foreign persons currently working in other countries who are adding to the quality of life of the citizens. That is the only time it is sensible to allow migration. There are also many foreign persons working in other countries who are unskilled yes, but still working for a living. The problem is that if millions of foreign persons are allowed into a country, some will fill skilled job vacancies, some will fill semi-skilled job vacancies and some will fill unskilled job vacancies, but, there are then those who will not work or are not able to work and will become a drain on the taxes of the hard-working citizens of that country. And with the extra millions introduced to swell the population, degrade the infrastructure and confuse the operation, the authorities won't have the time or resources to trawl the muddied waters and identify and deal with those who are costing the state, or the people, money. It's a very simple concept. One that's in plain view for all to see, except the Politicians.

Many foreign persons claim they are being "persecuted" in their own country. To "protect their Human Rights", the Politicians welcome them in with open arms, where many of them, who can't speak the language or are perhaps disabled or ill, then languish on benefits for the rest of their lives. All the while, our elderly have to struggle by, receiving state pensions which are significantly lower than the benefits these asylum seekers receive. It's shocking. This is especially the case in the UK. A Consolidist

Government would say, "If you really are being persecuted, we feel for you, but, we can't let you into our country because we owe it to our own citizens to run a tight ship, where no outside influences can ever be allowed for a second to even possibly to jeopardise the quality of life for them and their children".

There are those, mostly Politicians, who would say that the foreign workers who do semi and unskilled jobs help to boost and grow an economy. This is a totally flawed statement to make, if, you analyse it closely, from the different angle. It's incredible that the Politicians could pass this off to hide the fact that their non-existent immigration policies have resulted in millions of foreign persons either draining your taxes away or taking your jobs, be they skilled or unskilled. Let's say for example a Fast Food Diner is desperate for cooking and service staff. Is it good that foreign persons are allowed to do these jobs in our countries? Would these foreign persons be needed if there weren't so many people to serve? No. Would there be so many people to cater for, if we didn't already have the millions of foreign persons within our countries? No. It's so obvious, and such a simple concept. If we haven't got the extra people, we don't need the extra people to cater for them. That goes for fast food Diners, Retails Shops or Hospitals.

Our countries are currently awash with millions foreign persons. Wonderful Pakistanis, Chinese, Israelis, Brazilians, but, wonderful in their own countries. We love you all as fellow human beings, but we all have a duty to run our countries tight and streamlined, ensuring the health and wellbeing of our own citizens. They too owe it to their fellow Pakistani, Chinese, Israeli and Brazilian citizens. The clutter and confusion created by open migration is handicapping everybody.

If countries of the world had lived by the simple, singular Immigration policy of Consolidism, the level of debt within them would be trillions less than it is now. There are millions of foreign persons driving taxis, keeping shops, and running fast food takeaways in countries all over the world. They're taking the taxi fares and other business of the citizens of that country. These are not skilled jobs, and a Consolidist Government would ensure they're done by their own citizens. As the Politicians have it, currently in the UK, a 'British' Taxi driver takes hundreds fewer fares each year because of the thousands of foreign person taxi drivers in the country. The taxes she or he pays on their deficient wages are not invested in their healthcare system, but instead are used to pay foreign persons unemployment or disability benefits. To make it worse still, no doubt, due to the unmanageable numbers within the country due to the non-implementation of Consolidation and the permitted influx of foreign persons, some of the foreign persons driving the taxis are missed as also claiming unemployment or sickness benefits. The Politicians know this is happening, and would no doubt prosecute anybody caught defrauding the people, but, will they take measures to ensure it doesn't happen in the first place? Exactly. Why should they care? They earn good salaries. They have plush houses to live in. They have private healthcare. The foreign persons are not negatively affecting their lives.

If the Politicians were suffering as a result of open migration, do you think they'd do something about it? Let's take the analysis of this aspect of a UK society deeper. Thousands more taxi drivers than are necessary, means thousands upon thousands more gallons of fuel used up than are needed to. In a city, there may be a thousand fares taken in a day. If their taken by 100 taxi drivers, that will use up less fuel than if they're taken up by 200 taxi drivers, who are still driving around in their taxis all day. Even if they're sitting at a taxi rank, on a cold winter's day, they're running their engines so that they can switch the heating on. This unnecessary wasting of the world's dwindling oil reserves is not conducive to the avoidance of future wars or environmental pollution.

It would quite probably be the opinion of the Politicians that they allow the foreign persons in to boost the economy and do the jobs that the citizens won't do. Is this a sensible policy? Is it sensible to leave the millions of your own citizens unemployed as they are, then allow millions of foreign persons into the country, some to do semi and unskilled jobs? An element of the foreign persons will either immediately, or somewhere down the line, also claim benefits from the state. Is that 'Common Sense'? Or would it be 'Common Sense' to put a cap on your own population, not allow any foreign persons into the country, thus ensuring the running of the country stays manageable. Then focus on your unemployed citizens, training them and gradually sucking them out of the system until everybody is employed? It's not complicated and never should be. The Politicians over confuse things and we need to put an end to it.

Not only jobs and benefits, if millions of semi or unskilled British people went to live in Hungary, they'd all have a degrading effect on the country's infrastructure. With tens of thousands of extra British children in the country's classrooms, the quality of education, for Hungarian & British children, would be of a lesser quality. Is it easier to teach 3 children within a classroom or 30? It's plain to see that the more of anything you try to tackle, the more difficult it is to do a good job. A higher population inflicts more wear and tear on its transportation and healthcare systems. Who would have to pay for the repair and maintenance to the infrastructure? The State. In a country where the Proletariat pay taxes, that means you'll be paying for it.

An element of millions of immigrants, would no doubt break the law to some level, at some point, and are. This puts strain on the Police, Justice and Prison systems. Right across the board, free and open migration has a negative effect on absolutely everybody.

With a Consolidist Government, any holidaying or economy boosting foreign person breaking the law in that country, would be dealt with as they deserve. They'd be sent to a Consolidist Prison, then removed from the country and never be allowed to return. Due to the 'Phony Human Rights' the Politicians have us all singing to the tune of, foreign persons committing crimes are charged and lightly punished, but later allowed to stay in the country. It would be "a breach of their Human Rights" to deport them. And that's if they're caught committing the crimes at all, what with insufficient police numbers. In the UK, there are Muslim Preachers espousing hatred and promoting violence towards UK citizens. A UK citizen can be arrested in an instant for racial abuse, but, very often these Muslim Preachers, amongst others, are left to racially abuse British people. It's a double standard society where the UK Government looks after foreign persons before their own.

If the Politicians didn't conduct their business in this way, but instead were patriotic, which they absolutely should be. Also if they were supportive and proactive of their own over foreign persons. The foreign persons would scream "Racist!", and it would be "Politically Incorrect" to scream "Racist!". The foreign persons play on the Politician's fear, and subsequently passed down, our fear, of the word "Racist". With a Consolidist Government, evidence of a Muslim Preacher's crimes would be captured on film. If the person is of foreign descent, they'd be sent to a Consolidist Prison for however long their words deserve. Following that, they'd be removed from the country within 24 hours. Citizens of a country can say whatever they want within that country, but, foreign persons can't be allowed to openly incite violence against the persons of a country they're in. Especially when they promote the murder of those citizens. That's just 'Common Sense'.

In the UK in 2012, a Muslim couple were jailed for the Honor Killing of their daughter Shafilea Ahmed. The first obvious thing to say is that it's just totally unthinkable to any decent human being that you could murder your own daughter for absolutely anything, let alone for simply fraternising with people of another race. Looking at it from the different angle though. What do you see? Consolidism sees the fact that if the UK Government hadn't let Shafilea's parents into the country in the first place, because they had no reason to be allowed in. Shafilea would not have been able to fraternise with UK youngsters as she did, and would not have been killed by her parents. Yes of course it's totally and utterly wrong, and even evil, for her parents to even object to her associating with 'other religions', let alone murder her for it. But. We're all very aware that this kind of thing does happen within the Islamic Religion. It won't go away. Let's not fool ourselves that it will. So we have to deal with it. People suffer and even die because we're not taking the simplest of measures. We have to realise this and act to stop the egregious, extensive, unnecessary waste of human life. Secondly, far less important than the life of a beautiful young Muslim girl. If Shafilea's Parents were not allowed to settle in the UK, the British taxpayer would not be paying for their incarceration for the next 25 years minimum, which they were both sentenced to. Quite light for the murder of your own daughter. Would you agree? Why? The Government can't afford to keep law-breakers incarcerated. Costing approximately £45,000 per year to keep a person in prison, that means the British Taxpayer's children will not see £2.25 million pounds that they could of, if the Politicians had done their jobs and put some sensible immigration policies and measures in place.

★★★

'Phony Human Rights' are costing you quality of life, but, so too is 'Political Correctness'. One of the reasons foreign persons continue to take advantage of States and their people's taxes is because when someone cries 'Racist', everybody cowers, retreats and scurries away. It's not in the slightest racist to say open migration ruins countries. The sooner we all start to confront it, the sooner we can start to live better lives. It needs to be identified to be rectified. "If you're not deemed to be of use to us, we're sorry but you cannot be permitted to live in our country. If we do allow you in, the country will end up in a mess". This is the stance we have to take. For evidence that this is undeniably true, take a look at the UK in the year 2012. It's a shambles. Why couldn't the Politicians see this coming?

With a Consolidist Government serving the people, if foreign persons are deemed to be of use to the country, after a robust vetting and verification process, they're permitted to live and work within it. But, there would still need to be rules laid out which would provide insurance against the maintaining of its citizens' quality of life. Foreign persons will pay taxes equal to citizens of the country they're in. The foreign persons and their family will never be entitled to any State Benefits of any kind. A Consolidist Government would have no choice but to enforce this rule, which would ensure none of the citizen's taxes are used for anything but them and their families. If for whatever reason, the foreign person's employment is terminated, they will have to leave the country. It will be possible for them to remain only for the duration of a holiday visa, 1 month, if they so wish. The foreign persons have to pay for any healthcare they receive, if it's not a benefit received from their employers. Free healthcare is reserved for the country's citizens only. Any children of the foreign persons will be assessed, upon turning 18 years of age. If they have no skills deemed of use to the country, they will have to return to their country of origin. If they wish to partake in further education in a country, this will be allowed, but, all education, at all ages, must be paid for by the family.

Some may say those are harsh rules, but, unless we start enforcing rules such as this, our countries will remain overstretched and under-financed. The result, as is currently apparent, is that you the Proletariat are the ones who suffer. If you are a country that isn't modernised and technologically advanced. A country that needs skilled foreigners to develop itself, then 'Common Sense' would tell you that you may have to make some concessions on the above rules.

To maintain the essential definition and subsequent order in the world, any foreign persons working abroad who have children, should not be able to gain native passports for them. They should receive a passport from the country of their origin. It's unbelievable that somewhere down the line, Politicians have decided it's a good policy to hand out passports to any foreign person born within their countries. Who could have possibly been so very blinkered, that they did not foresee the problems this would cause by the blurring of lines and ever-burgeoning populations within our countries. It's just so obvious that if you allow open migration into your country, and, hand out passports as though they're tourist information leaflets, you will not be able to run your country as your people deserve. The UK serves as a perfect example of this. The citizens of the UK are suffering greatly due to the complete stupidity of the Politicians. A Consolidist Government would put an end to this. Is this racist? Consider this, 'The Chimibian Theory'......

A young, respectful, hardworking black couple from Namibia go to live and work in China. They're both specialist healthcare consultants who the Chinese authorities have deemed a use to the wonderful citizens of their beautiful country. After one year of working in China, the Namibian lady gives birth to their first child. She is the most beautiful black-velvet skinned, big white-eyed, little angel you have ever seen. After spending a week in hospital recovering from the birth, she and her husband take their baby to the local Passport Agency. At the counter, the father says "We've come to get a Chinese Passport for our newborn child". The Chinese man behind the counter looks down. In the black father's arms, a beautiful little new black life. Created by him and his beautiful black wife. Now they want a Chinese Passport for their child. Do you think this would be a sensible request? Exactly. It would be nonsensical for them to ask for a Chinese Passport. The authorities wouldn't consider it for a second. Not only would they not apply for the Chinese passport because it would be ridiculous. They probably wouldn't want to, because they want their baby to be a Namibian. A wonderful Namibian human being.

With this in mind, why have, for example, the UK Politicians issued British Passports to people who've come from all over the world? If a White American couple had a child in Pakistan, would it make sense for that child to be given a Pakistani Passport? Exactly.

It's not about race or colour or religion. It's about 'Common Sense'. It just makes no sense whatsoever to allow people to freely enter your country, and it's a totally insane proposition to provide their offspring with native passports. That can be spotted as trouble from a million miles away. The Politicians are so soft and foolish. They will never put an end to this highly damaging policy. If Politicians didn't allow this to happen, and took the other steps already laid out in this Manifesto, our countries would be operating on surpluses, and you would be living highly fulfilling lives. Instead, you're working your fingers to the bone. Scraping by, whilst the Government hands out your money to foreign persons who don't lift a finger. If you adopt Consolidism, your countries could soon be lending money to those that are still run by Politicians, and earning interest back which could be further invested in yours and your children's lives.

In light of how nonsensical it is to hand out passports to foreign babies born in a foreign country, a Consolidist Government would put an end to this practice from the time it entered Government. It would also hold a referendum to ask the people if they would see fit to repeal all passports handed out to foreign immigrants whose parents, grandparents or great grandparents had come from another country, and, people who are, in the current world climate, deemed a danger to a country's citizens. This danger will be identified in the Chapter 'Terrorism'. Only citizens whose previous four generations have native passports, would be eligible to vote in this referendum.

★★★

A Consolidist Government would ensure it has the punishments in place to deter people from illegally employing foreign persons without the proper paperwork. Anybody caught committing this offence, which is so highly damaging to our societies, will be sentenced to 10 years in a 'Consolidist Prison', have their business seized and 'handed over'. Not kept by the Government, but handed over to a patriotic citizen, who can then ensure the legal citizens keep their jobs, and more legal citizens can replace the imprisoned immigrants. Currently the punishment proposed by the Politicians is often just a fine. Does the 10 years sound too harsh? Would you ever consider employing an illegal immigrant at your gain, but to the detriment of society around you? Exactly. Then why should people who do, degrading the lives of you and your fellow citizens, only get a soft punishment if they're caught. It's ruining the countries we live in, and we have to take action. Only a country's citizens can work in non to low skilled jobs. This has to be the policy if we are to make an improvement to our countries and lives. There are plenty of non to low skilled jobs and plenty of unemployed citizens. With the subsidised wages, only offered with Consolidsm, it will be well worthwhile people taking these jobs.

Nobody will be allowed to enter a Consolidist country without having first made an application from their country of origin. Be it for a holiday or to work. As people enter the country, their paperwork and finances will be checked to ensure they are genuine tourists or persons there to take up legal employment. Thanks to the elimination of 'Catatonic Currency', Immigration Departments at airports would have hundreds of employees in place to ensure effective security at its borders. Prepaid hotel bookings, funds and travel bookings would all be 'properly' checked and verified to ensure a person does not plan to dissolve into society. Not only in the airport, but also in the towns and cities of countries, the security services and Police will have the powers to stop possible illegal aliens and check their paperwork, which will need to be carried at all times.

No healthcare, bank accounts, accommodation, or similar, would be provided to people without the proper paperwork. Does this sound too severe? Reminiscent of regimes of the past perhaps? It has to be done, or the misery of the masses will continue. The Proletariat will continue to suffer. These measures are not taken at present within our countries. As you go about your daily business, look around you. Tens of thousands of foreign persons either taking business away from your people or taking jobs that your people could be doing. It's not racist. It's happening and we have to stop it, because people are suffering. It may not be you, but there are those out there who are.

As you walk down the street, if you take the time to analyse those who go by, you will see many foreign persons who are not employable. They have to live somehow, but how? Off your taxes. Why would the Politicians allow them in? Why would they then provide them with free money and healthcare? Why wouldn't they stop them on the street, ask them for their paperwork and then quite possibly remove them from the country? You, the hard-working citizens deserve to have your taxes spent on You and Your families.

If we don't eject the Politicians from power, then start implementing these measures, we'll still be talking about the problem of immigration for decades to come. By this time, some of you will have passed away, having lived sub-standard lives due to the Politicians idiocy. We owe it to our children, grandchildren and all future generations not be cowed by 'Phony Human Rights' and 'Political Correctness'. We owe it to them to state clearly that this is a problem, then actually do something about it.

If you saw a 'stranger' in your home one day, would you leave them go about their business or ask them what on earth they're doing there? Would you be able to afford to let strangers wander into and around your home unchecked, eating your food, using energy to keep warm and bathe? Energy that you pay for. Would you allow a 'non-family member' into your house, stand them next to your child and say "Sorry son, I love you, but you can't have any food today, we have to give this woman the money instead"?

Effective preventions must be coupled with effective punishments to serve as deterrents. If you're found to be an illegal alien within a Consolidist country, any possessions and money you have will be seized by the state. Any 'precious' possessions such as family photos, jewellery and clothes will be stored until your release from prison, 10 years later. Upon release, you and your precious possessions will be returned to your country of origin. Anybody found harbouring an illegal alien will also be sentenced to 10 years in prison. Initially, these measures may sound too severe, though they really aren't. All over our countries, people are suffering because there are too many foreign persons in our countries. There are families living in tower blocks who can't let their children out to play in a garden. Not 100 yards down the road, a foreign family is provided with free state housing. Worse still, they can barely speak the language and are claiming state benefits of all kinds.

Does it sound impossible to implement such a tight, successful system? With the implementation of 'Consolidation' and the elimination of 'Catatonic Currency', as countries, we'll have the time, clarity and funds to implement these measures and better your lives. Not only will it ensure your taxes are spent on you. It will also create tens of thousands more jobs for you and your families.

In recent years, the UK Government have announced huge spending cuts to the education budget. Billions of pounds pulled from the educations of British children. Yet they continue to pay out billions in benefits and healthcare to foreign persons. Is this 'Common Sense'? Is this fair on you and your children, citizens of the UK? It's doesn't matter to the Politicians if it's fair or not. The vast majority of their children are in private schools. Paid for by their ample salaries, or even as a benefit of their job, which actually means you pay for it. They'll get a good education. The UK Government cut the education budget, but continue to spend billions on keeping the troops in Afghanistan, where some will tragically lose their lives. This is what the Politician is doing to your country.

If you feel like you're getting a bad deal from your Government, one of the major reasons, whether you'd realised it before now or not. Whether you're brave enough to say it out loud or not, are the lax immigration policies 'enforced' by the Politicians. A Consolidist Government would put it right, right away. Is it easier to effectively run a village of two hundred or a city of fifteen million? If you came home from work one day to find your favourite vase broken, would it be easier to get to the bottom of who did it, if you had two children or fifty children? If we continue to let unnecessary foreign persons swell our population numbers, our countries will continue to live in debt. It's a simple concept that the Politicians either seem to be completely missing, or be lacking the gumption to do anything about. Or a mixture of both amongst them.

There are certain peoples within our societies who have become established in their right to live in certain countries. There was a time though, when they arrived from far-off shores for the first time. When they weren't established. In those days soon after their arrival, the 'native' folk would have felt disgruntled that these 'outsiders' had infiltrated their borders, took their jobs and possibly started committing crimes within their communities. As an example, Great Britain has had no right whatsoever to colonise and subjugate the countries they have done across the world over the centuries. Gradually their Empire has been reduced as countries take back their sovereignty. And so rightly so. There are though, large contingent British Communities still residing in various countries across the world. 'Established' Communities. How would, and how do, these Communities, or any similar 'foreign' Communities, react when Migration results in 'different peoples again' entering those countries and living amongst them in great numbers? They feel resentful that 'outsiders' have been allowed to enter 'their' country and live amongst them. Taking their jobs and affecting their lives negatively in other ways. It's hypocritical in the extreme. When races mix, injustice occurs. When races mix, people die. When races don't mix, injustice occurs and people die. The world will never be perfect. But if we can avoid unnecessary injustice and murder by maintaining defined borders, we owe it to all on Earth to do that.

CHAPTER 4

State Benefits

Every morning, you wake, rise and leave your homes to earn a living. You expect no help from others. You take complete responsibility for yourself, your children, your household and your lives. You use the money you earn to pay for your own house, your own car, your own sustenance. In your lives, you only have as many children as you can provide for. That means as many as is possible without having to depend on handouts from 'The State'. And let's be under no misconception, money from 'The State' is not money from the Government, it's money from your pockets. The pockets of the Proletariat. The amount of money taxed from your salaries every year is currently far higher than it should be. Would you agree? Amongst other reasons, already detailed thus far in the Manifesto, your taxes are higher than they should be, so that your Government can give free money to people who didn't try in school, quite possibly due to poor upbringings. Or to people who are too lazy as adults to go out and work for a living. If it's a lack of effort in school, by parent or child, or both. This has resulted in them only being able to earn a low wage, and subsequently they refuse to work for such little money. Many of them openly state this, but still, the gullible, gutless Politicians do nothing to protect you and your money.

They hand your hard-earned cash over to people who choose a layabout life of Alcohol abuse. Or to people who choose to create more children than they can provide for, both in terms of finances and the quality attention a child requires to become a productive member of society. If someone was unfortunate enough to be brought up in one of these homes, with the amount of children outweighing the finances, there's a very good chance they will not have gained a good education and will have a low paid job. They too may well have gone on to have multiple children of their own. It's highly likely that each of these children will have sub-standard upbringings, compared to if parents can focus all their money and attention on just one or two children. What happens when a low income family's house is filled with the chaos of 5 arguing, screaming children? These children don't get the focus and attention from the parents that they need. They don't get the encouragement to do their homework and get good grades. Their education and upbringing suffers. As they reach child-bearing age, the cycle begins again.

The above never-ending cycle is plainly obvious as being a dead weight around society's neck, but, what have the Politicians done about it? Nothing. Why do people continue to have as many children as they do? There are two reasons. Firstly, the Politicians have not implemented 'Consolidation', and secondly they provide a safety net of free funds and provisions which enables people to continue their irresponsible ways and create more children than they can afford. We have to start limiting the amount of children people can have, and stop rewarding those who have more than they can afford with free money. If we don't do this, the problem will endure. Never going away.

You get out of life what you put in. Do you believe in that? A Consolidist does, and a Consolidist Government would make sure that those who put no effort and responsibility in, get absolutely none of your hard-earned taxes handed over to them. There have to be consequences in society, for being a lazy Alcoholic, for not having made an effort in school, for having more children than you know you can afford. At present, a Politician sees the solution to this highly visible problem, one even they can see, as allowing anybody to have as many children as they want, whether they can support them or not. If you don't have the means to provide for these children, because you didn't gain a good education due to your parents having had more children than they could afford, they'll give you the money of the hard-working people for free. It's insulting. Not only do they not do anything to put the problem right, they encourage the irresponsible behaviour by rewarding it with free money. It's crazy. How will the problem ever end if this is how we let the Politicians handle it? Pandering to the lazy and saying, "We have to give them free money now, or else their children will suffer." This encourages and engenders the irresponsible behaviour, ensuring it remains as a draining reality in our societies. If we set our stall out as society saying, "You're not going to get anything, people will then think a little harder before they have child after child.

As previously discussed, poor educations are also partly the result of the overcrowding of our education systems, both with our own and children of foreign persons. Again, overpopulation is the building block of a 'House of Pain'.

At some time in our lives, we've all seen people on television who say "Why would I go out to work when I can receive more in benefits from the Government than I can earn?". Absolutely the Government should be doing everything it can to make sure a person is better off working. The elimination of 'Catatonic Currency' would enable a Consolidist Government to subsidise wages to a good level, encouraging people to cease being a drain on society. A Consolidist Government absolutely has sympathy with citizens who are stuck having to face low wages due to the Politicians spending billions on foreign persons, foreign wars and allowing 'Catatonic Currency'. Why should they then be expected to toe the line and except a pittance as a wage? Still, there are people out there who have the inner-decency to work for a low wage instead of claiming benefits. To those who currently do choose to claim benefits instead of work, a Consolidist Government will make sure you are able to earn a good wage if you work. It will be worth your effort. If you still choose not to work, then you will be rewarded accordingly, with nothing.

We all have to remember, life is about giving and taking. It's ridiculous to see, for example, the rioting youths in the UK, who've quite probably put no effort into life, and continue not to do so, complain that they've got nothing out of the Government. With Politicians in power, there is a big element of truth in the fact that the Government could be doing so much more for them, but still, it needs to be openly identified that they have quite probably put virtually nothing in. Therefore, they can't then expect to receive a huge salary for an unskilled job.

'If' after the balancing of the jobs to people ratio, the elimination of 'Catatonic Currency' and the subsidising of wages, there are still those who choose not to work, 6 months unemployment benefits would be available to them. These benefits would then be stopped until a person has worked for a minimum of 1 year. If after 1 year, a person loses their job, they would be entitled to another 6 months unemployment benefit. It's not that a Consolidist government doesn't want to help people out if they're genuinely searching for work, but struggling to find any. It's just that, as is plain to see by the debt our countries are in, it's not sustainable to provide free money for people over long periods of time. There are many who take advantage of the Politician's current system, 'and will do for as long as it's in place'. This is a key point. The Politicians say continuously that they'll get tough and enact change to reduce the amount of your taxes that are spent on benefits. Have they?

If we don't put 'effective, robust, concrete' measures in place, such as only providing 6 months of benefits, we will never solve the problem of state-dependent people. It's plain to see. We can't allow people to drain your taxes away from you, the hard-working, by claiming benefits all their lives. It's a nonsensical, unworkable system that has to change. In certain countries, certain persons seem to think free money in the form of benefits is actually their right, and become aggressive and indignant if their benefits are not paid to them on time. It's nonsensical that the Politicians have let societies form where people are of this mindset. After implementing 'Consolidation', balancing the ratio of people to jobs and helping people to acquire subsidised, well paid jobs. Close monitoring, again made possible by 'Consolidation', would ensure people are not trying to play the system by getting themselves fired after 1 year so that they can spend the next 6 months receiving free money. If this is seen to become a pattern, they will receive no benefits. To avoid revenge attacks against employers who have had no choice but to fire an employee, the Government would be the ones who make the judgements, deeming people to be purposely incompetent or tardy.

A Consolidist Government, on behalf of you, your children, your family and your money, would not allow the lazy and irresponsible to continue to cheat you out of your money. If a Consolidist Government won power, the 6 months benefit window would start from the day it came into office. If this 'incentive' was in place, the dishonest among us would soon start to make an effort to look for a job. They'd start to do what is expected of them. Dress presentably, hit the streets, handing out resumés to prospective employers. Searching the internet and reading papers, actually looking for work, instead of sitting home, perhaps drinking alcohol all day. With the Politician's current promise to continue benefits their whole lives, why wouldn't people make no effort whatsoever to find a job? It's a no-brainer to some. The Politicians constantly babble on about how they're going to get tough on people who take advantage of the system. Do they live up to their promises? Do you ever see anything change? Exactly. A Politician never lives up to any of their promises. The day a Consolidist Government won power, lifetime benefits claimants would be history. Rejecting 'Political Correctness', we have to start taking real measures and adopting frames of mind which don't see us all dancing to the tune of the irresponsible and lazy, but instead saying, "You provide for yourself, like all of us have to. You will get nothing for free". Would you support this policy?

★★★

With a Consolidist Government at the helm, Child Benefits would cease to be paid. Does this sound unfair? The payment of Child Benefits results in the hard-working element of society losing out when their higher than should be taxes are handed over to support children that people couldn't really afford to have. Why would you pay a portion of your tax to receive it straight back in child benefits? An element of the taxes from your salaries is paid to both you in Child Benefits, but also paid as Child Benefits to the lazy, lifelong benefits claimants with more children than they can afford to provide for. A Consolidist Government would reduce your taxes and allow you to spend that money saved on your children. Receiving no free money for each child they have, people will be forced to think hard about actually how they would support any children they plan, or don't plan to bring into the world. To analyse it further, it's wasting time, money and effort to take tax from you and give it straight back in Child Benefits. Beaurecracy that could be cut out of our systems and lives, moving us towards a streamlined, highly efficient country. The Politician's can see none of this with their blinkered, trite minds.

At the moment, the Politicians pander to those who are totally fouling up the societies we live in. This may sound too strong, but it is the truth. By pandering, we're actually exacerbating the problems that are crippling us, and ensuring they endure. If we confront the elements of society that are holding us back, with what 'should' be their self-inflicted reality. Those who are growing up behind them, will be far less inclined to tread the same paths.

This fear we all have of being pointed at and labelled "Politically Incorrect" is a major problem, and the Consolidist Party believes we need to highlight it. This will enable us to avoid falling foul to the unnecessary problems and burdens it creates. The Politicians believe in saying they'll do something, but then, being held back by the reins of 'Political Correctness', they continue to allow the lazy and irresponsible to take society for a ride. They give them free money to spend and free houses to live in. They pay their utilities bills and give them child benefits. On occasions, they'll receive sickness benefits for illnesses which everybody can see don't stop people from working, but, nobody can say this out loud because of "Political Correctness". Even if, for example, there are people who've made the wrong choices and become a victim to the world's most dangerous substance, Alcohol. You can't be signed out of society as 'sick' for the rest of your life, as the Politicians allow. There are many non-dangerous jobs that can be done, if we all reject 'Political Correctness' and say it as it is.

Alcoholics can get out of bed in the morning, take some substitute medication if needed, then go off to work, sweeping the streets, earning more money than a Popstar for doing so. The exercise will be beneficial to healing their bodies and minds. Somebody who keeps our communities clean is far more important than a Popstar, so we must empower them and reward them more. If, as the Politicians allow, you're just signed off as 'sick', what else are you going to do other than drink all day. You're condition and frame of mind will just go downhill. It's so obvious that this is what will happen. As a society, we have a responsibility to look after the money of the people who haven't decided upon a lazy life of Alcohol. If we take the above steps, everybody wins, including the Alcoholics and currently lazy, as they earn good money for their contribution to society.

There are people out there who need help due to their disabilities, and a Consolidist Government would absolutely help them, but, in the vast majority of cases, we can all see those who are deserving and those who are taking advantage. The 60 year old woman in a wheelchair with Arthritis and Osteoporosis will receive sickness benefits. The Alcoholic will receive nothing. For those you do pay sickness benefits to, a Consolidist Government will do their duty of checking up on people to ensure the lives they're leading are consistent with that of somebody who is asking to receive other people's money to support them. 'Consolidation' and extra funds due to the elimination of 'Catatonic Currency' would make this infinitely simpler. It will be much easier for the newly employed surveillance personnel to identify benefit cheats in countries that aren't overcrowded.

State-provided housing is a policy currently supported by the Politicians of some countries. This policy has the absolute opposite effect to that which the Politicians believe it has. They would say it provides housing for those who can't afford it. What it actually does is exacerbate and encourage the problem of dysfunctional households and upbringings which produce the next generation of state dependent people. If the safety net is there, why would people limit the number of children they have and subsequently take the time and effort to bring them up properly, encouraging them in their pastimes and education?

There are many living in public housing that are 'highly' respectable, hard-working people, contributing to their upkeep. Through subsidised wages and lowered taxes, these fine citizens would benefit greatly from Consolidism. The problem is those who are unemployed, with many children and no means to support them. A Consolidist Government would advertise and educate people from a very early age to the fact that we all have a responsibility to each other to limit the number of children we have. Then to raise properly those we do bring into the world. Would this be better than advertising Alcohol on television? Would this be better than filling the television with hours of talentless Popstar videos advertising the message that you have to be the sexiest, coolest and toughest? We all need to spend quality time with our children, helping them with homework, teaching them about respect.

At home, in school, on television, we all need to be reminded that we need to be mindful of society and what effect we have on it. That we get absolutely nothing in life if we're not responsible and don't make any effort. These are the kinds of issues we should be concerning ourselves with every day. Not idolising people who play ball games, and, making them millionaires as we gullibly hand over our money.

With a Consolidist Government, there would be no free housing. The hard-working, what used to be 'low earners' under the Politicians, wouldn't need any help from the Consolidist Government. Due to their much increased subsidised salaries, they would have more than enough money to pay for their own houses. For those who are unemployed, there would be 'Shelter Halls'. A single person will be provided with 4m x 4m of partitioned space in the middle of a large hall. In it will be a bed and the one trunk allowed for personal possessions, no more. All around, other people or families in their partitioned spaces. A couple's space and bed will be slightly larger, but still, there's one possession trunk each. A couple, with children they couldn't afford to have, get a slightly larger space again and an extra bed. This is the maximum provision that a Consolidist Government would allow your taxes to be spent on. If a person or a couple have 2 or 8 children, they'll all have to live within this maximum provision space. The practice of rewarding the irresponsible in society has to end. If it doesn't, the irresponsibility will not end. It's that simple.

In the 'Shelter Halls', people will be kept warm and dry. They'll be given basic food and hygiene provisions. None of the responsible people's taxes will handed over in the form of free money. If people haven't had the decency of mind to make the decisions in life which would have put them in better positions. Why should they expect the Proletariat to bail them out and provide them with luxuries that should only be attainable for those who deserve them? People staying in the 'Shelter Halls' will be helped to find a job, which there will be enough of, due to 'Consolidation' having balanced the ratio of people to jobs. Undoubtedly, the position people find themselves in, living in these most basic Shelter Halls, will encourage them to find jobs for themselves. Having this provision in place instead of free housing, will result in many fewer people relying on the state for accommodation. With the implementation of 'Consolidation' resulting in manageable operations, through available funds, education, advertising and deterrents, we can achieve the elimination of the irresponsible mindset in society, and move the manageable amount of people to being self-sufficient. If we just let the population grow unchecked, it's plain to see that we cannot achieve this, however hard we try with education and deterrents, which would not be forthcoming under the Politicians anyway.

The 'Shelter Halls' will be filled with Communal Area CCTV Cameras. Any lack of respect or irresponsibility toward others in the facility will be captured and recorded. Three of these transgressions will result in a person being evicted and never again being allowed to take up accommodation at a 'Shelter Hall'. Will this result in some people having to turn to a life of crime? With all the money in society, as has already been identified, the streets would be flooded with Civil Security Personnel, and, once they're inevitably caught, Consolidist Prisons await.

No Alcohol, drugs or tobacco will be allowed inside the 'Shelter Halls'. Regular tests would be conducted. If someone is asking for the help of others to be fed and housed, they cannot be allowed to hamper their efforts to stand on their own two feet by consuming substances which could negatively affect their body and mind. Does this sound like 'Common Sense'? Clothes, bedding etc will be washed by hand, by each person or family. Cleaning of the Communal Areas of the 'Shelter Halls', will be the responsibility of each person or family. Rotas would be drawn up to share these duties fairly. 'Genuinely' disabled persons will be exempt from these duties. Those able-bodied will share the responsibility of washing the disabled person's clothes. A selfless act, not too much to ask of somebody who's accommodation and food is being paid for by others. It should go without saying, but seemingly can't in a

Politicians world, that if you ask to stay in 'Shelter Halls', you should have no children, or, no more children until the Consolidist Government has helped you back into well-paid employment. If you do have children, or more children, as a punishment, you will have to do a greater share of the tasks around the 'Shelter Hall'.

Does all this sound too harsh? Anachronistic perhaps? How many chances do we have to give people? If an unemployed, unskilled person, in 10 years finds themselves living in a 'Shelter Hall', it will more than likely be the case that the parents didn't have the sense nor responsibility to bring them up properly. Despite all the messages in school, on television and within society, they didn't have the inclination to make the right choices in life, so they've only got themselves to blame. Worse still, there will be some who add to the list of bad choices, as they bring children into the world, knowing they can't support them. We have to move away from this soft, gullible mindset that the Politicians have poisoned us with. It is killing us from within. Do you agree with how soft your Politicians are on state-dependent people?

There is one last point to make on 'Shelter Halls'. As a further safeguard for the Proletariat's taxes, a person is only eligible to stay in a 'Shelter Hall' if they have no other family to stay with. If they have parents, or perhaps an Aunt, Uncle or Grandparents, they will have to support their family member. A Consolidist Government would provide the dependents with food and basic hygiene provisions every day, thus slightly reducing the burden they are upon their relatives. These rations will available for collection at the local 'Shelter Hall'. This too would serve as an incentive to go out, find work and support oneself. Will the relatives be indifferent to having people sleeping on their sofa every night? Absolutely not. They'll be 'tremendously supportive and encouraging', pushing the dependent to find a job and live by their own means. Not only will this strategy give them incentive, it will also result in the relatives instilling values and morals within the person.

As the Politicians have it now, the unemployed get free money and houses in which they can party all day, perhaps drinking Alcohol to their heart's content. Why would they have the inclination to go out and find work, if the Politicians are willing to give them your money for free? If a person really wanted to drink Alcohol every night, that's allowed, but you have to go out to work to pay for it, and responsibly realise that you have to be in work the next day. If you do start missing work, you'll lose your well paid job and will receive the hard working people's taxes only in the form of the provision of a 'Shelter Hall' space. Consequence & Incentive. Welcome to a Consolidist World. Would you say it's unfair for relatives to have to support people if they're unemployed? At the moment, the Politicians think it should be you who takes the burden upon your shoulders. You, the totally unrelated stranger across the other side of the country. That's unfair. Would you wake up every other Monday morning, get dressed, leave your home, walk down the street and hand 120 of your currency to the man who sits in his house all day drinking Alcohol. Of course you wouldn't. Thanks to the Politicians, you don't need to. They do it for you. A Consolidist Government wouldn't give the state-dependent a dime more than is required to keep them fed, dry and warm.

We have to put an end to the cycle of overcrowded houses, poor upbringings and lifelong dependency on 'your' money. Right now, the Politicians are saying "You keep making as many children as you want, don't worry about it. We'll take money from these people over here and give it to you, despite your irresponsibility. You didn't try hard at school, you don't go out to work, but here's a free house. There's some money to spend too. If you want some beer, there you go, take it and buy yourself some beer". It's insanity. Even if you've come from the most dysfunctional family, there are those in life who still make it. They have the decency of mind to realise it's the right thing to do. They realise that hard work and effort will benefit them. It's this decency of mind our societies are missing.

For those who unfortunately don't have this moral fibre, we as a society have to ensure effective encouragement and deterrents are in place to bring it about. In the vast majority of cases, it's completely the choice of the individual. Work hard or lay back and live off the state. The latter won't be an option with a Consolidist Government running a country, and everybody would be constantly reminded of this through advertisement and education. This strategy may seem a little strange and excessive at first, but that's because it's new. It's a new, firm and focused effort to change our societies, to the benefit of 'everybody', even the currently state-dependent. If we can empower and effect change within the mind's of millions of children with television adverts, 'Respect' teams & lessons in school, and effective deterrents and incentives. Is that so strange? So leftfield that we have to reject it? Not only the minds of the children, but the minds of the irresponsible adults amongst us will be constantly 'reminded' of their responsibilities towards society. Do you ever tell your children, you get out of life what you put in? You tell them that because that's how it should be. That's how you see society, because that's 'Common Sense'. That's exactly how Consolidism sees society. The world can't operate properly if millions of people are dependent on others. That is evident right now, as we bare witness to our broken countries, containing hundreds of many more millions than we can cater for effectively. In your home, if your children were irresponsible, unruly, lazy, disrespectful, abusing Alcohol, would you reward them with free money? Would that be backward to the goal of producing a harmonious, hard-working household? Exactly. Then why should we let people in society behave like this? Our countries cannot function if we continue to allow the Politicians to pander to the lazy, dishonest, talentless and foreign persons.

How long have our countries been forced by the Politicians into continually debating how costly our benefit's systems are? Does it frustrate you? We always have been having these discussions, and we always will, unless we actually do something about it. Do you let potentially financially damaging problems linger around your household, or do you put them right? You put them right because you have to. If you didn't, you and your family would go under. Do you see the Politicians putting our 'houses' right? Why can you do it and they can't? For one, they don't have the intelligence and/or intestinal fortitude to enact what at first seems like drastic change. Secondly, you find it easier to enforce measures for your smaller, more manageable operation. It's easier to run a household of 4, than it is a country of 40 million.

The vast majority of the elements of society talked about in this chapter, do have somebody who can support them before you should have to. But as it is now, if they stamp their feet, the Politician-run Governments give them what they're blubbing for. How do you treat your kids when they stamp their feet? Do you give in to their unreasonable demands? Of course not. Your house wouldn't function if unreasonable demands won over. You explain to them why what they're asking is unreasonable and the negative affect it would have on everybody should you give in. You stand absolutely firm in your resolve, because you know in the long run it will benefit them and everybody around them? Does this sound accurate and sensible?

There are many countries around the world 'functioning' without benefit's systems. Why in countries like the UK, do the Politicians not have the courage to stop benefits going to the irresponsible? In other countries, the families have to take care of each other, which offers great incentive to contribute and instils values. If in these countries, they also implemented 'Consolidation' and eliminated 'Catatonic Currency', they'd be functioning very close to perfect. With a Consolidist Government, anybody who fails to make something of themselves, and fails to bring their children up responsibly, will only have themselves to blame. If you're willing to put the effort in, you will benefit massively from Consolidism. For those who choose not to make an effort, the absolute minimal help they receive from the people's pockets, will be as a direct result of conscious decisions they have made. All a Consolidist

Government asks, all the people ask, is that you work to support yourself and exercise respect and responsibility. After receiving your much better quality education through Consolidism and all its effective strategies, if you are of basic intelligence, Consolidism will ensure that you are subsidised and living good quality lives in towns that are regenerated and free from Anti-Social Behaviour and Crime. This is where society's money should be invested.

Unemployment has been a recurring theme as a problem throughout this chapter. The way the Politicians are attempting to solve this problem is completely wrong, as is evident by the fact it's always been a problem. We've already discussed that firstly, the most important thing to do is put a cap on population numbers and gradually train and draw the unemployed out of the benefit's system and into work.

The Politicians are also wrongly focusing all their attentions on the prospective employees, instead of at least focusing half their efforts also on the prospective employers. In our countries, there are millions of unemployed, but also, at least many hundreds of thousands of vacant jobs. Some of these vacant jobs lay dormant for many months. There must be many applying for these jobs, but the employers don't manage to find anybody 'suitable'. The employers need to be encouraged to give people a chance, without worrying about PC & Phony, unnecessary Health & Safety. Without worrying how a person looks and if they're 'highly effective communicators'.

We need to cut the facade, jargon, bureaucracy, egos and personal preferences within our societies and just get on with the task in hand. A Consolidist Government would pay the wages of newly employed people to be for the first 3 months, if, they were deemed to be difficult to employ by virtue of the way they look or their history. If someone has turned over a new leaf, Consolidism believes they should be given a chance to prove themselves. In general, if you're eminently employable, but somehow struggling to find work, a Consolidist government would also pay your full wages for the first 3 months, thus encouraging an employer to give you a chance. People are much more likely to feel empowered and want to work if they are seeing the rewards.

In contradiction to this, the UK Government currently encourages employers to give unemployed people jobs, but they then only receive their unemployment benefits as a reward for their work. It's obvious that thousands will fall out of love and not abide by this system due to the measly remuneration they see at the end of the month. What will happen? They'll get themselves fired or come up with some excuse. Then, due to 'Political Correctness' and the UK Government's softness and unwillingness to take a tough stance and effective measures, they'll be back unemployed and claiming benefits, draining societies money away, with no end to the problem in sight. If left in power, Politicians will continue to take diluted measures that will never improve our lives. It's a fact. We need and deserve a major improvement in our lives. Major improvement cannot come about without major action. We have to remove the Politicians from our societies and lives. They are a disease that is crippling us.

As the Politicians currently have it, we're all wasting time and effort looking at each other thinking "She hasn't got that certificate" or "As an employer, he's not asking to see this card proving he can do that. This is just irresponsible". We have to start rejecting time-wasting issues. As an example, in today's PC, PHR, Red-Tape societies, someone may be refused a job if they don't have a 'Food Hygiene Certificate'. Fifty years ago, there was no such thing. Were people dropping like flies from food poisoning? The world functioned back then without all this time wasting, Politician-Implemented bumph.

Sometimes people are refused jobs for as little as "I didn't like the way he answered that question" or "She wasn't dressed quite right". These are personal preference issues we need to drop if we are to get to where we need to be as societies. Employers should be encouraged just to give people a chance. If it turns out they can't do the job, then we'll have to try them at something else, but at least they had the chance. Of course, giving people a chance won't be possible with all jobs. Some are skilled and some will require 'genuine' skills and knowledge to ensure safety among their fellow workers and possibly the public. Though, we have to persuade employers to empower people by giving them jobs. Sometimes it's just this single chance they need to improve their frame of mind and become productive members of society.

We have to look into people's eyes and say "We want you to succeed". Instead of looking them in the eye and saying "You haven't ironed your shirt. I'd never employ you". Does an unironed shirt really matter? If we give them the chance, they won't be a drain on society, and, if we absolutely feel the need to, we can ask them to iron their shirt ready for when they show up for work the next day. This would make more sense and be much more conducive to eliminating unemployment.

We need, no, we have, to cut the Red Tape and Bumph out of our job's markets, economies, personalities and lives. It is holding us back. Job advertisements that require "Smartly dressed, focused, driven, self-confident people with excellent interpersonal and communication skills" are just wasting all of our time and efforts. What about "As long as you're not stinking dirty, don't shirk and can talk to people if necessary, we'll consider you for the job"?. We're all disappearing up our own behinds every day because of this rubbish and our La Di Da Societies. 40 years ago, people used to walk onto a building site, ask for a job and could well get one. Nowadays, you need cards, certificates, badges, training and be dressed in Personal Protective Equipment as though you're just about to board a rocket to the moon. This kind of garbage is holding us back. No doubt, some of the measures are necessary and keeping us safer, but much of it is way over and above, and we're only adopting it because we're all watching each other, encouraged by the Politicians. Anybody who doesn't support all the certificates and badges is deemed incompetent and unsafe. We need to look with great 'Common Sense' at situations and judge them as they are, without worrying about all the baggage of society's unwritten rules and personal expectations. To do this we need guidance and directives from the people who make the laws. But this won't be forthcoming with the Politicians in power.

★★★

Would you lay around on benefits, drinking Alcohol all day? Could you ever see yourself putting so little effort into life that you became dependent on others for free handouts, whatever form they take? Not in a million years would you even contemplate being that way. So why should we as a society allow people to get away with being like that?

If we implement Consolidation and control the population numbers, we could really focus on reducing the number of people dependent on the state. We could focus on mobilising and empowering people's minds, ensuring they have the drive within themselves to become good people who make a contribution to society. If we did this, there wouldn't be anywhere near the amount of money spent on propping people up. If we didn't have to spend so much money on supporting so many more people, your taxes would be lower. If your taxes are lower, you've more money to spend, thus stimulating your economy. On and on, the positive effects flow right through our societies if we adopt 'Consolidism'. If we stand firm and refuse to pander to the irresponsible, eventually we won't have to, because there would have been a complete change in how everybody views respect and responsibility. We have to speculate to accumulate.

If we don't get tough, people will not clean up their acts. A Consolidist Government would get tough, not just talk about getting tough, like the Politicians have done for the past several decades.

CHAPTER 5

Healthcare

Access to free, swift, good quality healthcare is a basic human right for every human on the planet. One which would be pursued and protected with great vigour by a Consolidist Government. Without the implementation of 'Consolidation', this simply cannot be achieved. That is an undeniable, unavoidable fact. As the population numbers grow, the free, usually slow, 'good quality' healthcare systems which are in place now, will gradually deteriorate until they suffer total collapse. To use the term 'free' is a little misleading. A 'free' healthcare system is funded by the hard-earned taxes of the Proletariat. With such hard earned cash being used, should it not be spent wisely in justifiable ways?

Consolidism believes that in every aspect of life, we should help those who choose to help themselves? Should the money within our societies be used to provide healthcare for those who have spent their lives abusing Tobacco and Alcohol? Is that really money well spent? Perhaps they have paid their taxes all their lives, but those taxes should be used to try and better our societies, finding cures for the at-present incurable diseases. Not to simply stave off self-inflicted illnesses and diseases. Should we not try, as a race, as a being, to reach a state of consciousness where we don't feel the need to ingest chemicals and substances that we know full well are negative for or health, aswell as in some cases negative for our societies? How do you think the travelling aliens would view an Alcoholic who spends all their living days ingesting a pure poison?

It's not quite normal to most of us, but it doesn't seem nearly as insane as it would to somebody who was witnessing a human being for the first time.

Those of you who do live clean, healthy lives. Who don't drink or smoke at all, or, who enjoy substances responsibly in moderation. Some of your taxes have to be wasted on the treatment of people who've knowingly brought their diseases upon themselves. That's money that could have been used to provide more Police on the housing estate where your elderly Mother fears to go out after dark. Very often, the 20 years of treating someone due to the effects of smoking costs more than the person paid into the system. Sometimes their illnesses render them unable to work. At this point, they become a 100% drain on society. Hospital Treatment, Hospital Stays, Consultations, Doctor's Appointments, Medication, Community Nursing. It all adds up to massive amounts of absolutely unnecessary, but absolutely avoidable spending.

"You help yourself, then we will help you too"? Is this one of the key life-lessons you teach your children as they grow up? Or perhaps you teach them, "If you choose to do nothing to help yourself, we'll help you anyway". 'Is' that kind of ethic, making for productive people and societies? So why, for example, do the Politicians say exactly that to those who for example, drink and smoke 'heavily' all their lives? Again, the fact that there are absolutely no deterrents in place, means that billions of currency, your money, is being spent treating those who have made the conscious decisions to steadily degrade their health. A Consolidist Government believes that if you're a lifelong heavy drinker or smoker, then you should have to pay for your healthcare, through your own funds. Either a One-Off payment or through insurance policies. A Consolidist Government proposes that every 6 months, tests would be carried out on every citizen to determine the levels of Alcohol, Tobacco, Cholesterol, Drugs etc in their bodies. If excessive lifestyles are evident, treatment for any illness which could be as a result of the conscious choices they've made, will have to be paid for by themselves. If at the next test, a pre-determined improvement has been made, they will then again be eligible for full free healthcare.

At first, this may seem to extreme and oppressive a strategy, but, hopefully we all would realise, having reached this point in the Manifesto, that unless we start taking actual measures to rectify the problems within our societies, we will all continue to suffer as a result of them. These regular tests for the whole population may seem like an almighty task, one totally impracticable to implement. As the world stands now, perhaps. But with the implementation of 'Consolidation' and the elimination of 'Catatonic Currency', it's easily achievable.

In order to 'effectively' avoid people playing the system by detoxing immediately before their tests, there will also be additional random tests carried out. Refusal to yield, or to put it another way, to cheat yourself, your children and society out of money and lives they should be leading, will result in you having to pay for 'any' healthcare required that could be connected to poor diet and lifestyle. Does this sound too extreme? A system you wouldn't support? A Consolidist Government would hold a referendum on this major issue. Whether it is supported or not, unless we actually put some kind of system and deterrent in place, we'll forever see the Politicians on our televisions talking about the need to improve our failing healthcare systems. It will go on forever and a day.

If you put the above measures into place, implement 'Consolidation', effective Immigration policies and eliminate 'Catatonic Currency', we can all have access to healthcare systems that are as close to perfect as they could ever be. This is how clear and straightforward a Consolidist sees the situation. How does a Politician view it? "Welcome immigrants, come on in for free healthcare, paid for by the Proletariat's taxes. Irresponsible citizens, it's no problem for you to abuse your bodies all your lives. Society will pick up the tab, you go ahead. Talentless people of society, you keep the billions dead in your bank accounts, when it could be put to use, providing our citizens with swift, good quality healthcare. Everybody have as many children as you care to. It will eventually result in the collapse of our healthcare systems, aswell as our countries, but we're not going to do anything about it". At the moment, the world is upside-down, inside-out, flawed, illogical and insane.

★★★

Would you let 10 total strangers, who had grazed their knees, into your home and help them with treatment? Your child too, has the same injury. Before you see to your own flesh and blood, as she sobs in agony, with tears rolling down her cheeks, you say "I'm just going to see to these 10 strangers, then I'll get to you in maybe 20 minutes, okay darling?". Not in a million years would you do that. A Politician has no problem in allowing this to happen in our hospitals all over our countries. But why should they care? It's not their health that's suffering. They've got immediate private healthcare. When a country's doctors do get around to tending to their own citizens, the service they receive 'can' be sub-standard because the doctors are exhausted from having to work in overstretched systems, i.e. run a bigger operation. This is key to improving our lives. We have to look after our own and make our operations manageable in size, otherwise our problems will never go away.

As is effectively conveyed in the above example, the "Caring for your own" policy is not about race. It's not because you would dislike black, white, yellow or brown people. It's just that you just can't afford to take care of other 'families'. Just like you don't let total strangers into your house and look after them at the expense of your children. We can't let foreign persons into our countries and look after them at the expense of our citizens. In the Middle East, there are some extremely rich countries. Those countries shouldn't let outsiders get free healthcare in their country, and they don't. The UK for example, will give free healthcare to anyone. They "won't let anybody suffer and will ensure the 'Human Rights' of everybody". Rather disgustingly, the people whose human rights are being ignored the greatest as a result of the Politicians' open door policy of treating anybody for free, are the citizens of the UK. Taking it further, even the foreign persons suffer due to having to rely on an overburdened healthcare system for treatment. If our countries don't adopt Consolidism, and have open doors, everybody suffers, including the immigrants, and Consolidist Governments don't want anybody to suffer.

★★★

If a citizen can't pay for the treatment of their self-inflicted illnesses, because they have no money, or, perhaps they've never paid into the system, and are ill due to maybe abusing Alcohol, any family they have will have to pay what they can afford for the healthcare of their relative. Does this sound too harsh? At the moment, the Politicians are making you pay for it. You, someone who lives in a different city. Someone who doesn't even know this person. Someone who's never smoked or drank Alcohol in your whole life. That's harsh. If they have no money, no family members and the person is a citizen of the country, they will be treated. People will not be left to suffer if there is absolutely no way the bill for their irresponsibility can be footed by someone other than the Proletariat. If they do return to work, which they'll be pushed to, they will have to repay the people for providing them with the healthcare they required. If a foreign person in a country requires treatment, but has no travel insurance. Depending upon their condition, they will either be returned immediately to their own country to receive treatment, or the bill for any urgent treatment will be sent to their Embassy.

★★★

People can drink, smoke and take whatever they want in a Consolidist society, but they have to take ownership of the responsibility and repercussions of their 'own' actions. You can't be irresponsible, get yourself into trouble, then front up to others begging for help. If we continue to step in and bail people out, where's the incentive for them to live clean, healthy, responsible lives? It doesn't exist. So, the clean, healthy, responsible lives won't exist. It's a very simple concept. If we 'effectively' educate the kids from an early age, there would be far fewer people smoking, drinking, overindulging in substances and eating unhealthily all their lives.

'Effective' education involves showing graphic footage of the results of excessive drinking and smoking. Blackened lungs and livers will leave an impression with the children that will dissuade many of them from a life of unnecessary addiction. There are many who propose that addiction is a disease, hereditary, and handed down through genes. This theory may be true, but, the addictive tendencies are sparked off by, for example, trying alcohol initially. If you were a person living in a remote jungle where alcohol and drugs were not known of, and you had addiction in your genes, would you have the desire to indulge? It's an impossibility.

Addiction can only come about if you're in a certain place, at a certain time, and, most importantly, make the decision to initially try alcohol or drugs. With early, hard-hitting education, many of our children, who currently would be inclined to try alcohol or drugs, would refuse them if offered, due to their minds having been effectively educated to the fact that if they can't control a habit, they could end up with degraded health, dead or in a Consolidist Prison. If trying drugs just once sparks off addictive tendencies, would it be a good idea to make drugs legal and available? On the surface no, but, even if they remain illegal, drugs will always be a part of our communities. That's a 100% fact. We have to make them legal, then use the funds generated for extensive, effective education, and provide a major deterrent against alcohol or drug-fuelled crime via an abundance of law enforcement personnel on our streets.

If there are alot of people taking the legal, Government-Provided drugs, the funds raised would be invested in alot of law enforcement personnel, to counteract any possible crimes that may occur. If there are not so many people taking drugs, there won't be the need or funds to invest in as many law enforcement personnel. It's a proportional, self-sustaining system that looks after itself. Currently, due to lack of early, effective education, there are alot of people taking drugs and committing crimes, but no money for effective policing. As part of the effective education, the Consolidist Party proposes that we arrange for Alcoholics and lifelong smokers to visit the schools. The children could see and hear firsthand what will happen if they make the wrong choices in life. As it is, the Politicians are peddling soft, watered-down 'awareness campaigns' that are having absolutely no effect on our children's minds. No change in their mindset, means no change in our societies woes.

At the moment, in most countries of the world, drugs are illegal. As has been mentioned in a previous chapter, with a Consolidist Government, all drugs would be made legal, should the people support it. In a Consolidist society, people would be able to do whatever they want, as long as it has no negative effect on any person around them. With a Consolidist Government, you can choose to be an Alcoholic, but you'll get no free money or healthcare if you do. If you choose to be a Heroin addict, that's fine, but you'll get no free money or healthcare from the state.

It's so hypocritical to have the Police in a country smashing down the doors of a drug dealer dealing who deals a drug that kills 40 people a year, but, 50 yards down the street, allow an establishment to sell 'drugs', i.e. Alcohol and Tobacco, that kill 100,000 people a year. Let's not be mis-guided by the Politician's flawed view on the world, and let's identify Alcohol and Tobacco as being drugs. The most destructive and damaging drugs that exist in our societies today. There are many who would disagree with this viewpoint, and genuinely believe that we should listen to the Politicians when they tell us Alcohol is acceptable in moderation, but all drugs are deadly, and therefore illegal. Would you be one of those people? If we should listen to the Politicians on issues like this, they also tell us that people should consume no more than two units of Alcohol per day, or it becomes bad for our health. How many times have the Anti-Drugs people in our society exceeded this limit, thus flouting the Politician's advice? Many will have to admit to having done this thousands of times, and this serves as a perfect indicator to the fact that what the Politicians say shouldn't be taken as gospel all the time, but we should instead analyse things for ourselves, being guided principally by 'Common Sense'.

There is a certain drug though, inflicting much harm and negativity on our societies and its health. The abuse of this drug results in promiscuity, violence and millions of lost work days, costing economies billions. Our towns and cities are turned into virtual war zones, with people fighting, swearing, spitting, shouting, and vomiting in the streets. This drug causes people to lose control of their bodily functions and often renders them unconscious. Their minds become so overpowered, they don't even know their names or where they are. What is the name of this drug? Alcohol. If this was any other drug causing this mayhem across countries, the people would demand it be illegal. So why is it legal and other 'drugs' aren't? To say drugs are bad and Alcohol is okay is blinkered and wrong, and we must start to say it as it is.

In the UK, the National Health Service (NHS) spends £3 Billion per year in the treatment of Alcohol related illnesses and injuries. In August 2011, there was a 900 per day increase in hospital admissions due to Alcohol related problems. Even just 900 admissions per day would be staggering, but this is an 'increase' of 900 per day to 1400. This substance is legal and the rest are lethal, so says the mind of a Politician. They have us living backward lives in an upside-down world. If you challenged a Politician with this evidence they'd say "We realise this is a problem and we are taking steps to deal with it……". On and on they'd drivel, but, they wouldn't say exactly what they plan to do, plus, they won't actually ever do anything that will actually eliminate or drastically reduce the problem.

All drugs, this includes Alcohol, are bad for you. Why do we feel the need to do this to our bodies? But if we are going to take substances, we should take them in moderation. Not everybody who takes amphetamine is a shivering, dribbling junkie. That's currently the picture the Politicians have firmly implanted into our minds. It's a falsehood. Take a look around as you go about your day. It's a guarantee that there will be somebody who you'd never expect, that takes 'drugs', but, they're still productive members of society.

A Consolidist Government believes drugs should be legal, produced and sold by the Government, thus making them safer. Effective, hard-hitting, unabashed education would be provided to all children from a very early age about how Tobacco, Alcohol & Drugs can negatively affect your lives and health if you lose control of your habit. The money generated from drugs would remain in society, to the benefit of society. Some of it used to educate people about Alcohol and drugs. As it is now, the Politicians allow a setup that means people take unsafe, underground laboratory drugs. It's soft and shy advertising campaigns are a total waste of tax-payers money. The drug warlords sit on billions of society's currency. Those who turn to drugs, many from the lack of education and poor upbringings, cost the tax-payers billions in the shape of funds the Politicians pour into the policing, the justice system and healthcare.

Worse still is that the penalties they put upon these people they call 'criminals' are lax and totally fruitless in effecting change in people's lives. They shouldn't be seen as criminals in the first place, but, they are by the politicians, who then 'implement' money-making measures that don't effect change amongst these 'non-criminals'. It's all such a continual waste of money. Politicians have declared war on drugs for decades, wasting billions of your currency. Has the problem gone away? This is the shoddy service the Politicians are providing you with, in exchange for their handsome salaries. As long as they bank that salary, they only need to pretend they care. They don't need to actually change anything for the better. This is what we've been letting them get away with.

We need to completely overhaul our societies in the way they function, or the problems, of all kinds, will remain. We have to at least give legalising drugs a try, bringing them out into the open, making it acceptable to talk openly about them, thus possibly helping people with problems which they would now never even dare to bring up publicly in today's societies. If drugs remain illegal, they will remain a problem for as long as humans exist. It's a 100% fact that if drugs are legal or illegal, there will still be hundreds of millions of people across the world taking them. So, we can either use 'Common Sense' and say we'll legalise them, make them safer and use the revenues generated from them, or, we can lose the hundreds of billions in revenue and continue to allow an ostracised element of our communities take unsafe 'underground' drugs. In modern parlance, it's a 'No-Brainer'. We legalise.

The Consolidist Party recognizes that humans have a need to release, to enjoy themselves and alter their state of consciousness. So it would propose we make all drugs legal, but, you have to pay for them yourselves and enjoy them responsibly. As societies, we can't have Alcoholics and drug-users taking us for a ride, as the Politicians allow. Currently, addicts get given all sorts of chances in the form of tax draining rehab programmes, medication and treatment. Some kick their habits, temporarily, then return to their addictions. How does a Politician deal with this? Exactly. They welcome them back with open arms, pouring more of your money down the drain paying for somebody's irresponsible, conscious decisions. What on earth is going on in a Politician's mind? Are they really expecting us to believe that they're trying to help us in the way their running our countries?

With a Consolidist Government, drink as much alcohol and take as many drugs as you want. It's not a Government's Right to try and shape people's minds about what they do to themselves. It should only step in once a person's actions are having an actual negative effect on those around them. With this in mind, if you've made the conscious decisions in life that have brought you to addiction's doorstep, and you then decide you want help to kick your addiction, you'll have to pay for it yourself. If you don't have any money, your family will have to pay for it. Let's not be cowed by 'Political Correctness' & 'Phony Human Rights' which allows people to suck money out of the system, as we can't say what we should be saying to them. If you want to stop drinking Alcohol, you stop drinking Alcohol, that's all it takes. If you want formal treatment, you pay for it. It's not the hardworking masses out there who decided to drink alcohol every day for the past 20 years. It was you. You have to deal with and pay for the consequences. Actions and Consequence. That's conducive to a Society in which the 99% receive their just rewards.

★★★

There are sometimes instances of malpractice in our hospitals. It's a tragedy, but unfortunately a reality. Mistakes happen. A Consolidist Government believes that people should be held accountable for their actions. If somebody is negligible, they should stand trial for it. How do the Politicians see this? They think it makes sense for people to be able to sue hospitals for malpractice. Is this a sensible policy? One which holds society's best interests in mind? Such a policy is enforced in the UK, where the healthcare is actually free. A free service someone can sue? Is this 'Common Sense'? What happens if a person wins a case? Funds leave the local Trust's budget, meaning that there must be cuts somewhere to the healthcare service provided for others. Is that a good idea? Exactly. The Politicians think so. "Human Rights" would they cry? It must be noted that malpractice and medical mistakes would occur with far less frequency if 'Consolidation' was implemented to produce a more manageable operation. Is it easier to provide quality healthcare for 5 people or 5 million people? Is it easier to provide for good quality healthcare for your citizens or for your citizens plus 2 million foreign persons? Also, the elimination of 'Catatonic Currency' would free up tens of millions in funds for training and monitoring of healthcare sector employees.

The way in which some of our hospitals are funded perfectly illustrates how broken our systems are, and how they need to be radically altered. Again, taking the UK as an example, the Government has for some time now being building hospitals through Private Finance Initiatives (PFI's). This is where a private investor provides the Government with the funds to build a hospital. The Government then pay them back after the hospital is built, plus interest, paid by taxes deducted from your salaries. The UK Government is running its country in such a way that it doesn't have to money to look after the health of its citizens.

Citizens of the UK. Do you think you should be made to pay interest via your taxes to receive your healthcare? A Politician does. There's enough money sitting in the bank accounts of the player's of the top 20 soccer clubs in the UK to build several hospitals. If you throw in the money sitting in the soccer club's owner's bank accounts, there's enough to build many many hospitals. Where have all those fortunes come from? Your pockets. And that's just soccer. What about all the other 'Sportstars', 'Popstars', 'Musicians' and Filthy Rich Businesswomen and Men? It's beyond belief that this is allowed to happen, but wouldn't be by a Consolidist Government.

When a country has to use PFI to build its hospitals, that would surely be the point at which the people running the country say "Hey, this isn't right. We need to do something differently to avoid this farce". Not a Politician. They just keep on heading down the same road. Not only are they allowing the billions in 'Catatonic Currency' to remain, they're allowing the owner of the construction company that builds the hospital to sit on the millions in profit she or he receives the project. Similarly, the private investor sits on millions. All the while, your taxes are higher than they should be to pay the 'interest' which the private investor adds to her or his fortune. Is this Common Sense? Top to tail, head to toe, your lives are being ruined by Politicians. Healthcare is just one ingredient in the recipe for disaster the Politicians call their "Capitalist Manifestos".

CHAPTER 6

Terrorism

Terrorism has emerged as a major threat to our countries in the last 30-40 years. This is arguably a more important issue than all the others that have been discussed thus far. It's not about quality of life, but life itself. Immediately, we can all identify that 'Consolidation' would aid us massively in the fight against terrorism. The fewer people there are to monitor for possible terrorist threats, the easier it will be to effectively monitor them. The more potential terrorists there are in a country, the easier it will be for some of them to slip the net. Is it easier to keep an eye on someone in a crowd of 5 or 5,000? A very simple concept.

To deal with this most serious of threats, once again, Politicians of the world are taking their usual softly-softly approach, aiming the resources paid for by you, in totally the wrong direction. You can bet your house on the fact that, just like all the other problems we see society riddled with, the Politicians will still be promising to stamp out terrorism in 100 years. It's a guarantee, unless, a Consolidist Government is given a chance.

As discussed in the "Crime & Punishment" Chapter, in the UK, the security services are always monitoring many possible or actual terror plots. When a report detailing this hits a Prime Minister's desk, does she orhe say "No need to worry too much. Just keep an eye on them"? What would you do if you held the lives of your citizens in your hands and that that report hit your desk? Exactly. You would do exactly as a Consolidist Government would do.

Record and collect the evidence that is enabling you to classify them as 'Potential or Actual Terror Plots'. Arrest the relevant persons, immediately. Present the evidence to your citizens, the courts, and let the justice system book them up for a very lengthy stay in a Consolidist Prison. If you have the inclination and desire to kill innocent people, the Consolidist Party believes you should be sent to prison and never come out. And it would provide Justice and Prison Systems that enable this to happen. With a Consolidist Government, life means life. How does a Politician see it? "Let the plot develop, because due to 'Phony Human Rights', we need to make sure we have way more evidence than we should need. It could be a dummy plot, leading us away from an imminent surprise attack, but, we're willing to take the chance because it wouldn't be us or any of our families killed or maimed. When we do arrest and charge them, we'll sentence them to 10 years in prison, but let them out in just over 5 for not misbehaving. That should do it". It's enough to make you physically sick.

Even if an early sneak attack ever killed just 1 person, that would be 1 person too many. What if it was your child? It would change your life forever. A Consolidist Government realises this and would not take the chance. Currently, if the security services are following plots, this means they're tying up resources which could be used to seek out plots elsewhere. Is that Common Sense? With a Consolidist Government, the perpetrators go to prison for life and the security services start looking elsewhere for danger, thus ensuring you and your family remain safe as you go out every day to work and school.

Through the elimination of 'Catatonic Currency', a Consolidist Government would ensure there are ample security services, with all the resources they needed to be effective in their efforts to protect you. This creates many jobs for you and your families. With 'Consolidation' and robust Immigration policies resulting in far less people to monitor, the ample security services could use their plentiful resources to keep You the 99% safe, as you deserve to be.

Highly effective surveillance and monitoring, decisive arrests and then heavy punishments in a hellish environment where their type are frowned upon. Is that Common Sense? That's how a Consolidist sees it. Those are some of the policies of the Consolidist Party. Policies that would have an effect. There is though an additional policy that would make your security absolutely watertight.

The 'facts' and figures show us that the vast majority of terrorism in the world is coming from one source, Islam and Muslims. We can surely all agree that this is not racist. It's simply a fact we all have to openly state if we're ever to eliminate the threat posed. Now, there are a very large percentage Muslims who are beautiful human beings, that would never even contemplate carrying out a terrorist attack, but, there are some who would, and are trying to as we speak. The problem is that we can't tell who's going to attempt an attack until they actually start planning it. With all the funds that would be poured into national security by a Consolidist Government, not even a trillion currency could buy us a mind-reading device enabling us to identify wannabe terrorists. With the tools we do have, it is 'possible' that we miss the planning and execution of a terrorist attack. They 'could' evade our radar.

Terrorist plots 'can' fully form only in the minds of the wannabe terrorists. There don't have to be discussions with others via telephone or email, or explosives to carry out a terrorist plot. All it takes is a gun or a knife and a busy high street for a tragedy to occur. There's no way of stopping this. As the terrorists are realising, because they're now moving towards plotting these types of attacks. A Consolidist Government would not be willing to take the risk, and would take decisive action to eliminate the chance of this type of undetectable attack occurring. All of our family members, friends and fellow citizens are far too important to us to take any chances whatsoever. Would you ever for a second jeopardise the safety of your loved ones, if you knew you could take action to absolutely ensure their safety? Exactly.

The Consolidist Party's Immigration policy has already been

described in a previous chapter. This on its own would have virtually eliminated the threat of terrorist attacks within our Non-Muslim countries. Taking the UK as an example, if a Consolidist Government had been in power for the past 70 years, the parents of the 7/7 attackers in London would not have been allowed to enter and live in the UK. The sons they had whilst living in the UK, sons that were given British Passports, would not have been able to carry out the suicide bombings they did. Simple and effective policies have highly effective results. 52 people died on 7/7. 52 dearly loved, dead and painfully missed because of the Politician's policies.

After those attacks, you'd think that the UK Politicians would take measures to ensure this doesn't happen again. 'Effective' measures. Not a chance. They continue to handout British Passports to Muslims born in the UK. Any Muslim from anywhere in the world can enter the UK for a holiday, or perhaps to even live, should they play successfully on the softness of the Politicians. A Consolidist Government in a Non-Muslim country would see this as ridiculous, and would have no choice, due to other people's conscious decisions, to never allow a Muslim, or anybody they deemed a threat, now or in the future, to enter their country. This is highly regrettable, but, absolutely unavoidable. You and Your family, our citizens, are too important to take any chances. If the Politicians continue to let potential terrorists into a country where there are already too many people to effectively monitor, eventually some of them will escape detection and successfully execute an attack. That's a fact. This Manifesto was written in 2012. Let Consolidism make a prediction. If the Politicians are allowed to remain in power in the UK, there will be another terrorist attack in which more of your loved ones will die. That's a 100% certainty. More than likely, the majority of the successful attacks will be 'low level' attacks.

In January of 2012, 9 Muslims with British Passports were found guilty of plotting terrorist attacks at the London Stock Exchange and the US Embassy, amongst other places. No doubt, the Politicians will allow them to be sentenced lightly, they'll then be allowed to remain in the UK to possibly plot more attacks. At some point, these people, or others, will be successful and kill somebody. When they do achieve this, they will have effectively been aided by the Politicians, who have the choice right now to take action, before the bomb goes off, or before a knife is raised in misguided anger.

Would you say it would be unfair or too extreme to ban Muslims, or anybody deemed a threat, from entering a country, to live or for a holiday? If you would, it's because you don't think a terrorist attack will ever affect your life, the lives of your children or your friends. This too, is the reason the Politicians don't take the steps necessary to ensure its citizens remain safe. "It's not going to happen to me". There is somebody somewhere in the UK right now who will be killed by a future terrorist attack. That somebody happens to be you. Is it too extreme now? Whether it be this year or in 10 years, there will be another attack. It's virtually certain that it will be carried out by another UK born Muslim, whose descendants are from a Middle Eastern country. The loved one who's sitting next to you right now. They happen to be the only death in this terrorist attack. Now how do you feel about not allowing potential terrorists into your country? It seems quite rational now doesn't it? If this was to happen to you, as it will happen to somebody, how would you feel about supporting the revocation of all the British passports the Politicians have handed out to foreign Muslims over the years, and very politely requesting that they return to their beautiful country of origin. The country that the terrorists are sullying the good reputation of. Would you do that in a heartbeat now, if it's you who's directly affected?

We have to realise someone will be affected and act on it, right now. We have to shed the mindset of not being able to appreciate how others suffer. The mindset of "It will never happen to me". What if it was a UK Politician's child who was to be blown in half by a bomb planted by a UK born Somalian Muslim? If they had the choice of that happening, or ejecting all Muslims, or any threat, from the country, which do you think they'd go for? Precisely. A referendum would be held to see if the Non-Muslim British people support the revocation policy.

Crossing the Pond. Would President Barack Obama allow an Americanised Pakistani Muslim to work as one of his Personal Secret Service Agents? Never would it be considered, even for a second. Though thousands who 'possibly' mean harm to Americans, are left to walk among you every day. The President has no problem with that. Why? Because you're not deemed important by those who are currently in Power. The Public Stance is that you are important, but, in reality, as long as it's not the Politicians or their families being harmed, they're not willing to take any action at all. Nidal Malik Hasan was allowed by the 'Powers' to work as a United States Army Medical Corps Psychiatrist at Fort Hood in Texas. He slaughtered 13 Brave American Soldiers. Secondarily he brought great shame upon his no-doubt highly respectable Muslim Family and the Great Religion of Islam. More Politician Errors of Judgement & Inaction, more Dead Americans.

Right now, the Politicians think it's Common Sense to allow non to low-skilled foreigners free reign to enter and live in our countries. They either take our citizens jobs or cost us billions in benefits. They degrade and overburden our public services. Some of their children, who the Politicians have handed passports out to, carry out terrorist attacks that murder our citizens. Is that Common Sense? It makes sense to a Politician. Whether it be Pakistan allowing British people to live and work in their country, or vice versa. In the name of security. In the name of a fair, prosperous society, it is a nonsense policy that is majorly detrimental to all our lives. The citizens and the immigrants. It's totally unworkable. The evidence is upon us.

There are those who will scream "Racist". A Consolidist would answer very calmly, "Common Sense". It's not about race. If you're white, black or Middle Eastern and we deem you a threat, through perhaps your religion, be it conspicuous or not, we have to refuse you entry into our country. Let the author of this Manifesto state that quite probably the most pleasant, generous person they've ever met in their life, was a Pakistani Muslim. A black man is the author of this Manifesto's idol. It is not about Racism. It's about 'Common Sense'. We cannot continue to allow ourselves to be bullied into submission by someone blurting that word out. It is used as a tactic to enable foreign persons to continue to take advantage of our societies, money, and infiltrate us to carry out terrorist attacks. If we continue to allow this to happen, we are all responsible for the suffering and deaths of our fellow citizens. We have a responsibility towards each other to stand firm. A Consolidist Government would do just that, and, do whatever it takes to look after its precious citizens.

A Consolidist Government would have the Common Sense to recognize the highly conspicuous threat posed by Muslims in any country. It would realise that another attack will happen somewhere down the line, and that one of your family members, or you, could be the victims of that attack. A Consolidist Government would realise the traumatic effect it would have on you. Through a referendum, it would ask you the citizen, if you would feel safer with all threats having been returned to their country of origin. The country of origin whose hardworking, law-abiding citizens the terrorists have brought shame upon.

Should the people support this policy, there would be no choice but to achieve this by not allowing the threats to take up employment, gain education, rent or buy accommodation, receive healthcare or hold bank accounts. This is not the fault of the citizens of a country, but the terrorists who have already committed, and will commit, atrocities in the name of their religion and people. Let's not dodge this most important of issues. We have to say it as it is if we are to remove the threat. It's not racist to politely request that a threat leaves our countries.

Would you ask somebody who's posing a threat to you and your family, to leave your houses? The unavoidable facts and dangers are there for all to see. A Consolidist Government wants to ensure your safety as a people. Would 7/7 have happened, if after 9/11, the UK Government had held a referendum and subsequently, at the request of the people, politely asked all Muslims to leave the country? Exactly. But they didn't do it. They didn't have to do it or care about it, because none of their family members or they were injured or killed in the 7/7 attacks, and it's exactly this that was in their minds, "In the years following 9/11, there could well be an attack in our country, but, the chances of it affecting me or my family are slim to none, so there's no need to go through the hard work of doing anything". That's what goes on in a Politician's mind. A Consolidist Government would act, immediately, for your protection, should you vote in favour.

It is not the hard-working, decent human beings who decided to kill innocent people. So when we could possibly ask a threat to leave our 'home', let's not all enter into the charade of having the threat accuse us of being bad people. And let's especially not, as fellow citizens, allow this to happen by cowering to 'Phony Human Rights' & 'Political Correctness'. If and when the threat return to their country of origin, amongst themselves they should strive to encourage and educate each other to the fact that terrorist attacks bring only hardship upon their people. That decent human beings would never ever contemplate such acts. Until your people have rejected it completely, we cannot allow you to possibly harm our citizens. That's the Consolidist Message.

In a Non-Muslim Consolidist country, if you're a genuine citizen of that country and you want to practice the wonderful Islamic Faith, which encourages many to be good, wholesome people, you can do so, but in your own homes. It is 'Common Sense' that when murder such as that witnessed on 9/11 has taken place in the world in the name of a religion, you can't allow that religion to be advertised, 'possibly' resulting in more murder. The identification of the measures we have to take to cure the problem are so simple, but, the Politicians are just not willing or unable to make it happen.

Citizens of a Consolidist country would be advised against

travelling to any country where there are great numbers of potential terrorists, or any country which doesn't adopt the 'Common Sense' policy of not allowing threats into their country. Again, sorry, but it's just necessary. Regrettably, following the terrorist attacks on our people, the only dealings which can be safely had with threatening countries, are at ports in order to continue trade and ensure jobs are protected.

The action which needs to be taken may at first seem quite drastic, but it's absolutely necessary. How many people do we have allow to be maimed or murdered before we act? For Muslim countries that adopt Consolidism, all the previously discussed policies, which result in people living bountiful lives and feeling like they matter, would virtually eliminate the possibility of people lashing out through terrorist attacks. That's all it really is. Terrorists are people who feel hard done by and want to make their voice heard. Consolidism and its style of Government gives people a good deal in life. It makes them feel as though they're living the best lives they possibly can. Good Muslims deserve good lives. Consolidism will provide those good lives for you, peaceful and respectful people of Islam. Embrace Consolidism. It's got nothing to do with religion, but rather ensuring You and Your beautiful little Muslim children are cared and provided for by your Government.

★★★

Would you let 10 total strangers from the same 'family' come and stay in your home indefinitely? They're not of any particular colour, creed or religion, just identified as strangers. They don't have skills or jobs. You have to support them at the expense of your children. One of them decides one day to set off a bomb which cripples your child. What do you do about this? Do you eject this person from your home, but allow the other members of the 'family' to continue to live there? Then one day, another of the family members openly states that they believe your family should be murdered in the name of their religion. Or to put it another way, 'in the name of a fictional book they've become attached to'. Do you allow them to stay in your home? Thousands of miles away are other members of this 'family' who are brainwashing people, telling them that you and your family are evil and deserve to die. To tackle this problem you let the dangerous strangers remain in your home, then spend all your money, at the expense of your children, to travel thousands of miles and fight the people brainwashing and recruiting others to their twisted, flawed cause. In the process of fighting, you get killed, leaving your crippled child without parents for the rest of their lives. Would this be Common Sense? A Politician thinks so. All along, all you had to do is say to the strangers, "You can't come into my home". Even if initially you allowed them into your home, then they became a threat. Instead of travelling the thousands of miles to fight and die, all you had to do was say "Please leave my home". If we remove the threat from our countries, we can bring our troops home.

Is that such a complicated theory? Why can't a Politician see how insane their policies are? Or perhaps they can, but are gutless imbeciles, too timid to take the right action. The understanding a Consolidist Societician would have on this issue, is that if you thought for 1 millionth of a second that somebody could be a threat to you or your children, you wouldn't let them into your home in a million years. Would that be a correct interpretation of your thoughts? It's time to act.

Just as the Politicians play right into the terrorist's hands, so to do the media in the most ridiculous, but subtle way which should be avoided. If you were an impressionable young Muslim, without your world views having yet been formed. If you were an individual looking for a voice in the world, as all humans are, wanting to be most important and the centre of attention. Incidentally, this selfish, inherently human individuality is one of the main reasons there's so much conflict and violence in the world. Would you be inspired to join a group of people being described on mainstream media television channels as "Insurgents"? What if these people were instead called "Enemies of Islam"? Is that as attractive a label to hold? It may not have a major effect, but, why encourage people at all, by making the cause seem romantic and epic? Can't the news channels see they're fuelling the fire?

If the truth be told, the terrorists kill and maim more Muslims than any other religion. Innocent, suffering Muslims, we feel for you all, but until you have cured the disease which currently exists inside your religion and people, we can have very little to do with you, or any other people or religion who threaten us. A Consolidist Government would of course allow free media and wouldn't dictate to news channels that they had to call these people not "Insurgents", but "Enemies of Islam". What it would do though, is speak up on issues such as the above, identifying, with no fear of PHR or PC, that it is farcical to romanticise the cause of the murderers.

Let's be under no illusion. Let's say it as it is. The reason these young Muslims, and others, decide to become terrorists is not because of what "the West" has done to them and their fellow Muslims. It's because they live in dusty desserts, under corrupt and oppressive Governments. It's because they have very little in life, and, if they do have access to a television, they see Las Vegas, London or Paris, and become jealous. Their lives and the way their treated and not provided for by their governments, results in them being desperate to have their voice heard. They're desperate to make themselves feel of worth and importance, with purpose to their lives. They then start to lash out at either their own governments or "The West". As already discussed at length, in Las Vegas, London and Paris, the people's quality of life is far below that what it should be thanks to the Politicians. But, in comparison to the environment the Muslims live in, plus taking into consideration the added brutality and oppressiveness of their Politicians, the "West" offers a better existence. One they become jealous of.

★★★

The Palestine & Israel problem. Has that been solved by Politicians yet? This is a perfect illustration of how ineffective Politics and Politicians are. Partition is the answer to this problem. Two separate countries. If there are people who are a threat to you, you have to remain separated from them. You can't hurt each other if you stay completely separated. There is the problem of the Palestinians firing rockets randomly into Israeli cities, but, we've all witnessed the far worse carnage that's occurred when Palestinian Suicide Bombers have managed to get amongst crowds of Israeli citizens. Why won't Israel agree to the demands of the powerhouse that is the USA? It's because the USA make reasonable demands upon Israel, but at the same time tell them if they don't yield, they'll stick by them anyway. Our societies and world are riddled with this approach to all issues, major and minor. It is killing us in every way, shape and form in our lives. No deterrent equals no progress. It's unfair to have good people like the Palestinians oppressed, but, just the same it's wrong for Israelis to be terrorised. Complete separation is the answer. This will not be achieved until the USA get tough with Israel. And this will not be achieved until 'Consolidism', and its tough stance on deterrents being present, is adopted. Israel and Palestine should be given one chance by America, and the world, to make reasonable concessions that decent human beings would realise have to be made in order to solve such a long and major dispute. If they continue to act like they're 7 year olds in the school yard, they should be left to it, instead of pumping so much effort and money, your taxes, into a situation that will obviously never be resolved until there's a big change in approach and policy. There's only so much effort that should be made before you have to say, "If you're not going to help yourselves, then we're not going to help you. Good Luck. So Long".

Analysing it further still. How did the Israel/Palestine problem come about in the first place? If certain startlingly simple Policies had been implemented by Politicians long ago, could we have avoided it altogether? The Answer is Yes. If Consolidist Policies were implemented. What Policies? Let Consolidism explain. Israel became a State in 1948. This following a series of 'Aliyahs' which began in

1882. 'Aliyah' is a term used to describe the Migration of Wonderful Jewish People to what is now known as Israel. Over the years, as the number of Migrant Settlers grew, both Jewish Migrants and Foreign Politician-Led Governments, called for the Jewish people to be able to form their own State. And as we all know, they did.

As has been discussed at length in this Manifesto, Consolidism believes that we should all largely remain in our own countries of origin, limit population numbers within those countries, then Consolidate. If we don't, as has been clearly identified, problems will ensue. The Migration of Jewish Peoples to what is now Israel and the subsequent forming of the State of Israel, would never have happened if Consolidism, the force for the people, had been present as a Socio-Political Ideology all those years ago.

Migration & Immigration causes Friction and Major Problems. Whether we're Jewish, Muslim, Christian. Whether we're Black or White. To avoid Conflicts and the Suffering of both the Migrants and Natives, we all need to remain within our own Borders. It's the only possible way World Peace can ever be achieved, and endure. Sadly it's inherent within Human Nature for many to dislike other peoples just because they're different. Of course, we'd all love for this not to be the case. But it is a reality. A reality that needs to be identified, and measures taken to avoid all our people's lives being sullied by the difficulties which occur from such a mindset. It's a mindset that will never go away. So let's not fool ourselves that it will. We have to work sensibly with what we've got. If we don't, our woes will be ever-present. Just look at the Tax-Draining Gang Wars that rage within the Prisons of the USA. The division between the Gangs is centred solely around race. What about The Ku Klux Klan, who are totally unjustified in the violence they use to express their displeasure at other races of human beings having been allowed into their society. The cause of the chaos, hatred and murder that goes hand in hand with elements such as the Prison Gangs & The Ku Klux Klan? Migration and the mixing of races. It doesn't work. Sad? Absolutely. But oh so very real and true. Lives are lost when races mix. If just one life can be saved by simple and clear Immigration Policies, wouldn't it be worth implementing them? Life is precious. 'All' Life.

Not only, as a result of Incompetent Politicians, is the World currently burdened with this incredibly difficult Palestine/Israel Problem, but, we've still got Politicians in power, and they are the ones charged with solving the Problem. As we all know, they cannot solve even the simplest of our problems. Thanks to the Politicians, millions of good Muslims & Jews have died and will die, and millions will continue to live lives of great hardship. Not only Muslims and Jews, but people of all colours and religions all over the world.

★★★

Islam is in many ways a wonderful religion, with the majority of its followers being highly respectful people of great compassion. Many countries in which Islam is the main religion, haven't fallen folly to some of the flaws of Western countries, such as how television results in talentless people becoming idolised and rich. There are aspects of the religion that are expedient in creating prosperous, orderly societies, such as its abstinence from alcohol and drugs. In other ways though, it is not a pleasant entity. It treats women as though they're second rate beings, which is totally disgusting. How women being second rate beings could even exist merely as a discussion point in Western countries is beyond comprehension. Worse still, is how Islam has been affected with the disease that is terrorism. With great regret, a Consolidist tells it like it is. From a Non-Islamic State's point of view, you are a danger, so we must separate ourselves from you. A Consolidist believes that it should separate its people from any threat. It's not about Religion, Racism or Xenophobia. It's about Common Sense. If Christians started committing Terrorist Acts in Islamic Countries, Consolidism believes that the Muslims of that Country should ask the Christians to leave. Full Stop.

Take a quiet moment to yourself. Close your eyes. Imagine you're a coloured human being. One living in the United States of America perhaps 50 years ago. Now imagine the feelings and emotions coursing through your veins if you found yourself in the following position. Your hands are tightly tied behind your back. Imagine how the rope feels on your skin. You've been battered virtually unconscious for an hour by a mob of unjustified angry white folk. Smell your blood. Taste it too. How do their burning torches smell? Can you hear the mob screaming abuse at you? Just because of the colour of your skin. Kneeling at the base of a tree, a rope is placed around your neck and pulled tight. You're about to be hauled up by the neck. The rope will tighten and tighten, until you can breathe no more, and life leaves your body. If somebody, at that precise moment time, just before you were to leave this earth, offered you the chance to change the course of history in such a way that your people had never travelled to America, or you found yourself in America, but returned to your home country at the earliest opportunity. So that you were not about to be murdered in cold blood. Honestly. Would you take that chance? Because there are thousands, or even millions of good people, who have found themselves in such a terrifying beyond words situation across the world throughout history. Without Migration, we can avoid anybody ever having to suffer such a fate due to their race, religion or affiliation. It's not just about being Black. Through the centuries, millions have been murdered because they are 'different' from the people they find themselves living amongst. It's happened to White people, killed by coloured people. It's happened Black on Black, in the name of religion or perhaps tribal affiliation. And it's happened White on White. It will continue to happen, possibly to you, if we don't face reality and fully accept the harsh truth that the notion of all races & religions living together in peace & harmony does not work. It sounds romantic, but, it happens only in fairy tales. We live in a real world. Not in a fantasy world.

CHAPTER 7

Defence

After considering the Consolidist Party's policies on Terrorism. Has it really been necessary to send our precious troops halfway across the world to die in dusty hell holes, in the name of 'The War on Terror'? It could have been easily avoided. There was an easier solution to the problem. One which was simple to identify, if you're not a Politician. In Iraq & Afghanistan, thousands of our precious soldiers have perished. Killed by the bullets and bombs of 'Enemies of Islam' yes, but, equally responsible for their deaths are the Politicians. Their brazen disregard for our soldiers and their families is all too evident, when at the nod of a head they unnecessarily send them to their deaths, thousands of miles from the precious love of their families. Whether the enactment of the solution to avoid their deaths would have been simple or not, if it makes sense to do it, then it is done. That is how a Consolidist's mind works.

If the US Politicians had not allowed Muslims to remain in their country when there were whisperings of the hatred towards them pre-9/11, 9/11 would never have happened. More than whisperings, what about the 'World Trade Centre' bombing in 1993. Was that not a loud and clear indicator that America and other countries cannot allow certain people to be among their citizens? Not to the Politicians. That's nearly 4,000 people that would still be alive and enjoying their lives with their families. That's nearly 4,000 families whose lives would not have been irreparably traumatised by their loss. Thousands more would not have had to have been sent to their deaths in the name of the "War against Terrorism". How idiotic can a Government be to choose the option of sending troops to their deaths, over removing the threat from their countries? It beggars belief.

The following observation is quite probably the best indicator that could ever exist of the total insanity that is a Politician's decision making process. More innocent people from their respective countries have died fighting the terrorists since 9/11, than died in the 9/11 attacks themselves. It is staggering that the Politicians have made decisions that have brought about that eventuality. It's so tragic that, up until now, our populations have had no choice but to allow Politicians to ruin their lives.

December 7th 1941. The Japanese launched a surprise attack on the US Naval Base at Pearl Harbor. What was the Politician's Solution? Prepare and 'advance' their forces to defeat the Japanese. The result of this policy? Approximately 111,000 dead. Over a quarter of a million injured. That means limbs blown off. Physiological & Psychological Issues that the Txpayer will be paying for until the end of the brave soldiers lives. This when there was no reason to 'go' into action in the first place. What would the Consolidist Solution have been following the Japanese attack? Shore up your defences. Bring in Warships, Hundreds of Thousands of Soldiers, Aircraft, Airmen, Resources, until there's such a show of force, the Japanese wouldn't have dared come back. They only attacked initially because they were able to sneak a surprise attack. USA, if with all this might on your shores, the Japanese did decide to come back, then you should have asked your countrywomen & men to fight. If the Japanese did return, would there have been fewer casualties than there were after the Politicians ordered the advance? Tens of Thousands fewer for sure. A fraction of the 110,000 deaths. The Politicians have no regard or idea of the fact that when they order their armed forces into action, people get killed and maimed. They can't seem to appreciate it, at all. They seem to think they're playing some kind of game, without any feeling of conscience weighing on them whatsoever. So why did the Japanese launch the attack in the first place? They wanted to take back Asian land from the White Man who was gradually spreading their footprint across the Pacific. This takes us back to Consolidation & Immigration. We should all stay within our own countries and cap our populations, or else it shall 'forever' result in War & Suffering. The growth and spread of humans brings about problems and eventually wars.

Politicians always talk about protecting the lives of the innocents in conflicts, and this is undoubtedly commendable. In the recent Iraq and Afghanistan wars, there has been a more innocent party than the wonderful law-abiding Iraqi & Afghan citizens. Who are these most innocents? It's the soldiers who have been sent from the USA, UK and many other countries to fight and die in the name of serving their country. The Iraqi & Afghan citizens are innocent of course, but, in future it has to be made clear that if any dictators want to rear their ugly heads, and military action against them is deemed necessary, it is you the dictator that has brought suffering on your people. The reason action has been taken in Iraq & Afghanistan is because of events such as 9/11 & 7/7. It's actually reaction, not action. There are some who try to make out that the "Allies" are out there killing for fun or for religious purposes. This of course is absolute rubbish. The people of the USA & UK don't want to be spending time, money, or more importantly lives, executing wars in far off deserts. Wars that the Politicians are executing in entirely the wrong way. This in keeping with the wrong way Politicians deal with every issue they encounter.

If military action needs to be executed, in future, it should be carried out in such a fashion that results in not a hair on the innocent soldier's heads being put out of place. If that means going directly for the dictator using remotely fired weapons, then so be it. The innocent soldiers are more innocent than the innocent civilians of the offending country. Politicians are far too footloose and fancy free, packing our soldiers off to far flung places to defend us, or defend the people of another country. A country's soldiers should never be injured or die in the protection of citizens of another country, unless they are 'great' allies, and the circumstances are exceptional, such as an enemy country 'actually' invading. We're sorry to see people being treated unfairly and perhaps dying or being killed, but, we can't send our precious soldiers to their deaths for your cause. Remote weapons we can use to help you. Soldiers on the ground? No. They're just too important to us. Are your loved ones too important to you? Do you think your soldiers should be sent to protect people in foreign lands? What if it's you, your wife, husband or child who's to die protecting foreign persons across the other side of the world? Because somebody dies when we send our troops abroad to fight for us. We have to realise this. Leaving the Earth. Leaving your body. Death. It's a massive, virtually incomprehensible event. Politicians just don't seem to be able to fathom or appreciate this.

A Consolidist Government would only ask soldiers to fight if absolutely necessary, and that's not the Politician's definition of "absolutely necessary". The wars in Iraq and Afghanistan were not necessary at all. Removal of the threat from our countries was the first action to take. Secondly, the allies should have gone directly for Saddam Hussein and the Taliban leaders using remotely fired weapons. If we do this, we will only ever have to ask our troops to fight, if another country is massing upon or pouring over our borders.

What's the reason Politicians have no qualms about sending our soldiers off to fight? It's not them who has to experience bullets whizzing inches past their skulls. Or one entering their skull at 2000 metres per second. It's not the Politicians who have to lace up their boots every morning, knowing there's a strong possibility that this could be their last day on Earth. As lucky citizens, sat safe in our homes, I don't think we could ever fully appreciate what it feels like to have this thought running through our heads every morning you wake a 6 month tour of duty. The reason everybody turns a blind eye to it, is because it doesn't affect them. But it affects somebody. Being acutely aware that it's You and Your loved ones who fight, and sometimes die for your countries, should any 'Non-Remotely Fired' military action be required, where You and Your dearly important family members will be put in harm's way, a Consolidist Government would hold a referendum, allowing 'You' to decide if 'You' deem it necessary for the sake of the safety and security of Your country. The Politicians don't have the right to make these decisions. Admittedly there are far more Non-Military families than Military families, so there is still an element of some choosing the fate of others, but, generally, a population, The 99%, is vastly more in tune than a Politician on how people actually die in military conflicts. Due to their pompous disconnect, as they languish in their ivory towers, with their bulging bank balances, Politicians just don't seem to get it. The people, who have to live, or die, by policies and decisions, should be the ones who make the policies and decisions. It's the only fair way to conduct the business of our countries.

The USA & UK could have fought and destroyed the Taliban with remote weapons, 'after', removing all threats from your home countries. But no, because the Politicians won't remove the obvious threat, they have to attempt to implement "Regime Change" in Afghanistan, which you're paying for with the lives of your soldiers. Do you think that's Common Sense? Would one of the Politicians be willing to lay down their life to achieve "Regime Change", as opposed to removing the threat from their backyard? Precisely. If it was them who had to go and fight, do you think the Politicians would still have decided to go to Iraq or Afghanistan? Never. They would have removed all the threats from their countries in an instant.

We have to stop allowing the Politicians to destroy our societies and kill our people, 'and people of other countries', by spending billions on unnecessary wars. Consolidism would have proposed that we asked all threats to leave our Countries. That's a peaceful solution in which nobody gets killed. Do it the Politicians' way, and hundreds of thousands perish. It is a fact that more of our troops will die before they leave Afghanistan. Knowing this absolutely, why wouldn't the Politicians make the following 'Common Sense' call, "Let's get out troops out of there, and instead remove the threat from our countries". What if it was one of the Politicians who was to die in 1 month's time in an Afghan desert? Would their policies change? In a heartbeat. If it saves just one soldier from here on in, we should do it. If it needs to be done, it's done. That's how a Consolidist sees it. But the Politicians won't do it, because they'd lose face.

If a Consolidist Government deemed it absolutely necessary to effect regime change in a country, this shouldn't be done with troops on the ground, unless the people sanction it. The people who will have to send their family members into harm's way. It should be done using smart weapons, fired from a great distance. In Iraq & Afghanistan, airbases should have been set up in neighbouring countries, or only aircraft carrier launched planes used. Compare this to the cost of putting troops on the ground inside enemy territory, not only financially, but most importantly in terms of lives lost. The air campaigns, focused on taking out the dictators and their mob, could be intermittently sustained for 100 years, with the money it's cost to put troops on the ground inside these countries for just ten years. It's not the case that if you stop air strikes for a long period of time, you're not winning. You stay there, with minimal financial outlay, waiting for the dictators to slip up, then take them out. Modern military aircraft can fire weapons from 100 miles outside cities, reducing the threat to our personnel to virtually zero. Would the Politicians say "Air Campaigns can't achieve regime change". First of all, if this Manifesto has achieved nothing else, it's identified that undeniably we can't believe a word a Politician says. Secondly, if an Air Campaign won't do it then, there you go Mr Politician, there's some boots and a gun. What would they say to that? "Uh. Let's try the Air Campaign anyway".

Would the billions of 'Catatonic Currency' be better spent on preventing our troops from dying by having as many of these smart weapons as is necessary, or sitting in the bank accounts of 'Celebrity TV Chefs' and other 'Society-Created Celebrities' that currently exist in this mad world? Why would we be a creature whose society is set up in such a way that a person can become a millionaire for cooking and talking about food? Not just that, but they're regarded as highly impressive geniuses.

If you're in the business of trying to win wars using troops on the ground, it costs lives. Lives which are thought to be invaluable by a Consolidist Societician, but not worth a penny to a Politician. If the majority of a people support their dictatorial regime and its policies of harbouring and nurturing terrorism, the air campaign should also focus on their country's infrastructure, until a leader steps forward in the country and says "We reject terrorism and are going to run our country like responsible adults". Once this occurs, we don't send any of our troops in, because of the obvious dangers. We help them at neutral borders with supplies and expertise to bring their country forward and have them prosper. It has to be said, that as a prevention before a cure, air campaigns against another country are mostly avoidable if we simply remove the threats from our countries to begin with. The Politicians are sending our troops in, knowing some of them will get killed, when they have the weapons to get the job done without ground troops.

We also have to think about the financial implications of jetting off around the world to fight wars or save the day. The US has spent over 1 trillion dollars in Iraq and Afghanistan. The vast majority of this being totally unnecessary expenditure. Whilst people back in the USA can't leave their homes for fear of being shot, robbed or stabbed, their taxes are being spent on implementing policies which ensure the deaths of thousands of their soldiers. Not only the trillion dollars, but the security of the armed forces are badly needed on the streets of America. Currently, especially in the USA, the Politicians have brainwashed the people into thinking it's everything to 'Serve your Country'. As soon as that statement is uttered, the soldiers march forth like brainwashed zombies. Yes, it is noble to serve your country, but only if it makes sense to. 'If' the Politician's reasoning for action is sound. If there's absolutely no other way of tackling a problem. Then, and only then, should the brave women and men 'Serve their Country'. Though, the Politicians reasoning for action would never be sound. They'd always send the soldiers to their deaths before taking alternative, obvious action. Action which protects 'their' soldiers and 'their' citizens in equal measure. The soldiers are not expendable They deserve protection too, in the form of sensible decision making. They're not there simply to die. "They're a soldier so if they die, hey it's not so bad". That's what a Politician seems to think.

There will be trouble in Afghanistan indefinitely. If foreign troops stay there, the trouble will be worse. The Taliban were defeated long ago. This is another mistake the media make, empowering the terrorists. They still call them the Taliban. The Taliban were a governing organisation. You can only be deemed Government if you sit in buildings of Government. If you 'manage' budgets and the affairs of the country. Any bunch of cave dwelling murderous criminals can call themselves the Taliban. Why would the media continue to give them the respect they don't deserve by calling them the Taliban? The 'Allies' defeated the Taliban a long time ago, but, as long as the foreign troops are there, the straggler terrorists and bombings will keep coming for the next thousand years. Until there are no attacks or bombings for many years, you can't claim to have won the war? That's the spin the Politicians are putting on the situation out there. How long? This will quite possibly never happen in Afghanistan. At least not for decades, following the events of the past ten years. Do the Politicians see this? No.

Just due to the nature of the Geography and Layout of the Towns & Villages of Afghanistan, you can't Govern or Police anywhere near all of it. You'd need to bring its infrastructure 200 years forward from where it is now before you could leave it behind as a secure, policed and responsible country that doesn't harbour terrorists. Is the West planning to stay there that long? A remote town of fifty people can be cleansed of the Taliban, but, your forces have to leave it some time. They may leave five Police Officers behind to maintain law and order, but they're not going to put up much of a fight against fifty wandering Taliban. The Politicians couldn't see this, at all! The worst thing is that the reason they continue to leave our troops in the country, is that extraction now would result in a "loss of face". They are leaving our loved ones to die in a country so 'they' don't have to suffer loss of face. It's all about them. These are the people who we are letting run our countries. They're like 10 year children in a playground fighting over a soccer ball. 'Somebody' out there in the USA. Consolidism feels for you. Your husband will die in the next 2 months because the Politicians don't want to lose face. How does that make you feel about Politicians? A Consolidist has more respect, an infinite respect, for the life of your warrior wife or husband.

★★★

Having not found any "Weapons of Mass Destruction", do you think America was wrong to have taken action against Iraq? "We didn't find any so yes it was wrong". That's probably what a large percentage of people would say. If we view from a different angle, and use an analogy, you see it in a whole different light.......

Imagine you arrive home from work one day to find a man on your front lawn holding a knife to your daughter's throat. "I'm going to kill her, I'm going to kill her", he screams, then drags her into the house and slams the door. All the evidence is pointing towards the fact that he is going to kill your daughter. Would you agree? Do you do nothing? Or do you do something? Do you rush inside and confront the man? Do you call the Police and wait for them to arrive? It would probably be safe to say that if all the evidence pointed towards an imminent crime, whoever the victim was to be, you'd do something. Inside the house however, if the real truth be known, the man may have no intention whatsoever of harming your daughter. Can you see the correlation? All the evidence pointed towards Saddam Hussein having WMD's. He had used them before. Couple this with the emergence of terrorism in a big way, action had to be taken. It doesn't matter a jot that nothing was found. The evidence compelled that action had to be taken. It must be noted, that 'evidence' could be genuine or falsified. Throughout this Manifesto, the Politician has been proven to be a devious creature. Can we trust 'their' evidence'? We'll never know. One thing's for sure, evidence would never be fabricated for any means by a Consolidist Government. If the evidence was genuine, action should have been taken in Iraq, but, the first action should have been removing all threats from our countries. Threats who could have got their hands on Saddam's WMD's to use against us. Secondly, we should have used only airstrikes and Cruise Missiles to destroy potential WMD sites and the Iraqi Leadership. Would Tony Blair and George Bush have sent troops into Iraq if they were the vanguard? Can you picture them with their helmets and guns, leading the charge into Baghdad and Basra? Exactly. They're cowards.

★★★

On the issue of Iraq, Afghanistan, and the killing of Osama Bin Laden, why is that people point towards the brave decisions of the Presidents or Prime Ministers? How difficult is it to say "We're going in". It's a joke to say that's brave. What's brave is the troops who actually put their hands up, volunteering themselves into action. Let's never fall under the impression that George W Bush deserves praise for starting an Arab Spring in the Middle East, or that Barack Obama deserves praise for approving the raid that killed Osama Bin Laden. All the credit lays with the troops, whether they were sadly killed or are still alive. If countries do deem it necessary to attempt to start an Arab Spring in the Middle East, it should be done without thousands of their troops having to lay down their lives. Why would the people of the West want to start an Arab Spring at the cost of their wives and husbands? They don't is the answer. That would be the guess of a Consolidist. It's the Politicians who do. The people of the Middle East stay over there and the West stays over there. That's the solution. A solution where nobody dies.

After the troops have returned home from fighting for us in these unnecessary ground wars, how do the Politicians reward them? In the UK in 2011, the Government announced that 10,0000 army soldiers would lose their jobs in a measure to reduce the deficit. Not only is that jobs lost, but National Pride too, as the UK's Armed Forces shrink and are gradually emasculated. Why does the UK Government cut the soldier's jobs but continue to pay for the unemployment, housing, sickness & child benefits of thousands of people in their country who could possibly be terrorists? Why do they continue to pay for the education of thousands of children whose foreign person, possible terrorist parents, don't pay into the system?

★★★

As a parting example, let Consolidism leave you with one final perfect illustration to best prove the importance of its central policy, Consolidation. It is now March 2012. For some years, the majority of the global community has been speaking out against the danger posed by Iran and its Nuclear Program. Iran says it's for peaceful, energy oriented purposes. Perhaps it is, but, it's plain to see that if Iran, or any other country, rogue or not, develops the ability to produce nuclear power, they would obviously then go just that extra mile to obtain nuclear weapons. That goes without saying. Another No-Brainer.

The USA, and Israel especially, have been poised to attack Iran for some time now. In the last few months, a key event in the timeline. The IAEA finally going on record, making damning statements against Iran and the alleged shielding of some of its nuclear activities. De Ja Vu? Iraq approximately 10 years ago? Is it the USA behind the scenes, pushing the IAEA, thus justifying their imminent military action? The USA, quite probably with Israel, will conduct air strikes against Iran in the coming few years. If they don't, Iran will have nuclear weapons in its arsenal. With Russia and China siding with Iran, who knows how quickly American and Israeli air strikes could escalate into World War 3? Other enemies of the USA, Israel and the West could become involved, Syria, North Korea, Venezuela, all no doubt willing to team up with powers that would give them a fighting chance to bring 'The West' to its knees.

So analysing it now, from the different angle and wavelength discussed. How does the world now find itself on the brink of World War 3? Would Iran have got away with announcing to the World that it's not going to develop nuclear energy capabilities, but simply move straight to developing a nuclear weapon? Not even Russia or China would have accepted that.

Iran does need nuclear power technology for peaceful purposes. It's true. Why? To support a growing population. If their population wasn't growing, they wouldn't need the nuclear fuel, and wouldn't have the facade to then surreptitiously develop nuclear weapons. The USA & Isarel would have no reason to take military action against Iran, and the world would not be staring World War 3 in the face.

The Non-Implementation of Consolidism and Consolidation is the absolute root of all the world's problems. We have to realise this and act on it before it's too late. Why can't Iran be allowed to develop Nuclear Technology? Here's the ultra-simple 'Consolidist Style' explanation that the Politicians can't seem to communicate with. A Nuclear War would kill hundreds of millions of people. The chances of a Nuclear War occurring, increases each time an additional country acquires Nuclear Weapons. A Statistical Fact. Conclusion? No more countries can be allowed to develop Nuclear Technology. It's for the safety and security of everybody, including the country trying to develop Nuclear capabilities.

That doesn't for a second mean that every country is going to agree with and abide by that statement, but, the first step to resolving disputes and problems is speaking the simple truth. Making unequivocally, uncomplicated, clear, succinct statements, free of Politician Time-Wasting Waffle and PC Timidity. Put the simple truth out there immediately, and start to move towards a solution immediately. These statements leave everybody being immediately aware of where they stand and are subsequently conducive to reaching a solution quicker.

★★★

We may not like it, and some may not believe it, but it is a reality that the glut of major and minor issues discussed in this Manifesto, have combined to create a perfect storm in which our civilization is slowly suffocating and dying. Whilst the position of our collective consciousness has contributed, it's the Politicians that have had the biggest bearing on the direction in which we are headed.

We humans will never all agree on every issue in our lives. We'll never agree on all the issues discussed in this Manifesto. But. Do you feel many or some of them make perfect sense? Do you feel some of the proposed measures are too extreme? You probably do. Why? We're so used to viewing the world being 'run', and fouled up, by politicians' soft, ineffective policies. If things are proposed, or done, differently, this would naturally surprise or even shock us. That's human nature. Consolidism is not telling you that you'd have to simply accept all the discussed measures should you support it. Through referendums, Consolidism believes you should be able to adopt as many or as few of the discussed strategies as you like. But 'You' get the final say on the major issues.

Politics and Politicians have never, aren't, and will never, do their job, do their part, and do what they have the power to do to solve our problems. We've all had to suffer the consequences of their empty promises for far too long. The Solutions to our problems are very simple indeed. Thus far, the Politicians have fooled many into thinking they are not, as they purposefully complicate situations in an attempt to blind us to their incompetency, or, divert our attentions away from the fact that their decisions are made in the interests of themselves and the mega-rich. Do not believe a word they say. Not a single word. Life, our societies, our countries need to be simplified greatly if we are to improve our quality of life. We The 99% deserve better than to have our lives continually sullied by the politicians' incompetence, gutlessness & greed. Our sub-standard lives are passing us by. It's time to take action. Now. Consolidism believes, being the most important element that makes our societies and world tick, The 99% should come first. If Politicians are left in positions of power, The 99% will continue to suffer. The world situation will gradually worsen, until the complete collapse of all our societies and lives. Consolidism is the only way to halt the sands of time.